How to Get the Best Out of  TV

Before It Gets The Best Of You

How to Get the Best Out of TV

Before It Gets The Best Of You

Dale & Karen Mason

BROADMAN
& HOLMAN
PUBLISHERS

Nashville, Tennessee

Published by Broadman & Holman Publishers, Nashville, Tennessee
Acquisitions & Development Editor: Vicki Crumpton
Page Design and Typography: TF Designs, Mt. Juliet, Tennessee
Author portrait by: W. Scott Mitchell Photography
Printed in the United States of America

4262-83
0-8054-6283-X

Dewey Decimal Classification: 302.2308
Subject Heading: TELEVISION AND FAMILY
Library of Congress Card Catalog Number: 95-36266

Unless otherwise noted, Scripture quotations are from the Holy Bible, New International Version, copyright © 1973, 1978, 1984 by International Bible Society. Also used is the New American Standard Bible, © the Lockman Foundation, 1960, 1962, 1963, 1968, 1971, 1972, 1973, 1975, 1977; used by permission.

Library of Congress Cataloging-in-Publication Data

Mason, Dale, 1960–
    How to get the best out of TV before it gets the best of you / Dale and
Karen Mason
        p.   cm.
    Includes index.
    ISBN 0-8054-6283-X
        1. Television broadcasting—Social aspects. 2. Television and family.
    3. Television—Religious aspects—Christianity. I. Mason, Karen, 1961– . II. Mason, Dale. 1960–
Married to television? III. Title.
    PN1992.6.M374   1996
    302.23'45—dc20

95-36266
CIP

96 97 98 99 00 5 4 3 2 1

For Jesus, our Savior . . .
because He came
and is coming back soon!

and for April, Kristin, Analisa, and Taylor—
our four treasured "inspirations."
Your Creator has tremendous plans for each of you.
Trust Him; Seek Him. Frinkinlioblisk!

Contents

Preface

Television has a profound effect on modern society. Whether you own a set or not, whether you watch a little or a lot, it has a profound effect on you.

As we have spoken at churches and seminars, and for radio and television interviews, we have been impressed by the stories that others have shared with us. Some are humorous, and some, heart wrenching. These stories have regularly reminded us of how very important it is that families make an effort to "master the media." If they don't, relationships inevitably suffer, and the entire household soon begins to miss out on some of life's most precious joys. All too often, "average" media management has dire results.

You may be surprised, but it is not our goal to convince you to trash your TV—though that may in some extreme cases actually be the appropriate response. There are too many good potential benefits from television and its modern accessories to cause us to universally endorse that course of action.

So take comfort! We are not anti-TV. Rather, we are pro good TV management! This book takes a proactive stance and offers enjoyable strategies that will help you to benefit from the good that television has to offer, without being battered by the bad. Believe it or not, your TV can be a tool that leads to greater closeness and richer relationships in your family, even in your walk with God. We want to tell you how that happened to us!

Also, and this is very important, you will see that most of the stories and principles included here can just as easily be applied to other electronic media, including how you use a stereo, a multimedia computer, video games, and the Internet. So think about the modern gadgetry that most directly affects you and those whom you love.

Finally, don't allow your reading of this book to be just another entertaining mental exercise. The stories, statistics, strategies, TV alternatives, and video reviews that you are about to read will do no good if they do no more than enter your mind. They need to reach you at another level—the heart.

So take a minute and ask God to use something from this book to better equip you, and those whom you love, to live and serve as He desires and to have more fun doing it!

We are praying for you. God bless!

Readers may contact the authors by writing:

Dale and Karen Mason
"Growing Together" Seminars
P.O. Box 1700, Gilbert, Arizona 85299

or via EMAIL to: HISkidDM@aol.com *or* mail@eden.org

PART I

Our Story

1

Once upon a Broken Promise

" . . . Don't worry if you've suffered a bankruptcy. And don't be discouraged if all the other car dealers tell you that you have no credit. At Sonny J's Auto Mart, poor credit, even bankruptcy, is no problem. . . ." A used-car commercial flashed across the screen, interrupting the detective show that I had already seen once or twice before.

I picked up the remote control and pushed the mute button. Lowering my size-twelve feet from their perch on the coffee table, I rose from my well-warmed dent in the couch, walked the few steps across our small apartment, and quietly opened the door to our bedroom.

It was after midnight, and I wanted to be careful not to wake my wife. But to my surprise, in the dim, dancing television light that slipped through the half-open door, I could see Karen kneeling beside our bed, hear her pouring out her heart to God. She was so deeply involved in her prayer that she was not aware of my presence. She did not know that I could hear her heart-breaking petition.

My wife was praying for me. She wasn't praying for my health. Nor was she praying for the concerns that I had shared through-out the day. No, with quiet sobs she was pleading, "Dear Lord, please help our family. We're hurting. We don't have our husband and father like we need him. Help him to *want* to give up this bad habit. There's nothing more I can say to make him change. It only makes things worse. You have to do it, Lord. God, I'm trusting you to help us. We need Dale. Please don't let him waste our lives by the way he watches television!"

I quietly backed out of the room and gently closed the bedroom door. Bewildered, I stood pondering what I had just heard. After several minutes, I walked the few steps back to the couch and sat staring at the silent, moving pictures. *Is she really serious?* I asked myself. *I enjoy watching TV, yes, but I'm not that much different than any average guy. I watch the same basic programs as everyone else.* But the prayer echoed in my mind and slowly began to touch my heart.

ADVICE UNHEEDED

I thought back to a day in a Marriage and Family college course when an amiable professor had shared his own bits of married wisdom. The experiences that he communicated easily held the attention of the idealistic group of soon-to-be-unleashed newlyweds. With an air that suggested the wisdom of experience, he voiced a deeply held personal conviction that now filled my mind again. "Don't have a television in your home during your first year of marriage. Establish communication and closeness without the strains that a poorly managed TV can bring."

I had fully intended to follow that advice. In fact, my fiancée and I had even discussed the idea after class that day and determined to take his advice. We would be TV-free for one full year. For Karen, this decision was a very welcome and, I believe, a very easy one. She was used to life without TV. But for me, it was a cautious, somewhat timid decision. My habitual viewing was more than relaxation. It was a way of life whose roots extended back to my early childhood.

Like most youths, I longed to hear the loud ringing of the final school bell of the day. I would run home, raid the kitchen pantry, and then flop down on the family-room floor in front of the television for an afternoon of kids' programs. Both my first and last thoughts of the day were molded by TV. And as I "matured," the hours I spent sitting or lying in front of the set shifted to a late-night concentration.

Over the years I graduated from "Leave It to Beaver" to "Happy Days." My infatuation for "Captain Kangaroo" switched to "Star Trek's" Captain Kirk. I'm embarrassed to admit it, but my early college days even found me addicted to a daily intake of one of the sleazy afternoon soap operas.

For me, a decision not to purchase a television for at least one year was a very big one. But the idea seemed good, so I agreed. (Besides, we didn't have enough cash to purchase a set anyway.)

So, Karen and I entered wedded bliss without the most standard of entertainment appliances. We returned from our honeymoon to a cozy little apartment free of the sounds of sirens, gunshots, canned laughter, and referees' whistles. We enjoyed evening walks and bicycle rides. We invited friends over to play board games at our dining-room table, and we spent time reading God's Word and praying. I was enjoying activities that I had never given serious thought to before. But I was aching, also. I remember looking at my watch at around 10:30 each night and craving to tune into "M*A*S*H" or one of the late-night talk shows. I missed my old "friends," but I was genuinely enjoying a newfound sense of freedom.

A WELCOME VISIT

Enter one very well-meaning widow. About six weeks after Karen and I had set up home on our own, we received a visit from Karen's mother. She had driven two hundred miles to our small, college-town apartment. She carried with her some belated wedding gifts, miscellaneous household items, and a strong desire to please her new son-in-law.

She didn't know of our decision to start our marriage without TV. Therefore, she couldn't appreciate the mental gymnastics taking place in my mind when she enthusiastically offered to buy us a television set as a wedding gift. I reasoned to myself, *Well, I've got a pretty good handle on my TV habit now, I'll be OK. . . . Karen won't want it though! She's not much of a TV viewer. But . . . this is her mom . . . I know! I'll tell Karen that I feel obligated to accept the offer, so as to avoid any hard feelings. . . . Besides, I'll only watch the news anyway.*

"Wow! That'd be great," I responded, trying to subdue my enthusiasm enough to be able to build a credible story to Karen once her mom had gone.

How God Works

As I stood outside our bedroom that night, the decision—to add a TV to our home without ever having been trained to use it properly—haunted me. The woman that I had married only two years before was, at that very moment, requesting God's intervention to help realign my priorities. Little did my beloved Karen know that, even as she knelt on the other side of the apartment wall less than ten feet from me, God was already beginning to answer her prayer!

Because God had allowed me to see the woman that I dearly loved distressed and at wits' end, I seriously began to reevaluate the use of my time. I didn't tell Karen that her words had been heard by someone in addition to God. My pride wouldn't allow me to do that. But with her prayer echoing in my mind, I began to seek God's help and to try earnestly to find alternative activities in which to involve myself. I sorely wanted to impress her with actions that would prove that my free time could be spent on something other than watching television.

As I began to pursue non-TV activities, I became much more aware of articles that reported or explored the subject of modern society's use of television. As I read, and as Karen and I observed the habits and attitudes of friends and relatives, we became increasingly alarmed and concerned for the millions of other Christian families who—knowingly or not—are in a situation similar to ours.

My desire to delve further into this subject intensified. I read everything I could get my hands on that discussed television and related topics: newspaper articles, magazines, books, research papers, and newsletters. Now, rather than staring blankly at a glass screen all evening, I was researching the very subject that I was also struggling with. God was using the materials that I was reading to cultivate within me the desire to change. He was showing me, indisputably, that uncontrolled and untrained use of TV can and often does have distressing consequences. And the more

I discovered, the more I yearned to share the information with others.

One fact that both comforted and concerned me was the realization of how similar my habits were to the myriad of TV viewers. I watched the same amount and basically the same types of shows as the rest of society.

But I also discovered that most viewers—including homemakers, factory workers, business executives, pastors, lawyers, mechanics, doctors, and teachers—are somewhat ashamed of and even frustrated with their own use of TV and all the other electronic media. More than just being dispirited by the programs, they are concerned about how their loved ones, or they themselves, use these technologies. Most of us want to see change, but the solution eludes us.

Hopefully, the "media-survival kit" that you are holding will provide the tools and answers that so many have begun to seek!

PART II

Television's Impact on the Family

2

How TV Affects
Communication and Closeness

Karen opened another packet of crackers and handed the two square saltines to one of our anxious, "vocally uninhibited" toddlers. I, meanwhile, charted a course back to the table. Balancing my second helping of lettuce and "fixins" from the all-you-can-eat salad bar, I dodged a hurrying young waitress, then stopped to let a busboy and his load of dirty dishes go rolling by.

As I laid my overflowing plate on the placemat, I noticed a cozy table for two to my left. Through the branches of an artificial tree, I could see a husband and wife who were out together, enjoying Sunday dinner.

That's nice, I thought to myself. But as I sat down I sensed that something was odd. Upon second glance, I noticed that this couple was together, but only in terms of proximity, for sitting between them was a two-inch TV.

Oblivious to his surroundings, a thirty-something gentleman that I'll call "Fred the football fanatic" sat with an earphone crammed in one ear and a finger in the other. I quietly chuckled. However, the humor of "Fred" and his little TV quickly subsided when my eyes fell upon his sullen wife. She sat within arm's reach, alone.

Apparently finished with her half-eaten meal, "friendless Fran" stared out a window, silently waiting for the next commercial when she could again have sixty seconds to try to share a feeling and hope for a spark of concern. From my vantage point behind the artificial tree, it was clear that watching TV had taken priority over communication in this couple's marriage.

For many viewers, TV has a damaging hold on their lives. We tend to sit so close to our little screens that we can no longer see the big picture. Few viewers recognize that their TV habits may actually need some fine-tuning—or in some cases a complete overhaul.

This chapter presents some very intriguing and important statistics. It examines the price we pay for the way we use TV, and it encourages each of us to take a few steps back and look at our lives from a more enlightening vista.

THE TV HABIT AND THE CHRISTIAN

I wonder if we realize how much television has changed our culture? We have an entire generation of children and young adults who choose TV (or computer and video games) almost exclusively over other after-school and evening activities, young people who have never been mentored in the life skill of how to find satisfying media alternatives and who seem to have all but forgotten how to interact with family and friends.

The daily routine of passive TV viewing monopolizes the free time of both children and adults. "Research shows [that] people don't respect themselves for watching television, don't enjoy it much, and by and large wish they could quit."[1] At the very least, indiscriminate television viewing is a bad habit; and for many, it is a very real addiction. "Millions of Americans are so hooked on TV that they fit the criteria for substance abuse in the official psychiatric manual."[2]

Let's face it. How often do we settle down in the evening and breeze through the channels until we find what appears to be a sufficiently entertaining program—regardless of the content or morals displayed?

The typical Christian attends church faithfully, singing with sincerity the desire to have God take his life and let it be committed to the Lord Jesus. But that same Christian then returns home, turns on the TV, and plops down to share the same vicarious, sexually suggestive, violent, and often profane experiences as his non-Christian neighbors.

As Christians are naively sucked into responding on cue to prerecorded laugh tracks and crude talk-show hosts, conversation and commitment seem to be forgotten. (Or maybe they were never really learned by the generation labeled "Baby Boomers" and the children of baby boomers.)

Although startling evidence continues to be released regarding the negative effects of indiscriminate or large doses of TV, few have made personal application of the abundant advice offered by godly experts. There is an alarming degree of spiritual indifference regarding television. Seldom do we discuss with our families how the on-screen action contradicts the biblical norms by which we are instructed to live. Nor do we realize the number of hours TV is viewed in our homes.

Unfortunately, neither has there been any significant improvement in *quality*-control efforts to determine what shows are allowed into our homes. In most households, the TV schedule dictates the evening agenda, rather than a careful scheduling of preselected programs or non-TV activities. Often, without even questioning the content of the shows that are about to enter our living rooms, we zap a bag of microwave popcorn, pull the tab on a cold diet soda, and relax both body and mind in front of the nearest television set.

WHAT THE STATISTICS REVEAL

At first glance, Americans appear to be busy—so busy that hardly another activity could be jammed into our schedules. Some of the many things that fill our week include: full and part-time employment, church services and activities, sporting events, bill paying, schoolwork, housework, yardwork, grocery shopping, telephone conversations, auto maintenance, food preparation, eating, sleeping, personal hygiene, computer "hacking" and CD-ROM games, reading newspapers and magazines, and the list goes on.

However, the average family still finds time to tune in the TV for fifty hours each week—more than a normal workweek, or an average of more than three hours *per person*, per day.

While most of us complain about the increasing amount of violence and immorality portrayed on television, we "stay tuned" nonetheless. The immediate-gratification box has become an indispensable appliance in American households. We strate-

gically place TVs throughout our homes for ease of use and undisturbed viewing. We arrange our living-room furniture, our mealtimes, bedtimes, even our bathroom breaks around television. In fact, it appears that we find television more essential than indoor toilets! Televisions are found in 98 percent of American households, while indoor toilets have been installed in only 97 percent of homes.[3]

After a live interview on a midwestern radio station—during which we shared this rather humorous "toilet statistic"—the female talk-show host told us that TV isn't handled very well in her own Christian home. With an embarrassed grin, she went on to divulge, "When our TV went on the blink, my husband ran out and bought a new one as quick as if we were out of toilet paper!" Unfortunately, her family's amusing TV dependence is the norm, not the exception, in modern society.

One summer evening, while stopped at a busy intersection, I noticed a young couple in a small car pulled up next to mine. They weren't paying any attention to each other; neither did they seem to be aware of the beautiful sunset blazing across the western horizon. Then I noticed that both occupants had their eyes fixed on a small object resting on the console between them. Plugged into the cigarette lighter and glowing in the dim light of evening was a portable TV.

It seems that as more programming becomes available, the more we feel obligated to look at TV. The easier it is to take a TV set with us during our daily activities, the harder it becomes to say no to its availability, or its immense impact on our lives and attitudes. Sadly, most parents choose to buy a second (third or fourth!) television set, hoping to buy some peace by avoiding some of the inevitable irritations that arise from disagreements about what will be watched. Rather than exerting control and responsibility, they take the path of least resistance.

An evening stroll through almost any neighborhood reveals that, in many homes, parents watch TV in the living room while the kids watch, unsupervised, in their own bedrooms, the kitchen, or the family room. As "personal" television sets become more popular, the less we strive to engage in meaningful, much needed conversation. Instead, we march to our designated section of the house and allow the writers and producers of visual media to dictate our thought patterns and to shape our worldviews. Watching television has degenerated "from being a family affair into a solitary experience. . . . solitary TV watching marks the height of alienation" in modern, industrialized society.[4]

While well-meaning parents may be "keeping the peace," they are also forfeiting precious, never-to-be-repeated opportunities to nurture lifelong family relationships.

THE COST

For five decades television has been *mis*represented as one of the least costly forms of personal and family entertainment. Its proponents argue that, once a set is purchased and planted in its own little corner, it costs only about a dime a day for the electricity required to empower it.

While TV may be one of the least costly forms of entertainment in monetary terms, it is one of the most costly entertainment choices in terms of opportunities lost.

Within a generation of the creation of commercial television, the medium deeply entrenched itself into our lives. All too often we forget that when we choose to watch TV, we are also choosing *not* to do something else.

It is important to realize that the problems associated with TV are not directly caused by the electronic invention itself.

Think about all the centuries before 1950. People did not sit idly in their cottages or castles waiting for television images to appear. No, they filled their lives with activities and people. As the hours of viewing have multiplied, though, the time and attention left for people have vastly diminished. Too often we become guilty of child neglect, spouse neglect, friend neglect, and God neglect.

Consider the evening dinner hour. It used to be a time for the family to "connect." But how often is this important portion of the day now accompanied by watching TV? One observant writer has noted that "once upon a time, television was a dessert, something couples shared after dinner, after daily chores, after talk time. But today . . . it has become the whole meal, and benumbed silence has replaced loving conversation."[5]

The cost of TV? High indeed! When improperly managed, it amounts to paying for an electronic sedative that is voluntarily and habitually injected into both adults and children. Its side effects: the erosion of personal and spiritual relationships and the thoughtless waste of a priceless, nonrenewable, supernatural resource—time. Where something else once was, television now is.

Even if everything funneled into our homes via the television was good, we would still need to weigh carefully the merits of sitting idly in front of the screen against the other good activities that TV replaces.

The Buck Stops Here

It is important to realize that the problems associated with the use of TV are not directly caused by the electronic invention itself. A TV set does not require our full allegiance from the day that we bring it home. It doesn't yell across the room and sternly demand that we give it the majority of our free time. Its presence only suggests that we begin watching. And we do!

We begin to stay up too late watching TV on Saturday nights. We begin to choose network programming over evening church programs. When unsupervised, children begin to pay just a little more attention to afternoon reruns than their schoolwork, a good book, household chores, or even active outdoor play. And, of course, adults happily accept the never-ceasing assertions that we deserve a break, looking to TV and its mindless game shows, soap operas, sporting events, situation comedies, and late-night talk shows to relax us from the tensions of the day.

However, we cannot cast all the blame for the problems that arise from immoral television programs upon unregenerate media executives. After all, no one forces us to watch the programs they present.

While secular writers and producers must certainly accept responsibility for their large contribution to the moral decline of America, Christians have been guilty as well. Ted Baehr, a member of the board of directors of the National Religious Broadcasters, contends in his book, *The Movie and Video Guide for Christian Families*, that what he calls the anti-church, anti-American, anti-everything attitude prevails in Hollywood today because churches have retreated. In many ways our passivity and lack of interest has been as much of a contributing factor as that of Hollywood's continually degenerating moral code. We still sit down and view the questionable programs. We have become callused to the increasingly amoral, anti-God programming. We still purchase the products that make the shows profitable. Responsibility for the problems that arise from violent, immoral television programs rests as squarely on the shoulders of those who habitually and carelessly push the "on" button as it does on the program providers themselves.

The vast majority of us no longer benefit from the positive aspects that carefully selected TV programs and videocassettes can provide. We Christians have slowly fallen into the trap of indiscriminate, misuse of TV. Whether a bad habit or an actual addiction, we need help.

There is no better time than now to reconsider our relationship to TV (and all the other electronic media) and commit to a fresh, new stance based on consistent Christian principles. The best first step that I can think of is to identify what God's Word says in relation to our TV-viewing habits.

3

How TV Affects Spiritual Reality

Since the late 1940s when TV sets first began to appear in large numbers on retail-store shelves, Christians have had to decide how to deal with this marvelous, yet mesmerizing communication tool. The simple solution, "Don't purchase a set," proved to be no solution at all. Media abstinence was a short-lived option for most Christians. Surveys as early as 1953 confirmed that TV ownership was almost exactly the same in evangelical households as it was in the general public.

By the mid-1960s, TV ownership had become so prevalent the *Moody Monthly* included an article that stated: "The local church is undoubtedly affected in a definite way by TV competition. . . . Excessive Saturday night viewing makes an appreciable difference in attendance at Sunday school and church on Sunday morning. . . . The Sunday evening service finds itself competing with one of the most glittering entertainment arrays of the week. Midweek activities likewise suffer from the pull of the easy chair and the television set."[1]

That same statement applies, and even more so, today. TV increasingly gets the best of our prime time. It's just so easy.

One of the clearest of Christ's instructions is found in Mark 12:30: "You shall love the Lord your God with all your heart, and with all your soul, and with all your mind, and with all your strength" (NASB). In other words, we are to cling to and give ourselves wholly to God; we are to give Him priority above all else, submitting our thoughts, desires, and goals to His loving care and the principles and commands of His Word. If our lives are truly to be lived according to His plan, we must learn to see the world as God sees it. The only way that we can gain God's perspective is to filter our media choices through His guidebook, the Bible.

However, Christians are, for the most part, no longer people of the Book. Surveys indicate a disappointing lack of knowledge about our faith. And secular news reports continue to reveal an even more disappointing lack of *adherence* to that faith.

We don't live out what we profess. "Virtual reality" has replaced the truth of spiritual reality. By this I mean that many who once were thrilled by a vibrant relationship with Jesus have allowed a passion for the Bread of Life to be replaced by a craving for the visual smorgasbord of television and its related technologies.

Somewhere there is a balance that avoids television gluttony. But it won't be found while sitting with the remote control in your palm. Let's take a few minutes to discover some of what the Bible has to say with regard to television and other visual media.

SCRIPTURAL DIRECTIVES

In spite of the fact that television wasn't developed until the twentieth century, God's Word is far from silent with regard to its use. The Bible's clear guidelines relate either directly or indirectly to all areas of everyday life. Our use of television is a small barometer reflecting our personal application or disobedience of these guidelines.

For those who doubt that Scripture has anything to say about mastering this assemblage of wires and circuitboards, consider the following passages with your favorite programs in mind:

> *I will walk in my house with blameless heart. I will set before my eyes no vile thing.* (Ps. 101:2b–3)

> *Be imitators of God. . . . Among you there must not be even a hint of sexual immorality, or of any kind of impurity, or of greed, because these are*

improper for God's holy people. Nor should there be obscenity, foolish talk or coarse joking, which are out of place, but rather thanksgiving. . . . Have nothing to do with the fruitless deeds of darkness, but rather expose them. . . . Be very careful, then, how you live—not as unwise but as wise. (Eph. 5:1, 3–4, 11, 15)

For the sinful nature desires what is contrary to the Spirit, and the Spirit what is contrary to the sinful nature. (Gal. 5:17)

The acts of the sinful nature are obvious: sexual immorality, impurity and debauchery; idolatry and witchcraft; hatred, discord, jealousy, fits of rage, selfish ambition, dissensions, factions and envy; drunkenness, orgies, and the like. I warn you, as I did before, that those who live like this will not inherit the kingdom of God . . . Those who belong to Christ Jesus have crucified the sinful nature with its passions and desires. . . . Let us keep in step with the Spirit. (Gal. 5:19–21, 24–25)

Therefore do not be foolish, but understand what the Lord's will is. (Eph. 5:17)

Whatever is true, whatever is noble, whatever is right, whatever is pure, whatever is lovely, whatever is admirable—if anything is excellent or praiseworthy—think about such things. (Phil. 4:8)

The hours spent with television are not simply hours of easy and well-earned relaxation. They are the terrain on which a spiritual battle is fought. Hour by hour, sitcom by soap opera by sporting event, we are choosing whom we will serve. Will we demonstrate our love and obedience to the God who created us, or will we submit ourselves to the entrancing glow of the lesser god?

MODERATION VS. OVERLOAD

None of this means that television, the appliance, is inherently bad. *When used in moderation,* it can be an educational, a cultural, and even a spiritual benefit.

One study indicated that children who watch *some* TV (about one supervised hour per day) do slightly better in school than children who never watch it. "Actual medical studies, done separately at Stanford University and the University of Southern California, show that programs like television situation comedies can have amazing health benefits. . . . Watching comedy shows can reduce harmful stress, relax

It's time we learned how to get the best out of television, without letting television get the best of us.

muscles, stimulate the heart and respiratory system and improve circulation."[2]

Also, certain groups within our society have a greater "need" for the benefits that TV can bring. Elderly and homebound men and women look forward with great anticipation to family-oriented programs, since they often provide a feeling of companionship. (Of course that may mean some of us should just turn off *our* TVs and visit these folks occasionally.)

Single parents left alone to fill the roles of mother, father, chef, chauffeur, spiritual leader, playmate, breadwinner, homemaker, disciplinarian, nurse, and auto mechanic find the ability of TV to temporarily occupy the kids to be a much-appreciated asset. Used in moderation and with sharp discernment, television can provide the overextended single parent with some free time during which she (or he) can retreat and attempt to accomplish some of her many tasks. Unfortunately, humans are not exactly well-known for moderation or self-discipline.

When at last our days on this earth are over, and the accumulated years we spent watching TV are tallied against the few weeks or months we invested in one-on-one time with God through prayer and reading His Word, most of us will hang our heads in shame for allowing this electronic distraction to rob us of so very much time.

It has been estimated that the average reader can easily read through the Bible in only seventy hours. What this means is: if the average adult TV viewer, who watches three hours per day, would substitute just twenty-four days of the TV diet with Scripture reading, he could journey through the entire Bible! Even slower or more studious readers would have no trouble getting from Genesis to Revelation in double or triple that amount of time. But there is one catch. *Discipline.* The viewer must resolve to temporarily replace some or all of his TV viewing with a different kind of input.

A more realistic challenge would be to cut your daily viewing by just one-sixth (thirty minutes) to two-and-a-half hours (or less) a day. At the same time, schedule at least thirty minutes per day for Bible reading. By doing so, you can read through the entire Bible in less than twenty weeks! And better use of future free time is an almost certain by-product.

The enigma is that Bible reading requires effort. Why choose an activity that requires effort when we can grab a soda and the remote control, settle back into an overstuffed couch, and relax both body and mind in front of the TV? God's "still, small voice" can be conveniently drowned out by the chase scenes, rude remarks, shoot-outs, and sexual liaisons of an average TV day.

A PERSONAL APPRAISAL

Look at the world around you. Do doctors acquire and maintain skill at practicing medicine simply by attending an occasional seminar? Or by graduating from years of medical school? No. On the contrary, they practice what they have been taught, and lifelong study to remain current is required. In the same way, to develop a vibrant personal relationship with Jesus Christ, we must dedicate significant periods of time to serious study and application (practice) of the Scriptures.

What about you? Do you make time for serious, uninterrupted prayer and praise? Or are you among the millions of "normal" Christians who invest an hour or two at church each week and in ritualistic Bible reading, but twenty or more hours in front of the TV? Does the spiritual climate in your home more closely resemble the warm, lushly growing tropics of South America or the barren lifelessness of Antarctica? Has infatuation with the TV set replaced more important priorities in your everyday life? Has your television been elevated to the position of a new type of "family altar"?

We can't be naive. Our adversary is extremely cunning. Satan has been very successful in his unceasing efforts to titillate us with the things of this world; and TV, in its very proliferation, is perhaps one of his most effective snares in modern society.

While we cannot become recluses, simply sitting in our bedrooms reading the Bible all day, neither can we ignore the need for godly, responsible media management. It's time we learned how to get the best out of television, without letting television get the best of us. We need to use different standards than those set by Siskel and Ebert and their contemporary counterparts for that which we allow into our minds, our hearts, and our lives.

Whether you give too much attention to the television, a set of well-used golf clubs, your home computer, or even a pair of lightning-fast knitting needles, remember: too much of even a good activity can be detrimental if that activity comes between you and your spiritual health.

4

How TV Affects Your Worldview

It is an amazing statistic; one you may never have considered. Only a few hundred entertainment industry executives decide what 250 *million* Americans, and nearly a billion additional viewers around the world, ultimately will or will not see during TV prime time this week. How these men and women choose to represent issues can dramatically transform the moral and ethical attitudes of viewers. Here is one disturbing example.

TRICKED INTO BELIEVING

We were angry, disappointed, and frustrated. Although we had only seen a few episodes of the new "family" TV show, our guard had quickly been let down. The prime-time production was superbly written, a stirring combination of out-of-the-ordinary characters and intellectually arousing situations. In this episode, the plainly dressed Amish family was having some difficulty in adjusting to the modern technologies and social differences of "civilized" America. But their strong reliance upon and devotion to God was often very evident. As a general rule, the writers of this show had chosen to treat God fairly. He was not mocked. In fact, He was held in very high regard.

Recently, though, things had been changing. The previous week we had watched as religious concepts of the New Age movement were carefully interwoven into the plot. Still, we did not think that, overall, it was bad enough to cause us to alert the kids. So we just shrugged it off and kept quiet.

This episode, however, this blatant attack on biblical morality, could not be ignored. A premarital act of fornication between one of the stars of the show (a recently widowed young woman) and a man whom she had known barely more than one week was, at first, met with righteous anger by the young widow's mother-in-law. We watched anxiously to see how this woman of God would help her lonely, beloved daughter-in-law to acknowledge and ask forgiveness of God for her sin.

But it was here that the story took an alarming twist. The widowed girl's non-Amish mother encouraged her immoral choice. In a brief confrontation with her Amish mother-in-law, the young widow defiantly stated that she was not about to apologize to anyone. "I believe in what I did" (sex with a practical stranger). She accused her Bible-believing mother-in-law—and representatively, all Christians—of being unfeeling, rigid, and judgmental. The Amish mother-in-law then quickly made an unrealistic 180-degree turnaround by admitting the error of her ways and her need to "adjust" to a changing moral climate. The show ended with loving hugs and a warm-hearted acceptance of the girl's sin.

Apparently, if two people are intelligent and caring, they will put aside their outdated ideas—and the Book on which they are founded—and quickly accept this and other similar "social differences." The writers of this episode even went so far as to correlate the acceptance of premarital sex with progressing from the horse and buggy to the automobile.[1]

SUPPER HOUR AT THE HOLLYWOOD DINER

God is intimately concerned about our minds. We are to love Him with all our heart, soul, and mind (Deut. 6:5). We are to be transformed by renewing our minds (Rom. 12:2). We must guard what we feed our minds because "you are what you eat" or more accurately, you are what you *think*. Let's find out who is in the kitchen at the Hollywood Diner and what the chef is cooking up for supper tonight!

Does the Kitchen Staff Have a Hidden Agenda?

In his revealing book, *The Home Invaders*, Donald Wildmon documented the findings of the "Lichter and Rothman" study from the mid-1980s. In this well-known inquiry, in-depth surveys and interviews were conducted with 104 of the most influential professionals in the television industry. Among those interviewed were 15 presidents of independent production companies, 61 producers (26 of whom are also writers), and 10 network vice-presidents responsible for program development and selection. These individuals were identified by the Lichter and Rothman survey as "the cream of the television creative community . . . some of the most experienced and respected members of the craft." However, many alarming statistics about the prejudices of the people who decide what we are offered were revealed (and remember, this study was done over a decade ago). Among the findings were:

- 93 percent seldom or never attend worship services.
- 97 percent believe that the pregnant woman carrying an unborn child has the right to decide on abortion.
- Merely 5 percent strongly agree that homosexuality is wrong.
- Only 16 percent strongly believe that adultery is wrong.
- An astounding 99 percent believe that TV programs should be a little more critical of traditional Judeo-Christian values!

A more recent (1995) study, conducted by UCLA and *U.S. News and World Report* asked a much broader and less powerful group of 6,300 entertainmnent industry decision makers for their opinions on various moral and spiritual topics. As you probably already know, the "Hollywood elite" remain in a world of their own, substantially less conservative morally than the vast majority of Americans.[2] Secular television's architects, biased against Christianity and its essential moral guidelines, admit that they are not in it just for the money. They are trying to move their viewers toward their own ideal of the good society.

This group of television executives plays a major role in creating and shaping the programs whose themes and stars become idolized in our popular culture. In an article from the *American Family Association Journal*, Judy Price, vice-president in charge of children's programming at CBS, stated, "I think we've broken a lot of ground (in children's programs) where people would not have dared to go in prime-time." When questioned as to her motivation for taking control of the children's programming division she boldly responded, "I could get away with more."[3]

We must ask ourselves: "Are these the people we want to shape our thoughts and our children's attitudes?"

An Ever-Changing Standard

TV has become the ever-changing standard on which the morality of modern society is based. One step at a time, it has replaced the Word of God as the absolute guideline for moral choices in our lives. By touching the thought processes of millions of people every evening, prime time works to make the values of the coastline liberal elite the values of the nation. Habits, attitudes, and values that traditionally have been instilled by parents, or by the church, are now being taught by television. "It tells us . . . what is right and wrong, what is acceptable and unacceptable, whom to believe, whom to trust and not trust, and whom we should desire to emulate."[4] Secular television producers have gradually acclimated us to a make-believe world where there are no real consequences for sin. Even the most difficult personal problems can be successfully resolved in thirty to sixty minutes.

While researching for this book we were surprised to find that *Star Wars* filmmaker George Lucas once candidly confided his opinion that "the influence of the church, which used to be all powerful, has been usurped by film. Films and television tell us . . . what is right and wrong."[5]

Television has an awesome potential to shape and change almost every aspect of life. We can literally *watch* history change anywhere in the world via satellite transmissions (for example, the coverage of the war in the Persian Gulf, or the slow speed chase of O. J. Simpson in his white Ford Bronco). And the more a viewer watches, the more pervasive and believable the messages of the media power brokers become. Biblical truths begin to blur. Discernment begins to wane. Actions that were once out-of-bounds begin to be accepted, both on the screen and in society at large.

Tom Hanks, who has starred in such blockbusters as *Apollo 13*, *Forrest Gump*, and *Sleepless in Seattle*, received his first Oscar for his enthusiastic portrayal of a homosexual lawyer in the movie *Philadelphia*. At that time, he openly stated what most in Hollywood try to hide: "The film industry can capture an idea and make it glamorous and gorgeous, so that the audience isn't even aware that they're embracing something they would never have embraced before."[6]

With the "help" of skillful scriptwriters, our viewpoint mutates. Behaviors that we once found wrong are no longer perceived as such. We forget that television and film productions are not a true-to-life, balanced view of how the world really is.

WHAT IS *NOT* ON THE MENU?

Since our minds are of such great concern to our Maker, we must also consider if the TV menu promotes a malnourished mind. Take a look at a few of the important ingredients that television programming leaves *out*.

True Christians

What is missing from the TV screen? For starters, how about a decent individual with a sincere, biblically-based belief in God? For the most part, the only modern-day people on secular television that believe in God are kooks and fanatics. True Christians find themselves portrayed as oddities or relics from an era long past. It's no wonder our neighbors have such a distorted view of Christianity!

Belief in God has been edited, redefined, and replaced. By emphasizing the supposed self-sufficiency of man, TV writers and producers train us to ignore the hand of God, to deny His rightful authority over our lives. To put it simply, the standard television worldview ignores God.

Belief in the Creator

By what is left out of the programming, television teaches that the Creator does not exist and, therefore, His purposes and expectations are not important. In *Taming the TV Habit*, Kevin Perotta stated, "No made-for-television movie leaves the viewer marveling at how God worked out everything for the good of the characters who trusted Him. No television hero, in a moment of humility, admits his inability to right an injustice and calls on God to act. No news commentator reflects on the rise and fall of nations in light of the biblical prophets who spoke about the kinds of behavior which God rewards and punishes."[7] Created man, not man's Creator, fills the screen.

The television view of the world completely excludes an awareness of God. This ploy distracts people from thinking about who God really is. Instead, programmers fill our minds with man-centered stories and man-centered explanations for God's supernatural acts. Even the Corporation for Public Broadcasting (PBS/NPR)—which for decades has been substantially underwritten by all American taxpayers—unwaveringly promotes the theory of evolution as if it were irrefutable fact. Biased television producers effectively withhold from both news and drama the wealth of scientific evidences for biblical/scientific creation.[8]

It is of practical importance to every Christian to realize that as our Creator God owns us, and we shall therefore heed His directives about what we allow between our ears. We are to have the mind of Christ (1 Cor. 2:16). I'm afraid, however, that too often what we put inside our minds greatly dishonors Him.

Ordinary Living

Have you ever noticed that ordinary living is left *out* of the pseudoworld of TV programming? Gone are the daily routines, the self-sacrificial actions, and healthy relationships exemplified in the lives of millions of real people. We are given, instead, an illusionary world, which we welcome for its vicarious experiences. But we retire from our daily viewing with a new collection of unrealistic expectations to which we can never attain.

THE INGREDIENTS

Turn your attention to what *is* on the menu at the Hollywood Diner. Are the ingredients of the normal "TV dinner" fit for human consumption?

Covetousness and Lust

Let's start by discussing the appetizer—those all-too-frequent thirty- and sixty-second commercials that bombard us with images designed to whet our material tastes. They attempt to seduce us into buying everything from luxury cruises to gourmet dog food. They tell us what we are supposed to long for. If your car is not the latest model, with the smoothest lines, you don't have everything you deserve. Even more subtly, we are told that if our spouse is not the most beautiful, or adorned with the best body, he or she may not necessarily be worthy of our continued devotion.

In case you are sitting there thinking, *Yep. I agree. That's what commercials do. But I don't let them affect me,* think again! Why else do highly profitable advertising agencies continue to thrust these types of sales campaigns at us? And why would manufacturers continue to pay hundreds of millions of marketing dollars for these kinds of ads if they weren't accomplishing their intended

---

goal—to entice and arouse us to action? Let's not delude ourselves. We are being trained to covet, and to do so unabashedly.

One evening my family and I had opted to watch TV for a little entertainment. We found a purely wholesome special and were enjoying it immensely. However, a commercial break soon interrupted our relaxation by filling the screen with a provocatively dressed female slowly caressing and kissing her lover with all the seductive expertise of an uptown prostitute. "Click"—off went the tube until our chosen program returned. This isn't what we are training our pliable little girls, so vulnerable because of their innocence and naivete, to admire and eventually emulate. This isn't what I or my son need either. And I knew it certainly was not the kind of appetizer that God expected me to serve to my family.

Sexual Promiscuity

Increasingly, sex and violence are television's main courses. Sexual fornication, adultery, and homosexuality are dished up in heaping portions. According to a study released by Lou Harris and Associates, Inc., the three networks broadcast sixty-five thousand references to sexual behavior (in just one year), an average of twenty-seven references per hour. And that number continues to rise.

Sex is God's idea! In the intended boundaries of a loving marriage, it is an exhilarating and creative physical expression of human love.

Greg Lewis, in his book *Telegarbage*, stated that "references to intercourse on television, whether verbally insinuated or contextually implied, occur between unmarried partners five times as often as married couples" and "references to intercourse with prostitutes comes in second." And what about homosexuality? God calls it sin, but on network TV it is glossed over and presented as nothing more than a state of being that should be accepted as naturally as the pigment of one's skin.

Television is probably the greatest sex miseducator in the world today. Beware! Network TV would have us believe that sex is simply an activity to indulge in whenever, wherever, and with whomever one gets the urge.

The truth is that sex is God's idea! In the intended boundaries of a loving marriage, it is an exhilarating and creative physical expression of human love. Originating in the paradise of the garden of Eden, sex is a deeply intimate act created by God to physically and emotionally unite one man with one woman and to propagate humanity (Gen. 2:18, 24; Mal. 2:15).

Designed by God to react with amazing ease to the physical attributes of women, *men* are especially prone to sexual fantasy. Women, of course, have their own battles with impure sexual thoughts from time to time. But because men have been designed by their Maker as they have, discernment and self-control are most critical for males.

It is unnerving when one considers the extent to which the God-given wonder of sex has been prostituted to facilitate the sales goals of the corporate world. Television viewers from cradle to rocking chair are fed a lie that says, "Fantasize, enjoy, indulge, no one will ever know!" But God's Word says that sexual fantasy about someone you are not married to is nothing less than *adultery* (Matt. 5:28).

Violence

Murders, car crashes, explosions, and shoot-outs are the meat and potatoes of TV's police and detective shows (not to mention the after-school and Saturday-morning cartoons, which will be discussed in the next chapter).

Violence hardly causes us to raise an eyebrow these days. The more calloused we become through repeated exposures on TV and other visual media, the more it takes to shock us when violence is part of the nightly news. We are rapidly becoming desensitized to the point of apathy toward genuine misery and pain.

Then, consider the ever increasing popularity of horror films. Neighborhood video shops do a booming business in these shows where Satan and his works are glorified. The customers are not just teenage boys, either. These videos are also rented in large numbers to young girls for overnight slumber parties. To make matters worse, the already near meaningless age/rating guidelines established by the MPAA (Motion Picture Association of America) are not enforced at thousands of video rental counters. Whether the customer is nine or twenty-nine, most store owners operate by the philosophy, "If he's got the dough, he can watch the show!" Today, we have a generation fed by violence that embraces horrors that just a few years ago we could not have imagined being publicly broadcast.

> *Christians tend to claim some sort of immunity. We falsely assume that because we step into our Sunday-go-to-meeting duds, pack the family into the car, and attend church, televised impurities cannot corrupt us.*

Selfishness

Whether the appetizer, a side order, or the main dish, every item on the television menu is heavily garnished with humanistic selfishness. We are told that we can and should have absolutely everything we want—as soon as we want it. After all, we deserve what we desire. On TV, skilled scriptwriters have redefined sin to the point where an action is only wrong if it obviously hurts someone else, or if the one who commits an illegal act gets caught. Guilt, the natural result of wrongdoing, is presented as a mental distress that you pay a psychiatrist to help you resolve. There is no mention of repentance.

Lust, sexual promiscuity, violence, and selfishness are constant menu items at the Hollywood Diner. The normal network offering is poor nourishment for growing Christians. If anything, it will stunt our growth. No, contemporary television programming is not harmless entertainment bringing usually unoffending or humorous images into our homes. When we don't carefully select what we watch, TV fuels an ungodly way of looking at life. From adventures to sports, from soaps to the news, it delivers—by our own invitation—the images of a depraved and wicked world to our minds and hearts.

But It Doesn't Affect Me

How many of us are compromising God's guidelines for self-gratification and personal convenience? Many parents that demand their children adhere to a rigid nutritional regimen abandon those same children to consume hour after hour of visual "junk food," oblivious to the harm being done.

Sunday School vs. Superheroes

My wife serves as a children's Sunday School teacher at our church. I am always amazed as I observe her late nights of preparation. She carefully chooses the lesson concepts. Then she spends hours searching for just the right pictures to illustrate the Bible story. She designs the craft and song times to complement the story. All this is done with high hopes that the meager sixty minutes she gets with those impressionable little rascals will leave a lasting mark in the wet concrete of their minds. And she is sure that it does, to varying degrees. But she winces when considering the many hours of godless images that will capture their attention during the next six-and-a-half days. How much of Jesus' gentle footprint will still be identifiable after TV's superheroes and supervillains have repeatedly stampeded through the wet concrete that she had so little time to shape?

Christians tend to claim some sort of immunity. We falsely assume that because we step into our Sunday-go-to-meeting duds, pack the family into the car, and attend church, televised impurities cannot

> We must learn to carefully use rather than habitually watch TV.

corrupt us. But that clearly is not the case. We must recognize the awesome power and influence that television has in our lives and in the lives of those around us. TV viewing, which generally seems like an unimportant activity, often done out of boredom, is truly one of the most critical mental battles in which we can choose to participate.

Every time we turn to another daytime talk show or soap opera, a special movie, a sitcom, or even the nightly news, we enter a receptive communion with the images and messages of a blatantly anti-God culture. In the battle of TV viewing, most of us have chosen to lay down our spiritual armor. We have willingly abandoned our defenses and offered ourselves as unprotected targets for the arrows of the evil one. We have based our viewing decisions more on our own personal schedule and habits than on the basis of acceptable program content. And we resist, rationalize, and reject the thought of changing those TV habits.

The decision to love God with all our heart, mind, soul, and strength has practical implications for our use of television. We must learn to carefully *use* rather than habitually *watch* TV. We must train ourselves to be more discriminating in our program selection. And we must be biblically knowledgeable to discern that which honors God from that which shames Him.

If there is nothing on that truly merits the investment of your free time, ask God to help you to rise from your reclined position, walk across the room, and simply push the off button. Then you and your family can invest time in alternate activities that will better serve the Creator's purposes and help you to build a consistent, God-centered worldview.

Watching television through boredom or lack of imagination for other things to do denies the creativity God has given each of us, as well as the infinite diversity of His gifts to us.

5

How TV Affects Children

SEVEN SHOCKING REASONS TO WATCH WHAT KIDS WATCH!

This chapter is dedicated to grown-up kids. It is for those adults who feel that—since they freely watched television when they were young and don't think that they were too negatively affected—TV won't have a significant impact on their children, or on themselves as adults today.

The difference, though, lies in the nature of the programs that were prevalent in the fifties, sixties, and seventies, as compared to now. By and large, today's parents were brought up on wholesome or family-oriented programs that emphasized traditional, Judeo-Christian values. The most worrisome of the shows incorporated hard-to-explain "situation ethics" or just plain stupid (but fun) frivolity.

Today's most popular programs, however, include blatant sexual promiscuity, profanity, coarse joking, and glaring antifamily/anti-Christian plots and subplots. Occultism, extremely graphic violence, and self-indulgent materialism also permeate a huge percentage of Hollywood's offerings. Now more than ever, discretion is essential.

Although what you are about to read is a rather chilling revelation of the "bad fruits" that result from conventional TV management, it is important to remember that *not everything that comes through TV is bad.* Rather, it is overuse and a generally lackadaisical attitude toward the medium *by adults* that so often leads to regrettable results.

It is not our intent to alienate you from your TV. In fact, beginning in the next chapter, there are some refreshing, creative ideas of how you and your family can gain lasting control of and benefit from this valuable communication tool.

> *The average child between two and eleven years old watches over twenty-seven hours of poorly supervised television per week.*

You *can* transform the family TV from a menacing enemy into a beneficial ally! However, because the average child between two and eleven years old watches over twenty-seven hours of poorly supervised television per week, because "the only thing that kids do more than watch television is sleep,"[1] and because we are convinced that most parents are either unaware of or completely calloused to the indecent liberties that modern media take with our children, we implore . . . "*Your attention please!*"

INCREASING CHILDHOOD VIOLENCE

The American Academy of Pediatrics has thoroughly studied the issue of TV violence and its effects on children. As long ago as 1984, their research confirmed some long-assumed realities, including the fact that repeated exposure to televised violence promotes a proclivity to violence and a passive response to its practice. Also, the office of the U.S. surgeon general has investigated the negative effects of television almost as often as it has studied the consequences of cigarette smoking. A *USA Today* article reported, "The government has not insisted yet on labeling television programs with the warning: 'viewing may be dangerous to your mental health,' but that is the inescapable conclusion of massive research."[2]

We have all heard or read a news story about a life-shattering crime committed by some ten-year-old who saw it on TV and thought it would be "fun" to act out himself. It's probably safe to assume that none of the parents of these young terrorists sat their infants in front of a TV with the intention of training them how to kill and maim, rape and brutalize; but the messages were transmitted, and the children were there, antennas up, ready to receive.

Not even a strong Christian home guarantees immunity to violence. Christian parents—who, for the most part, allow the same shows into their homes as their non-Christian neighbors—need to remember that during a youngster's estimated twenty-two thousand hours in front of television by age fourteen (and thousands more in front of video games!), he has witnessed on TV alone the assault on, or destruction, of more than eighteen thousand individuals, usually without any negative consequences. Is it any wonder we see children "playing" violently, cursing, or fighting?

The early evening hours when the most family-oriented shows are supposedly on is really the most violent time on weekday television. Violent acts during prime time (over ten instances per hour) are now surpassed only by the number telecast for the viewing pleasure of impressionable youngsters during Saturday-morning cartoons—an average seventy-six incidents per hour![3]

Dr. Jay Martin of the University of Southern California found that "in a multi-year study of 732 children, conflicts with parents, fighting with peers, and delinquency were correlated with the total number of hours of television viewing." It is troubling to note—especially for childcare operators and parents who let their children watch moderate to large amounts of "only the good stuff"—that the "fundamental correlation is not between aggressive behavior and the viewing of violence on TV. Increases in aggression correlate with *viewing television*, not with viewing violent scenes."[4] While exposure to violent programs desensitizes viewers "to both real violence and victims of vioence,"[5] it is the process of viewing—the number of hours actually viewed—that correlates the main factor with negative behavior.

It appears that the best way to guard against overaggressiveness and interpersonal conflicts is a two-pronged approach. First and most importantly, cut down on the total number of hours viewed. Second, eliminate all violent programs from your TV-viewing diet so that a callousness to pain and suffering is not unnecessarily fostered in the hearts of your children.

DECREASING ACADEMIC PERFORMANCE

Thanks to TV, today's kids are exposed to more information than any other generation in history. But are they smarter for it?

Nationwide, reading scores continue their downward trend. The number of partially illiterate college students continues to climb. Classroom teachers around the world are finding it harder to establish a healthy learning environment, no matter for what age students they are responsible. They are frustrated because the children that they are expected to educate turn off very easily and seem restless and apathetic. Educators are in daily competition with the effects of television and other visual media. Unfortunately, many feel that they are losing or have already lost the struggle to adequately educate and equip tomorrow's leaders.

In a *Parade* magazine article entitled "Why They Excel" (January 21, 1990), author Fox Butterfield discussed the differences in academic achievement between Americans and Asians. Among many other thought-provoking statements, she referred to a study prepared for the United States Department of Education that compared the math and science achievements of twenty-four thousand thirteen-year-olds in the USA, Canada, South Korea, Ireland, Great Britain, and Spain. "One of the findings was that the more time students spent watching television, the poorer their performance. The American students watched the most television. They also got the worst scores in math. Only the Irish students and some of the Canadians scored lower in science." An observation shared by a student at Berkeley should cause most parents to seriously consider the situation in their own homes. This young Korean-American frankly stated, "I don't think Asians are any smarter . . . there are brilliant Americans in my chemistry class. But the Asian students work harder. I see a lot of wasted potential among Americans."

Recent studies suggest that North America is never going to gain ground in trying to catch up with the academic quality of our overseas neighbors by depending on "educational TV." While most parents assume that educational shows are teaching basic skills, and while this is correct to a very limited extent, children who watch these types of shows "tend to solve problems only on the basis of facts or concepts presented . . . whereas children who learn the same materials in a traditional manner solve problems more freely and individually. Decreases in cognition tend to occur whether the program is an adventure show, a comedy, or even an educational program. A broadcast whose subject is how to increase creativity is likely to *decrease* creativity in the viewer."[6]

Educational psychologist Jane Healy says that PBS's *Sesame Street* itself is far from the educational television show it purports to be. "It is truly amazing that everyone seems to have bought the notion that this peripatetic carnival will somehow teach kids to read, despite the fact that the habits of the mind necessary to be a good reader—language, active reflection, persistence and internal control—are exactly what *Sesame Street* does *not* teach."[7] She sees the program, which is "viewed by almost half of all American preschoolers on a weekly basis, as a contributor to a new and growing educational problem: the two-minute mind."[8] Her solution should be shouted from the rooftops: "Parents need to stop rushing lessons (pushing kids into early pre-school instruction) and plugging in to technology. . . . Instead, they need to find ways to involve their children in everyday activities" and "control the use of television in the home."[9]

While attention-grabbing newspaper headlines demand excellence in our nation's classrooms, the evidence that too much television has an adverse effect on scholastic performance is overwhelming. The bottom line is: the more television a child watches, the greater the negative impact on his or her learning and development. Our cries for educational reforms must be matched by reform on the homefront—in our TV-viewing and other electronic-media habits.

DISTORTED VIEW OF SEX AND SEXUALITY

Adults have watched as the minimum moral standards to which network programs must attain have continually declined. The decline has been great, but its effect has been slow enough that the vast majority of Christian adults are no longer shocked or outraged by programs network programmers would never have dared to transmit only a decade earlier. And, as adults become increasingly desensitized to casual sex, so are the children that God has entrusted to their care.

In an effort to broaden and obtain a better selection of programs, the majority of American households now subscribe to cable-TV services. But better control is usually the first benefit that cable-TV subscribers realize *doesn't* come with their monthly service fee. In fact, in a study of 450 sixth graders who watch cable, Oklahoma State University professor Godfrey Ellis found that a staggering 66 percent of the children watched at least one program a month that contained nudity or heavy sexual content.

Where do Christian children develop their weakened moral ideas? A substantial part of the blame can be laid to poor TV management. A child may attend Sunday school for one hour a week, church for two more hours, and never really hear about God's prohibitions regarding premarital sex. But when a child has unlimited access to the world's perspective at the rate of twenty-five to thirty hours per week, which ideas can we expect to have the most influence?

HEFTY INCREASES IN CHILDHOOD OBESITY

In 1984, medical researchers for the American Academy of Pediatrics documented a fact that had long been assumed: television viewing increases consumption of high-calorie snacks and the prevalence of obesity. Research in

While television has a lot to answer for, its exploitation of children may rank at the top of the list.

the 1990s has shown that, compared to the late 1970s, "there has been a 98 percent increase in extreme obesity among children. . . . Obesity has become a near epidemic" afflicting one out of every four youngsters, and about 30 percent of adults.[10]

Still another study—this one sampling 1,077 children between the ages of two and twelve—revealed to the American Heart Association a serious finding about children who watch two to four hours of television a day. For them, there is a *significantly* higher likelihood of high cholesterol levels (above two hundred) than those who watch less than two hours a day.[11]

And a researcher at Memphis State University, Dr. Robert Klesges, found that "children watching TV tend to burn fewer calories per minute—not only fewer than those engaged in active play, but also fewer than those who are reading or 'doing nothing'—in fact, almost as few as children who are sleeping."[12] And the heavier a child is, the more grave the effect. For children of normal weight, "TV-watching triggered a 12 percent (metabolic) drop. . . . The metabolic rates of obese children fell an average 16 percent."[13] Dr. Klesges suggested the obvious: "It seems prudent for people of all ages who have weight problems to curb their time in front of the tube and do something more demanding instead."[14]

COMMERCIALS: A CLASSROOM IN COVETOUSNESS

There are very influential and cunningly deceptive media power brokers out there, hungry in their insatiable desire to garner material wealth. They are obviously willing to sell our kids down a moral and intellectual drain in that process. While television has a lot to answer for, its exploitation of children through commercials may rank at the top of the list.

It is estimated that the average child sees twenty thousand commercials per year. Contrary to adults, who often mute out commercials, or who get up and make a mad dash for the bathroom during the 60 to 180 seconds that they are allotted, children like TV ads. They like to be told what to lobby for, and lobby they do.

When mom tries to pull a tasty, healthful box of cereal from the grocery-store shelf, her hand is held back by a whining, pleading child who is willing, at that moment, to sell his birthright in exchange for a box of colorful, sugar-saturated, puffed flakes. The child makes such an embarrassing scene that— although she knows it is the wrong thing to do—the poor mother finally gives in and throws the doubly expensive box and its "free prize" into the cart. (It lands on top of a plastic container full of vitamin fortified, fruit-flavored sugar water.)

Like their parents, children willingly dance to the puppet strings of Madison Avenue. They buy into and energetically promote the idea that ability and health are products of material consumption. Commercials are the place where sizzle overwhelms substance and where paid liars can get away with anything, provided they *look* honest on camera.

Unfortunately, commercials have all the best of advertising minds, plus frequent repetition going for them. Their lack of intrinsic importance becomes immaterial as these other elements create an overwhelmingly influential message. This is a good reason for Christian families to build a home library of distinctly Christian videos. At the same time, it is a warning to avoid letting children watch shows that carry a large number of commercials directed specifically at them, particularly the Saturday-morning cartoons, which contain about 25 percent more commercials than other programming.

If you are tired of hearing Junior whine all the way through the grocery store, tired of dragging him kicking and screaming from the toy department of the local discount store, *turn off Saturday-*

morning TV. Invest in several of the excellent Christian children's videos now available (see our video reviews and "Author's Choice" picks for suggestions), or go to the park, or just go outside and play a game with your children. In the long run, you have everything to gain and nothing to lose.

IMAGINATIVE PLAY BECOMES TV-PROGRAMMED PASSIVITY

A simple observation of children's free play shows that it is often connected to TV programs. It seems that every little boy wants to play with toys that are connected to popular, violent cartoons. Children run around blasting their friends with imaginary laser bullets through overpriced plastic weapons that they have learned how to use by watching TV.

Toys linked to television, "program" a child to play in a way that is fashioned after the show—whether violent or benign. Children no longer need to envision situations or new worlds; they simply replay last Saturday's cartoons. Imagination is crippled; inventiveness is stunted.

Television has completely altered the way children spend their time. Yesterday's children spent much of their days playing games and exploring the outdoor world around them, but today's children spend their time with their eyes glued to the television screen and their bottoms firmly planted on the living-room rug.

TV has often been identified as a sort of "plug-in drug." This description is really quite accurate. Television gradually narcotizes viewers into passivity. Youngsters who should be outdoors getting bruised, dirty, and exhausted, exercise only their blinking eyelids as they sit entranced, hour after hour, in front of the tube. Dr. Paul Fink of Thomas Jefferson University in Philadelphia has studied childhood viewing habits and concludes that obsession with TV causes children to be more passive and less creative.[14] Evidence also indicates that television interferes with the capacity to entertain oneself and stifles the ability to express ideas logically and sensitively. Television viewing replaces essential play activities with passivity rather than activity. These findings are generally true of adult viewers as well.

NO TIME FOR FAMILY TIME

Daddy won't be home on time tonight; he's working late at the office again. But that's OK; Timmy has the TV! The TV is always there to keep him company. Who needs Dad when the TV is in good working condition?

In his book *Family Issues*, Christian author Bob Larson revealed an alarming finding that should make even the most carefree father sit up and think. He shared that a "Michigan State University study revealed that when four- and five-year-olds were offered the choice between giving up television or their fathers, a third opted to give up daddy."[15] According to another study, "the average five-year-old spends [only] 25 *minutes* a week in close interaction with his father [but] 25 *hours* a week in close interaction with the TV set."[16]

> The girl was heartbroken by the way that television stood between her and her parents, and between her parents and God.

Parents often regret not spending more time with their children. However, in a survey conducted for the Massachusetts Mutual Life Insurance Corporation, "two-thirds of those surveyed say they would probably accept a job that required more time away from home if it offered higher income or greater prestige."[17]

In a *Saturday Evening Post* article, Marie Winn wrote, "The television set casts its magic spell, freezing speech and action, turning the living into silent statues. . . .Turning on the television set can turn off the process that transforms children into people."[18] Poorly managed television wastes opportunities for kids to learn how to relate to other people—including their parents and siblings, and relating with their families is a desire of today's youth. In a nationwide, ethnically balanced survey of 750 ten- to sixteen-year-olds, "three-quarters said that if they had a choice between watching TV or spending time with their families, they'd opt for family time."[19] Instead, in the strong words of one author, "Parents have abused their children in order to benefit themselves, turning the TV set into a constant and convenient baby-sitter."[20]

I'm convinced, however, that the family's loss of control of its time is one of the most perplexing of the problems faced by parents today. We recognize the fact that values completely contrary to those we want our children to absorb are being shot—rapid fire—through the TV set into the living room. We realize that, as the family supper table also succumbs to the chatter of TV noise, hope for a daily period of sharing, caring, and interaction is almost zero. Yet we stay "tuned in" anyway.

> When we put TV ahead of people, it reveals a lot about the value we place on others.

When one considers that the average family now spends almost fifty hours per week with the TV, yet Mom and Dad allot only 27½ minutes during the same week to focus in and talk to each other, it is little wonder that relationships suffer. And when families suffer, our entire nation sees and feels the results.

Children of all ages need adult contact. While a teenager's vehement verbal attacks may suggest otherwise, they need adult/child relationships for reassurance that they are loved and for instruction in the ways of adult society. Author/lecturer Josh McDowell has repeatedly stated that he often has teenagers come to him, convinced that their parents don't love them. When asked why they feel this way, many respond that they just don't feel important. Their parents don't try to spend time with them anymore. In fact, poorly managed TV has become one of the primary impediments to relational richness in millions of American homes.

After a lively meeting where we had been invited to challenge a large group of Christian teens about their TV habits, a teenaged girl shyly came to Karen. The girl was heartbroken by the way that television stood between her and her parents, and between her parents and God. She was convinced that she was not as important to her mom and dad as were their TV sets. This teen actually *wanted* to get closer to her parents. But the way that TV was used in her home made true closeness an all-but-impossible dream. Most disturbing of all, her parents would be surprised, even angry, if anyone were to suggest that maybe TV rated too high a priority in their average Christian family.

If someone in your home wants some uninterrupted time to share some problems or feelings, do you sometimes respond with, "Shhh, I'm watching TV"? That phrase is a strong indication that television is the basic presence, and all others are considered interruptive. When we put TV ahead of people, it reveals a lot about the value we place on others. Remember, children learn from parental example—whether that example is lethargy or caring involvement, love of TV or love of people.

Will you give prime time to your family, friends, and church? Make a commitment for just one or two weeks to change your viewing habits. The pages that follow are designed to equip everyone in your household to do just that. You will find useful suggestions, unique forms, intimate stories, TV-alternative activities, and helpful video evaluations. Now you can finally get the best out of TV, *without letting TV get the best out of you!*

Part III

The TV Habit Repair Kit

6

Evaluating Programs

HOW TO FIND THE GREAT SHOWS
. . . AND ACTUALLY GET YOUR FAMILY
TO CHOOSE THEM!

Most parents would probably agree that the innocent questions of a young child can be extremely convicting. As the father of four inquisitive youngsters, I have been reminded of this embarrassing fact on many occasions. One incident stands out in my memory.

It was the weekend. Time to relax. We had gone to the home of a relative for an evening visit. After a while, I stole away to the already occupied "TV room." Very soon my two-year-old daughter followed the sound of the television straight to where she knew her daddy had to be. She was wearing one of those "I found you!" kind of expressions. You know, it was the sort of victorious smirk kids flaunt once they have spotted a cleverly hidden playmate in hide-and-seek.

Cuddling up onto my lap and resting her tiny head against my chest, we settled back for a bit of visual entertainment. Before long we were both fully engrossed in a fast-moving, suspense-filled science fiction movie. About one hour, a dozen expletives, and several sexual innuendoes into the show, the screen was suddenly filled with a graphic depiction of torturous killing.

I was caught off guard, but I quickly remembered the presence of my tender two-year-old, and I shielded her eyes to protect her from this gruesome sight. Obviously frustrated, she turned to me and asked, "Why you put your hands over my eyes?" Intent on maintaining my composure I calmly responded—in my authoritative, daddy-sounding voice—"Because little girls shouldn't watch bad things like this." But without even a moment's hesitation this little child immediately asked, "Then why *you* watching it?"

Convicted and dumbfounded by the penetrating words and sincere expression of my own young daughter, I quietly responded, "Good question." Together we rose and left the room.

God used that simple experience to challenge me. My own personal TV-viewing selections were often far from wholesome, edifying entertainment. I knew that already. Yet, I also knew that there were positive aspects to some of what I watched. My greatest frustration, though, was with myself. I wanted to be a more consistent example to my wife and children. I earnestly desired to exhibit self-control and to be more discriminating in my program selections. But all the desire in the world did me no good until a simple one-word question could be answered: *"How?"*

SOUND FAMILIAR?

We hope that by this point you, too, are pretty well convinced that the TV set(s) inhabiting your home *must* be dealt with. But *how?* Initiating a battle plan requires practical help. Before you load your TVs into the family car and hurl them from the nearest cliff, learn to discern helpful entertainment from harmful entrapment. Whether you are eight, twenty-eight, or sixty-eight, it's not too late to learn how to benefit from the good that TV has to offer, without being battered by the bad.

DISCUSSING PROGRAMS

We will be best able to transform television viewing into a much more positive and useful experience if we view it with others and get into the habit of discussing what we are seeing, good and bad, in ways that enhance our awareness of the moral and other issues involved. While the thought of discussing TV programs may seem a bit awkward at first, it is well worth the effort. Many harmful effects can be neutralized or lessened when viewers openly discuss and question TV content with each other.

Candid discussions of TV programs often lead to many other opportunities for deeper conversations on a wide variety of topics that aren't likely to come up elsewhere. What begins as a simple comment or question on sub-

> By taking time to watch and talk about programs together, you exhibit loving concern.

jects like morality, corporate ethics, sportsmanship, marital infidelity, and consumerism become gripping discussions that can wonderfully alter what goes into the minds of those sitting in front of the TV.

PROGRAM EVALUATIONS

Envision a youngster pleading to watch a show that you suspect will fall far short of God's expectations for decency or purity. You decide to watch and coevaluate the program with your child. To emphasize the fact that *God* sets the standards (that this is not simply a clash between the "old-fashioned" opinions of parents and the "modern" opinions of a new generation) you turn to God's Word before turning to the channel selector.

Together, you read from such passages as Ephesians 5:3–12, where you are reminded of the need for Christians to remain pure, both physically and mentally. You hand the child a photocopy of the following Program Evaluation Form and request that he turn the show off if and when he feels that it breaches scriptural principles. Your young viewer will enjoy the sense of responsibility and will grow through the new challenge to do what pleases God, rather than himself.

Gregg Lewis, in his ground-breaking book *Telegarbage*, shared that "a junior-high son of one Christian father wanted to watch one of the more explicit adult sitcoms. His father hesitated, then agreed—if they watched it together and if the boy promised to keep a tally of every suggestive or shady line he noticed. Less than halfway into the show, the boy turned to his father and said, 'I see what you mean. I've counted fourteen already. Why don't we turn to something else?' They came to a joint agreement not to watch the program anymore."[1]

While discussion certainly won't remove every negative influence, a combination of quality and quantity control can help to change the family TV from an ominous threat into a much more positive force. By taking time to watch and talk about programs together, you exhibit loving concern. By reminding family members that God's Word (not yours) is the ultimate standard by which our everyday activities are to be judged, you reassure them that you are not simply intent on winning an argument. Rather, you are seeking to fulfill your own God-given responsibilities and to illustrate a practical application of God's Word.

USING THE "PROGRAM EVALUATION FORM"

If we are going to watch television, we must take time to determine the difference between the main plot and the subplots. When the messages are recognized, their power to influence us subconsciously is vastly diminished.

In a movie where the hero is involved in immoral activities, or where good is accomplished by deception, or crude jokes and profanity are used to make us laugh, we need to question the wisdom of watching such actions. We need to remind younger viewers that the actions or language are not appropriate or acceptable in the sight of God, even though the writers are trying to convince us otherwise.

You are encouraged to photocopy the following "Program Evaluation Form" for your personal use. Use an enlarging photocopier to increase the size so that it fills an 8½-by-11-inch piece of paper. Then, store copies in a three-ring notebook, or just keep a few near the TV. For the next several weeks, each time you turn on the TV, pick up an evaluation form. Then, judge the content of the shows that you watch. In a very short time you will see beyond the obvious storyline. You will be amazed at the subplots, biases, questionable actions, and values statements present in almost every form of dramatic media presentation. You will also develop a much greater degree of control over the television set.

However, before shoving a pile of evaluation forms at your family, it would probably be wise to evaluate a few shows on your own. Read the sample form that we have provided toward the end of this chapter to get an idea of what type of data can go in

---

each section. Get comfortable with the form before you try to interest others. If possible, try not to let anyone else know what you are doing.

Curiosity will soon get the best of not only your youngsters (if you have any) but also other adults who happen to be watching with you. Once this happens, respond enthusiastically. If they express interest, ask them to help you spot the items listed on the form.

Begin by outsmarting the advertising executives. Use the commercial breaks as "time-out" periods. Turn off the TV or mute the volume and share with one another exactly what is taking place on the program. Then you might try to evaluate the commercials. Often, they are even more sexually suggestive and materialistic than the program itself. For offensive advertising, write to the product sponsors. Tell them you find their ads tasteless or offensive and that, contrary to inducing you to purchase the product, the nature of the ad has made you determined to avoid it altogether.

Above all, try to be casual about your observations and discussions, especially at first. Try not to intimidate or bombard other viewers with too many questions. Go easy unless you are absolutely convinced that a program is harmful or blatantly inappropriate.

Be forewarned. There is bound to be someone who will complain that discussion while watching TV will intrude on the diversion usually sought by viewers. Be sensitive to this. At first, you may need to reserve in-depth discussions for the commercial breaks or until the show is over. However, use of the Program Evaluation Form, because it encourages the exchange of ideas and opinions, actually begins to *enhance* the pleasure received by all viewers involved. A fuller understanding of all aspects of a program will produce much greater fulfillment, even if the show is not too good.

Finally, there is a side benefit to filling out this form. Because you are actively evaluating the programs, your mind remains active and alert, engrossed in the project at hand. You will eat less junk food! So don't be surprised if you lose a couple of pounds in the first week or so!

WHY NOT JUNK IT?

Why not simply throw away your TV? This is a very good and logical question. In fact, many viewers have followed through with this line of reasoning in a very literal way. A pastor friend of mine once confided that when he was a young boy his father took him, his brother, a sledge hammer, and the family's only TV set into the alley behind their house. The boys watched as their father—at wits' end due to TV content—smashed the television into a shiny junkpile. (And that was in the early 1960s!)

However, the long-term solution to media-related problems does not seem to be that of bashing or banning TV altogether. While those few Christian families that have chosen to live without a television are to be respected for their strong standards, they should also consider the need to sit down with their children and explain their reasons for not having one. After all, a complete, legalistic ban on TV may just avoid or postpone the inevitable problems instead of dealing with them.

Children can usually visit friends to watch whatever they want. Many grow up, get married, and buy a TV for their own homes without ever developing discernment or good judgment on how to use or control it. (By the way, my friend's father eventually replaced the set that he had destroyed. In fact, the same father is now a retired grandpa with *five* television sets!)

> *Rather than junking our TVs, the best solution seems to be that of training ourselves and our children to exercise biblical, moral judgment and quantity control.*

Rather than junking our TVs, the best solution seems to be that of training ourselves and our children to exercise biblical, moral judgment and quantity control.

As TV reviewers, your family will learn to look carefully at the shows—and at other issues in life. They will begin to discern and discriminate and will have practice in putting their ideas into words. Best of all, they will start to realize that every statement, every hand gesture, every joke, is intentional. Every moment of TV content has been designed to communicate a specific message.

We've designed the following form to help you and your family to be alert enough to discern just what that message is—and the effect it's having on our society.

As promised, here is the sample Program Evaluation Form, completed by the authors during and after viewing *Baby Boom*.

PROGRAM EVALUATION FORM

THIS FORM IS DESIGNED TO AID IN EVALUATING THE CONTENT OF TV PROGRAMS, VIDEOCASSETTES, THEATER MOVIES AND LIVE STAGE SHOWS.

Title of Show: *Baby Boom*

Name of this Episode: —

Date Viewed: *1-23*

Evaluated and Viewed by: *Dale — KM, MT, AJ, KMM*

Time Began: *7:30* AM/PM

Time Ended: *9:20* AM/PM

If Film or Video (Rating): *PG-13*

If TV Show (Network): —

SECTION ONE: Complete this portion while show is in progress. Try to involve other viewers by asking for help in spotting the following items.

PROFANITY
Ephesians 4:29 & 5:4, James 5:12

1	2	3	4	5	6	7	8	9	10	11	12	13	14	15	16	17	18	19	20
✓	✓	✓	✓	✓	✓														

VIOLENCE
Psalm 101:3-4, Galatians 5:19-26

	1	2	3	4	5	6	7	8	9	10	11	12	13	14
FIST FIGHTS / KNIFINGS	∅													
GUNFIRE / EXPLOSIONS	∅													
RAPE / INCEST	∅													
MURDER / KILLING	∅													
OTHER VIOLENCE	∅													

Why are you still watching this lousy program?

SEXUALLY SUGGESTIVE CLOTHING (or Lingerie)
I Timothy 2:9

1	2	3	4	5	6	7	8	9	10	11	12	13	14	15	16	17	18	19	20

NUDITY or SEXUAL INTERCOURSE (Implied or Explicit)
Ephesians 5:3

– TYPE OF RELATIONSHIP –	1	2	3	CONTEXT(s)
PREMARITAL (Fornication)	✓	✓	✓	star w/ veterinarian,
EXTRA-MARITAL (Adultery)				w/ boyfriend, "nanny"
ALTERNATIVE (Homosexuality)				w/ sailor
RAPE				
WITHIN MARRIAGE				

OCCULT PRACTICES (Magic Spells, Witchcraft, etc.)
Deuteronomy 18:10-14, Leviticus 20:6

1	2	3	4	5	6	7	8	9	10	11	12	13	14	15	16	17	18	19	20

OTHER ACTIONS OR STATEMENTS OF DISRESPECT TO GOD, OR TO CHRISTIANITY
Galatians 6:7, Isaiah 45:23b-24

① Potential adoptive parents who refer to "pastor friend" (to align them w/ Christians?) are backward fanatics. ② Shows a potential nanny as weird Christian in a comical job-interview scene.

SECTION TWO: To be completed immediately after viewing, even if you are unable to complete Section One. Attempt to involve all viewers.

WHAT PROMPTED YOU TO VIEW THIS PARTICULAR SHOW?

_____ Unplanned. Just bored and flipping through the channels.

_____ This was a rented video tape. The label caught my attention as I browsed in the video store.

_____ Saw advertisement in newspaper or during another show.

✓ Pressure from family or friends who wanted to see this show.

✓ Recommended by a friend.

✓ Other _wanted to see a movie. This was recommended._

BASIC / SURFACE PLOT (most obvious storyline): _"Yuppie" female is forced to quit her great-paying executive position after she becomes bonded to "inherited niece. Leaves big city to live in the country. Meets man, starts successful business, decides to run her national enterprise from country home and be mommy too._

SUBPLOTS (the less obvious storylines or values statements): _① Sex before marriage is glorified. ② Living together is good ③ Don't feel guilty about selfishness ④ Christians are either legalistic, backward, fanatical — or all three!_

OVERALL GENERAL IMPRESSION	Ephesians 5.15-17. Philippians 4.8		
		YES	NO
1. Did you seriously consider an alternative activity before viewing this show?			✓
2. Would Jesus, your parents, or your spouse approve of your viewing of this show?			✓
3. Was this show "pure, lovely, praiseworthy"?			✓
4. Do you now think that you should have more earnestly pursued an alternative activity?		✓	

MISCELLANEOUS COMMENTS: _We took both of our young children based on recommendation of good friends that they "have never seen a cleaner show!" DECISION → Never take kids to a PG-13 film. There was no blatant nudity, but it was very effectively implied. Teaches godless morals._

OTHER SUGGESTIONS:

- COMPARE EVALUATIONS AND ANSWERS - Have each viewer complete a Program Evaluation Form as they watch the same show. Compare. It can be very interesting to see the same show, but to understand its messages differently.

- WHEN AT A THEATRE MOVIE - Try to sit far enough away from other audience members so that your writing doesn't become a distraction. Always complete Section Two as soon as possible upon completion of the show, even if there was not enough light to complete Section One while at the theatre. (Excellent discussion starter if you go out for refreshments afterwards!)

IMPORTANT! Trying to be careful about what they view, friends and relatives often ask for comments about theatre movies. By completing this form while the story is still fresh in your mind you will be able to give a much more fair endorsement or caution to those who ask.

PROGRAM EVALUATION FORM

THIS FORM IS DESIGNED TO AID IN EVALUATING THE CONTENT OF TV PROGRAMS,
VIDEOCASSETTES, THEATER MOVIES AND LIVE STAGE SHOWS.

Title of Show _____ Name of this Episode _____ Date Viewed _____

Evaluated and Viewed by _____

_____ AM/PM   _____ AM/PM   If Film _____   If TV _____
Time Began   Time Ended   or Video   (Rating)   Show   (Network)

SECTION ONE: Complete this portion while show is in progress. Try to involve other viewers by asking for help in spotting the following items.

PROFANITY   Ephesians 4:29 & 5:4, James 5:12

1	2	3	4	5	6	7	8	9	10	11	12	13	14	15	16	17	18	19	20

VIOLENCE   Psalm 101:3-4, Galatians 5:19-26

	1	2	3	4	5	6	7	8	9	10	11	12	13	14
FIST FIGHTS / KNIFINGS														
GUNFIRE / EXPLOSIONS											*Why are you*		
RAPE / INCEST											*still watching*		
MURDER / KILLING											*this lousy*		
OTHER VIOLENCE											*program?*		

SEXUALLY SUGGESTIVE CLOTHING (or Lingerie)   I Timothy 2:9

1	2	3	4	5	6	7	8	9	10	11	12	13	14	15	16	17	18	19	20

NUDITY or SEXUAL INTERCOURSE (Implied or Explicit)   Ephesians 5:3

– TYPE OF RELATIONSHIP –	1	2	3	CONTEXT(s)
PREMARITAL (Fornication)				
EXTRA-MARITAL (Adultery)				
ALTERNATIVE (Homosexuality)				
RAPE				
WITHIN MARRIAGE				

OCCULT PRACTICES (Magic Spells, Witchcraft, etc.)   Deuteronomy 18:10-14, Leviticus 20:6

1	2	3	4	5	6	7	8	9	10	11	12	13	14	15	16	17	18	19	20

OTHER ACTIONS OR STATEMENTS OF DISRESPECT TO GOD, OR TO CHRISTIANITY   Galatians 6:7, Isaiah 45:23b-24

SECTION TWO: To be completed immediately after viewing, even if you are unable to complete Section One. Attempt to involve all viewers.

WHAT PROMPTED YOU TO VIEW THIS PARTICULAR SHOW?

____ Unplanned. Just bored and flipping through the channels.
____ This was a rented video tape. The label caught my attention as I browsed in the video store.
____ Saw advertisement in newspaper or during another show.
____ Pressure from family or friends who wanted to see this show.
____ Recommended by a friend.
____ Other _____

BASIC / SURFACE PLOT (most obvious storyline): _____

_____

_____

_____

_____

_____

SUBPLOTS (the less obvious storylines or values statements): _____

_____

_____

_____

_____

_____

OVERALL GENERAL IMPRESSION Ephesians 5:15-17, Philippians 4:8	YES	NO
1. Did you seriously consider an alternative activity before viewing this show?		
2. Would Jesus, your parents, or your spouse approve of your viewing of this show?		
3. Was this show "pure, lovely, praiseworthy"?		
4. Do you now think that you should have more earnestly pursued an alternative activity?		

MISCELLANEOUS COMMENTS: _____

_____

_____

_____

_____

_____

OTHER SUGGESTIONS:

• *COMPARE EVALUATIONS AND ANSWERS - Have each viewer complete a Program Evaluation Form as they watch the same show. Compare. It can be very interesting to see the same show, but to understand its messages differently.*

• *WHEN AT A THEATRE MOVIE - Try to sit far enough away from other audience members so that your writing doesn't become a distraction. Always complete Section Two as soon as possible upon completion of the show, even if there was not enough light to complete Section One while at the theatre. (Excellent discussion starter if you go out for refreshments afterwards!)*

IMPORTANT! *Trying to be careful about what they view, friends and relatives often ask for comments about theatre movies. By completing this form while the story is still fresh in your mind you will be able to give a much more fair endorsement or caution to those who ask.*

7

Taking a Personal Viewing Inventory

HOW MUCH DO YOU REALLY WATCH?

Ask a mountaineer why he feels compelled to scale the face of a sheer precipice and he replies, "Because it's there!" Many TV owners turn the tube on for the same reason.

For the majority of TV viewers, habit dictates action. Chances are, you, and some of the members of your family, fit into this ever-growing category.

READ THE WARNING SIGNS

Honestly answer this simple test to self-inspect your TV tradition. A yes response to any one of the following questions should serve as a warning flag that improvement is needed. Answering yes to three questions strongly indicates that you should seriously reevaluate your viewing habits.

Most women are surprised after answering these questions. In fact, female viewers often need to improve their viewing habits even more urgently than the rest of the family.

While researching the viewing habits of women, I discovered the results of one survey that made me chuckle—momentarily.

QUESTION	YES	NO
Do I frequently turn the television on without knowing what I'm going to watch, flipping through the channels to find the most appealing show that happens to be available at the moment?		
Do I frequently fail to turn off a program that is uninteresting or offensive?		
Do I usually leave the set on when someone comes to visit?		
Do I sometimes keep the TV on during meals with others?		

Forty-one percent of the readers of *Glamour* magazine consider themselves to be "couch potatoes." In answering a *Glamour* survey, the women admitted that they aren't exactly positive role models in the area of TV management.[1] It is Mom that watches more TV (thirty-two hours a week) than anyone else in the family.[2] And according to Nielson Media Research, grandmas are the champion couch potatoes; they log an average of more than forty-four hours per week.[3]

And yet, positive role models are exactly what the younger members of our households so desperately need. Children are profoundly influenced by the adults in their lives. If Mom or Dad tends to watch television recklessly and/or extensively, the children will follow that model.

WHAT ARE YOU MISSING?

In one study, researchers mounted cameras on top of TV sets and recorded the amount of time viewers also read, talked, walked in and out of the room, and so forth. They concluded that viewers actually watch only 55 percent of what is on.[4] Television jabber often serves as a background during other activities such as doing homework, housework, cooking, or balancing the checkbook. In most homes, having the set on has become a routine, a habit.

The sheer amount of time spent with the TV on is important not only because of the potential harm, but also because of the many good possibilities missed. For most of us, our heavy investment in television viewing is a bad deal. It squanders our time. What we get in terms of entertainment and information does not sufficiently make up for what we give up in terms of ordinary life.

When the TV is on, we usually don't talk with family and friends in depth about subjects of great importance. Our reading—aside from thoroughly studying *TV Guide*—is distracted and superficial. We don't fix the roof or play softball with the kids outdoors. We don't spend quality time thinking or planning. We don't gather for family devotions. We don't benefit from quiet times with our Creator. First Corinthians 6:12 challenges us, "'Everything is permissible for me'—but not everything is beneficial. 'Everything is permissible for me'—but I will not be mastered by anything."

Regardless of who we are, we have duties to perform, people to care for, and our God to know better. It stands to reason, then, that if our lives and responsibilities are important, the time God gives us on this earth must be important too. We should frequently ask ourselves if spending time with the TV might be costing more than we should be willing to spend. If we are to experience the depth and richness of life as God intends it, we need to pursue the things that God might want us to do, rather than constantly pursuing the things that we want for ourselves.

> *We need to pursue the things that God might want us to do, rather than constantly pursuing the things that we want for ourselves.*

KEEPING A VIEWING INVENTORY

It is very helpful to have a visual "snapshot" of the way that TV is used in your home. This is where the Viewing Inventory Form can be so helpful. Adults usually underestimate the number of hours that they and their family spend in front of the set. Those who keep a running record for a week or more are generally surprised at how quickly the hours add up.

Admittedly, there are times when we need to just stop and do nothing, and television viewing certainly fills that need well. However, the question is: Do we need to do nothing for several hours every day?

Generally speaking, the following table defines your skills in TV management, assuming that you are reasonably healthy and that the only shows viewed are of a wholesome, scripturally acceptable nature. (Filling out a Program Evaluation Form from the previous chapter will help you to be better at deciding what is acceptable and what is not.)

HOW DO YOU RATE?

Hours spent per person per week with the TV on	Type of Viewer
0–7	EXCELLENT, provided that the shows you choose are wholesome.
8–14	ACCEPTABLE, but moderate cutbacks are advised
15–21	HEAVY USER, significant and immediate changes are needed.
22 or more	ADDICT! Bad news. For you, TV is more than a crutch; it is a wheelchair! You are missing out on the fullness of life as God designed, and probably causing others to miss out as well. Take this warning *very* seriously.

Although our chart classifies viewers who watch no more than seven hours per week as "excellent" TV managers, this in no way means that one must meet some sort of quota every day. If you find yourself feeling compelled to watch TV daily—even for just one hour—you may be controlled by it.

As the owner of this book, you have our permission to photocopy the following form for the use of your family. In fact, we strongly encourage you to do so! By using an enlarging photocopier and then posting a full-size (8½-by-11) Viewing Inventory Form in some prominent place—on the refrigerator, the living-room coffee table, taped to the TV set, etc.—you can keep track of every minute that your TV is on. Do this for at least one full week, preferably three or four. Heavy viewers (those who find themselves in either of the last two categories) will have to write small or use more than one chart to record *honestly* everything that they watch.

The simple act of consistently filling out this form encourages preselection of programs over channel scanning. It also helps to cut down on the amount of time the TV is on but not really watched.

After reading the next chapter and initiating some of the suggestions listed there, complete another Viewing Inventory Form. You will be encouraged at how quickly and dramatically even deeply entrenched viewing habits can improve!

The One Week

VIEWING INVENTORY
A DAILY LOG OF HOURS SPENT WITH THE TELEVISION ON

DATE		NAME OF TV SHOW (or video)	TIME BEGAN	TIME ENDED	TOTAL
	MONDAY				
	TUESDAY				
	WEDNESDAY				
	THURSDAY				
	FRIDAY				
	SATURDAY				
	SUNDAY				
		TOTAL NUMBER OF HOURS THAT THE TV WAS ON DURING THIS ONE-WEEK PERIOD			

HOW DO YOU RATE?

Hours spent per person
per week with TV on

Type of Viewer ★

0 - 7 _ _ _ _ _	**EXCELLENT** TV Manager
8 - 14 _ _ _ _ _	**ACCEPTABLE,** Moderate cutbacks helpful
15 - 21 _ _ _ _ _	**HEAVY USER,** Serious cutbacks needed
22 - or more _ _ _ _ _	**ADDICT! / Terrible TV Manager** Urgent restructuring necessary!

★ Assuming that all programs viewed are of a scriptually acceptable nature.
(Refer to chapter 3 for biblical guidelines.)

Your Name _____

8

The Withdrawal-Symptoms "Survival Guide"

TEN GREAT IDEAS THAT REALLY WORK!

If you have decided to begin restructuring your personal or family television-viewing habits, congratulations! You are about to join the ranks of a select group.

Only a small fraction of the scores of millions who need to change are actually willing to admit the need, even to themselves; but for those who have learned how to exercise better TV management, they consider the rewards—relational, emotional, spiritual, and financial—immeasurably worth the struggle it entailed. But consider this note of reality from one who has been there: it isn't easy, especially as your changes are being initiated.

For most of us, television is deeply entrenched in our lives. This didn't happen overnight; it took years. As a result, our habits regarding its use are not easily modified. In fact, Dr. Pierre Mornell, a California psychiatrist and knowledgeable researcher on this subject, says that if you are used to having the TV on several hours a day, "getting rid of it cold turkey is likely to cause a seizure."[1] While his overstatement may make us chuckle, almost everyone who has seriously undertaken to limit TV viewing to an average of about an hour a day has had to cope with the symptoms of withdrawal.

How long these symptoms last and how severe they will be is unpredictable. They assail in various ways, often showing up as: extreme nervousness, moroseness, depression, apathy, appetite loss, excessive withdrawal into sleep, and others.

While most adults can imagine these types of symptoms in children, they are not limited to youngsters. Several years ago, the Society for Rational Psychology, a German organization, paid volunteers to abstain from television for a year, and they discovered that adults also suffer TV withdrawal.[2]

During the period of readjustment, some families will experience more conflict, more stress, and more tension. But be encouraged. *The long-term rewards are well worth the short-term struggle!* And to give you the winning advantage, this chapter contains ten practical strategies to help ease the symptoms that we've just described.

PREPARING FOR VICTORY

Satan doesn't want you to be selective in your use of television. Remember, he's the prince of the power of the air—and, today, all too often the air*waves*. He has worked hard to cultivate a generation of remote control-clutching men, women, and children. Our adversary won't give up without a struggle. He knows that his years of striving to "hook" us on inane sitcoms, sexually explicit dramas, afternoon soaps and chat shows, weekend sportscasts, and violent or occult-oriented children's cartoons will be a failure if *you* choose to take the steps necessary to restructure *your* prime time.

At the risk of sounding overly spiritual, we encourage you to begin by resolving in prayer before the Lord (preferably as an entire household) that you will strive to watch only those programs that measure up to the biblical directives set forth in God's Word. Refer again to chapter 3 of this book and to the Bible references included on the Program Evaluation Form at the end of chapter 6 for help in establishing a biblical foundation for your use of the TV.

Next, and this is very important, ask someone you can depend on—your spouse, your parents, a close friend, Sunday school teacher, pastor, even your children—to pray for you. Give them a copy of this book. Ask that they read it and that they help you by holding you accountable, checking periodically to see how well you are doing.

If you are married and your spouse has not yet come to the same determination to restructure his (or her) television-viewing habits, politely, and in love, ask him to read this book. By doing so, your spouse will more fully understand why you are doing what you are and how he can best help you.

How My Life Has Changed

My own attempt to restructure a deeply imbedded TV habit initially met with frequent frustration. It has taken time, prayer, and a lot of searching for help in my struggle. Again and again, my good intentions have failed and confirmed the well-known adage that "old habits die hard."

> *Redirecting my desire to watch TV proved to be extremely difficult. Everything else seemed like work when compared to the effortlessness of sitting down with the remote control.*

I might go several days, even a week or more, but eventually a night would come when I would give in to the same old temptation. Following Karen to our bedroom, I would kiss her goodnight and assure her that "I'll be in in just a few minutes." Then, after creating a bountiful Dagwood sandwich, I would find myself drawn into the same selection of late-night viewing options as millions of others. *I'll just keep the set on until I finish my midnight snack* was my usual logic. However, when the snack was gone, all too often I would lay a throw pillow on the coffee table, prop my big feet where I knew they shouldn't stay, and tune in shows that I knew I shouldn't see.

Redirecting my desire to watch TV proved to be extremely difficult. *Everything* else seemed like work when compared to the effortlessness of sitting down with the remote control. I discovered that I had gotten so used to triggering the on button as soon as I came through the door at the end of each work day that I had all but forgotten the innumerable other, more rewarding, things to do. The problem was that the last thing that I was likely to do when I felt like watching TV was to get creative and try to think of something else. None of the books or articles I read had prepared me for the struggle that is experienced when a viewer begins to realign his or her evening and weekend hours.

But slowly—at first reluctantly—I began to insert other activities where TV once was. Rather than turning to the evening news as soon as I got home, God led me to a series of Christian novels that I began to read to Karen as she finished making dinner. Rather than running for the *TV Guide* as soon as the last morsel had been consumed from my dinner plate, I carried my plate to the kitchen. (I discovered that wives often give great hugs if husbands help clean up the supper dishes!) Then, rather than turning up the volume to quiet (or drown out) a bored baby, I found that unfolding the stroller and strapping in a diaper-clad damsel for a family walk usually calmed even the most frantic cries for attention. And those evening strolls eventually led me to a determination to exercise more frequently.

In effect, what I learned was that simply telling myself that my use of the TV should be restructured was not enough of an incentive to keep me true to my goal. Without more *appealing* activities, I inevitably fell back into the same old rut. I had leaned on TV to fill my "free time" for far too long, so I needed ideas for entertaining alternatives and reminders of responsibilities. Karen could sense this need and began to compile a list of "TV Alternatives" that we kept handy and could easily scan whenever we felt the urge to turn to the tube. Section 4 of this book lists some of Karen's ideas. We're sure you'll have more of your own.

Yes, we still watch TV. We strongly considered trashing it, but instead we learned how to turn it off—and to turn it back on only when a show that we especially want to see is scheduled to be aired. We thank God that TV is now a *tool* rather than a *crutch.*

WITHDRAWAL SYMPTOMS SURVIVAL METHODS

Because we know that the pull of the TV can be very intense, we strongly suggest that you initiate at least two or three of the following methods for surviving the initial symptoms of TV withdrawal. All of the ideas are viable, and most will cost you little or no money to do.

Method 1: Assemble a "Survival Kit"

This is the most basic and probably the most practical way to ensure victory as you struggle to modify the use of television in your home. Simply grab a cardboard box and fill it with as many of the following items as you have on hand. Organize it as neatly as possible and then place it in the TV room. Its very presence suggests that something other than TV be turned to throughout the day. Make sure that it is easily accessible (how about atop or in front of the TV?) and be sure to praise those who use it.

The TV survival kit suggested contents:

1. Coloring books
2. Crayons, colored pencils, or markers
3. Three-Ring notebook with sections for:
   - blank Program Evaluation forms
   - blank Viewing Inventory forms
   - "Fun Things to-do" lists with suggestions of activities that you know the members of your family will enjoy
   - "Chores to-do" checklists, reminding each child of required household duties
   - names and phone numbers of people whom you would like to get together with for non-TV activities
4. This book, with the "TV-Free Activities" section clearly marked
5. Craft projects
   - model car, airplane, ship, rocket, etc.
   - needlework, mending needs, craft kit
6. Craft and handyman magazines
7. Stationery (or other writing paper)
8. Envelopes, with stamps already attached
9. Tape recorder
10. Blank Cassettes (on which to compose "audio letters")
11. Recorded audio cassettes
    - Christian music
    - dramatized stories
    - Bible on tape
    - sermons
    - favorite speakers
12. Bible
13. Bible Study Workbook(s)
14. Christian novels (C. S. Lewis, Frank Perretti, Janette Oke, etc.)

15. Children's storybooks

16. Radio (pretuned to a Christian or other "parent approved" station)

17. Jigsaw puzzles (for various skill levels)

18. Board games

19. Raffle tickets (to be used as described in the "Twenty Tickets" section that follows)

20. Photographs and an empty photo album (Start filing some of those photos you never seem to get to!)

Method 2: Twenty Tickets

Dr. James Dobson, one of America's most prominent advocates for the family, has suggested—and we have modified—a system to help bring about better control of television. In *Focus on the Family* magazine, Dr. Dobson has repeatedly endorsed a very practical, easy-to-initiate plan to monitor the *quality* of programs that a family watches; regulate the *quantity* of television they see; and include the entire family in establishing a TV policy.

In essence, the enhanced "system" is this: first, adults sit down, with or without their children (depending upon ages, and personalities) and select a list of parent-approved programs and videos that are appropriate for each age level in the home. Use your local newspaper's TV schedule to help create this list.

Next, highlight the approved shows, or write them down and tape your list on the refrigerator or somewhere else where it can be easily referred to throughout the week.

Finally, buy a roll of inexpensive raffle tickets (large colorful rolls are available from any business-supply or party-supply store for just a few dollars) or make a stack of your own by using 3-by-5 cards. Issue twenty tickets to each member of the household each week for at least a month. It is very important that mom and dad participate too.

Each ticket can be used to buy up to thirty minutes of approved viewing. When someone has "spent" his twenty tickets, he has completed his television and video viewing for that week. The beauty of this system is that it reduces parental nagging and encourages individual responsibility. Viewers automatically become more careful about choosing what programs to sit in front of because they realize that they only have a limited number of tickets (and time) to invest.

Twenty tickets at thirty minutes each represents a maximum of ten hours per person, per week. That is a good target amount, but don't be too rigid or legalistic. And be sure that your younger children actually understand that the twenty tickets will be replaced with twenty more next week.

When Karen and I first introduced this system, our four-year-old daughter misunderstood the concept and thought that the initial twenty tickets were all she would get for the rest of her life! Unfortunately, I was oblivious to this misunderstanding. One evening early in the week, after my daughter had already spent two or three of her twenty tickets, I came into the family room where she was playing and I sat down to watch the news. (Yes, I paid a ticket!) Knowing that the rule was that *everyone* who watched a program had to pay a ticket, and not wanting to use another ticket from her "lifetime" supply of twenty, she *ran* to me and begged that I turn off the set. Once I realized that she was trying to budget twenty tickets over the next seventy years I was able to calm her. And all of a sudden, twenty tickets per week sounded extremely generous.

An added incentive for children not to use all the tickets is to "pay" them something for each one that is returned unused. The rewards could range from a nickel or so for each ticket (depending on their age), to a special dessert one evening, or an extra-special family outing (roller skating, bowling, camping, visiting a museum) for saving of a certain number of unused tickets over a two-, three- or four-week period.

Method 3: The Exercise Connection

Many families already have one. If yours doesn't, just visit a few rummage sales next weekend. It's an exercise bicycle! Slightly modified and connected to your television via an automobile alternator and twelve-volt car battery, you can pedal up some watts right in your own living room!

This has got to be one of the most unique (and harder to initiate) methods yet devised to improve the way that families watch TV. However, it is guaranteed both to encourage selective viewing and to improve the viewer's physical fitness! Every minute that the set is on must first be "earned" by riding the bike to store energy in the battery. The TV then draws its electric current from the battery.

A set of plans that explains the set-up is as close as your local library. Go to the reference desk and ask for the microfiche for the March/April 1981 *Mother Earth News*. On page 134 you will see an article entitled "Cycle Power, Part II." In addition to diagrams and parts lists, the article even describes how to build an exercise bike from scratch. This is a great way to "exercise" self-control for your family's TV-viewing habits. It is also a super science-fair project for any child who enjoys a challenge!

Method 4: The Switch

The switch is sure to be a discussion starter when friends come to visit. This is a nice looking, inexpensive, little key-lock device that you plug the TV power cord into. Special screws seal the back of the 3-by-5 inch unit shut and make this device almost impenetrable for the average child. And Mom and Dad get to hold an actual "key" to the TV (or to the stereo, video games, or computer). Once the TV—or any other small electrical appliance—is plugged into the switch, the appliance cannot be energized unless the key is inserted and turned to the on position.

While our own family uses the switch only rarely, we found it beneficial in our home in that it forced us to think twice before just habitually turning on the TV. Also, we've had friends share that they have locked the TV off when a new baby-sitter—whose TV morals they just didn't know much about—was coming over. The Switch is especially popular among parents of latchkey children—the kids who spend unsupervised hours at home before Mom or Dad return from work.

If this handy device sounds like a good idea for your family, or for someone you care about, contact the manufacturer for ordering information.[3]

Method 5: Two-Week Shutdown

It is often much easier to manage TV if it is initially completely out of reach for a reasonable period of time. Unplug your set(s), turn it toward the wall, even remove it to a closet, outdoor storage shed, or a neighbor's garage.

If you have children, be sure to have a family conference during which you explain why you are taking what will undoubtedly appear as a drastic step. Admit your own misuse (if applicable), and commit to your goal of being a much better example in the future.

When the TV is reintroduced into the household, limiting the amount of time it is on and determining what programs are allowed to be viewed will be an easier task. Going from no TV to some TV is usually much better than cutting back from limitless viewing to your totally new standards. Also, the family will know that it is actually possible to live without this modern technology and will probably try some new or forgotten activities.

Method 6: TV-Viewing Contract

I was excited to read about a grade school principal who organized an amazingly successful week of TV abstinence in her school of 270 students. Mrs. Pat Sumrow of Edison School in Elmhurst, Illinois, used a simple TV-Viewing contract that was sent home with her students. Almost 250 of her 270 students committed to stop watching TV for one week by signing the contract and by getting one of their parents to sign too. An adult signature space was included on the form so that teachers were assured that someone from home would help the young people stay true to their goal. The incentive for the students: a slumber party for all successful abstainers, chaperoned by PTA members and teachers. Over 99 percent actually made it through the week TV-free!

You may want to try to interest your child's teacher or principal in a similar challenge. Or, you can design a scaled-down version in which you try to interest your child's primary playmates. Offer to take your child and any of his or her friends on a weekend campout, water skiing, or some other activity if they can go without turning on the TV for any reason (including videos and electronic games) for, say, two weeks.

The positive peer pressure generated by a challenge such as this is very beneficial, especially if you initiate the "Two-Week Shutdown" mentioned previously. We have designed a suggested contract that is especially well suited for high school and junior high age students. It is included at the end of this chapter. Feel free to photocopy and use ours, or design your own.

Method 7: Inconvenience Yourself

If your TV is a lightweight or portable model, consider clearing a semipermanent place for it on a laundry-room shelf or in some other inconvenient location. Remove it from this spot only when there is a program on that is worthy of your attention. Return it to the storage place immediately after the show is over.

If the TV is too large or too heavy to move, unplug it, cover it, and use it as a table for a nice flower arrangement. This way you are forced to think twice before watching whatever happens to be on at that moment. If an on switch is not immediately available every time you enter the room, you will be less inclined to simply sit down and start watching.

Method 8: Bare "Essentials"

Unless you have an incapacitated person in your home, or some other very unique situation, you probably don't need more than one television set. Yet, an amazingly high percentage of us clutter the kitchen counter, the bedroom, the living room, even garage workbenches with a wide variety of TV sets. Some have stereo speakers in oak cabinets. Some are nothing more than cheap, neon-colored plastic, but all are capable of exerting almost inescapable magnetism toward those around them.

People give varying reasons for having multiple sets in the home. The most common justification is that additional TV sets are more convenient. But the bottom line is, do these extra TVs strengthen our fragile lines of communication, or do they further separate us? Do they tempt us to watch more TV than we should? Is any amount of convenience that they bring worth the price of the relationships in our home?

By selling all of your extra televisions and video players, the programs that enter your home can be regulated much more easily. Also, the money that you receive can be used to pay bills, donate to needy families, take the family on vacation, give to a ministry that is involved in strengthening the family, give to your church, or to reinvest in board games, books, wholesome videos, uplifting music tapes, and so on.

When you think about it, having TVs scattered throughout your home is about as foolish as a dieter stashing chocolate bars everywhere. You are destined to endure an undending struggle until the number of sets in your home can be counted on a single finger.

Method 9: Accountability

As mentioned earlier in this chapter, the act of making yourself accountable to a friend or family member can be very helpful. Let someone else know that you are setting out to change the way that you watch TV. Ask them to hold you accountable by:

- checking weekly to see if you are keeping track of the number of hours and types of programs you view
- ensuring that you are discussing with your children/spouse/friend the messages of the shows that you and they are watching
- talking about new activities you have tried during the week.
- sharing what you have learned through personal prayer and scripture reading that week

You may even want to ask your friend to join you in this endeavor to improve TV-related habits

Method 10: Keep This Book Handy!

This book has been designed to provide you with the essential tools (forms, TV alternatives, and video evaluations) for your ongoing endeavor to restructure your TV-viewing habits. Don't file it away on a bookshelf once your initial reading is finished. Keep it handy!

Finally, we designed the "TV-Viewing Contract" that appears on the next page specifically for use with older children and teens. Feel free to photocopy and use it as is, or use it as a basis upon which to develop one for your own situation (for example, include a personal computer or multimedia games if you deem it appropriate for the children in your care).

The Movie, Video, Home Computer, and
TV-VIEWING CONTRACT

I hereby promise that I will strive to be an excellent TV user.
In addition to viewing TV for no more than the number of hours
listed below, I will, with encouragement from the "witness"
signed hereunder, restructure my viewing choices to reflect
my commitment to live in a way that is
truly pleasing and honorable to God.

To that end, I, _____,
do hereby pledge before the undersigned witness that beginning on _____ and continuing for _____ week(s)
therefrom, I will take control of what and how much I watch, and
I will seek out and involve myself in TV-alternative/TV-free activities. I will view no more than _____ hours per week (0 to 7
hours).

I understand that this commitment includes not only television programs but also video movies and video and computer
games both at my home and at any other location.

Signature _____ Witness _____

Date _____ Date _____

AFFIRMATION OF CONTRACT FULFILLMENT

I hereby certify that (full name) _____ Age _____
has achieved fulfillment of the stipulations of this TV contract.

Signature of confirmor: _____

Relationship: _____ Date _____
Father, mother, friend, etc.

9

Changing the VCR from Foe to Friend

Five decades have gone by since TV ownership became afford-able for the average American. During that time, corporate research and development divisions have been very busy—and very productive.

The electronic technologies integral to TV and its related gad-getry have improved *dramatically*. Perfectly clear, full-color pic-tures have replaced fuzzy black-and-white haze. Full-wall visual-entertainment systems now dwarf the typical seven-inch TV screen of the 1950s. Digitized stereo cacophony has supplanted the crackling of the original in-cabinet speakers. Cable TV wires supplying dozens of channels now snake their way through our neighborhoods and into the living rooms of 70 percent of Amer-ican households; and ever-smaller satellite dishes, originally most popular in rural and mountainous areas where normal housetop antenna reception is poor, now dot the yards and rooftops of an ever-increasing number of urban residences.

Add to these marvels of human ingenuity the tremendously popular videocassette recorder (VCR) and video laser discs. These TV-top boxes are now wired between antenna and

Christian teens average the same fifty R-rated films per year as their secular counterparts.

television set in nine out of ten American households. This fact is disheartening as well as encouraging. On the negative side, Americans have almost unlimited access to sexually explicit and violent films. But to their benefit, with the VCR, families have the ability to control and broaden the selection of entertainment they watch on TV. If a Christian is going to have a television in the home, one of the best and most convenient alternatives to normal network fare is the videocassette player. However, because VCRs and laser disc players can be programmed with violence and raw sex just as easily as they can be programmed with uplifting materials, the viewer's ability to discriminate increases in importance.

VIDEO SEDUCTION

Most adults would never slink into a smoke-filled pornographic bookstore or an X-rated film theater. But millions now surrender to the temptation to rent the same explicit material and tote it home to the secrecy of their personal TV and VCR. They do so without the fear of being seen in the "wrong place."

One pastor, who chose to remain anonymous, wrote an extremely intimate and revealing article about his own video seduction. Finding himself the recipient of a VCR intended to help enhance his ministry, he took the machine home and hooked it up in the family room. He envisioned himself viewing messages by some of the most respected Christian leaders and purchasing some animated Bible stories for his children. He also wanted to "time shift" some of the better-quality children's shows and family-oriented movies to an hour more in line with his family's schedule.

Driving to the nearest video rental store, he walked through the front door intending simply to pick up a Disney classic. However, as anyone who has ever been inside one of these video shops can attest, his attention was diverted by the provocative posters and explicit video jackets used to draw attention to all varieties of ungodly productions.

At first he stood firm. But after a while, he began to note that many of his own congregation members were discussing the same films that he had been struggling to avoid. Eventually, he began taking PG and PG-13 dramas home for him and his wife to view after the children had gone to bed. There was profanity and occasional nudity, but the two of them felt firmly enough rooted in their Christian walk that such things wouldn't really have an effect on them. Or would they?

After a time, the once objectionable content of the films became commonplace. What was originally felt to be extremely violent or provocative was now only mildly so. One day he finally rented an R-rated movie. Before long he found the sexual scenes more enticing and less offensive.

This pastor continued his daily personal devotions, but he knew that it had really become a sham. His addiction and his cravings became ever more intense. He was finally jolted into changing his habit and asking his wife's forgiveness after a weekend when she had gone out of town for a women's conference. The author of this true story writes:

> This was my chance to view an X-rated film alone. I contemplated this decision for at least a week. I did not want to give in to the temptation. Yet I could not seem to get the film out of my mind.
>
> On Saturday night I went to the video shop, intending to get a family movie. But I found myself laying $3 on the counter for an X-rated (NC-17) movie. "It's just curiosity, not lust," I told myself. "Perhaps as a Christian leader I should be aware of what the world is consuming."
>
> What I saw that night was ugly. The film degraded men and women. The beauty of human sexuality as God designed it and as I had experienced it in marriage was absent. I felt empty, cheated, and defeated.
>
> It was at this point that God brought me to my senses. He had been calling me to repentance all along, but I had been ignoring Him. Shocked by my failure, I realized I was in danger of destroying my life and my ministry. If I hardened my heart and harbored this sin, what would entice me next?
>
> I did four things that night before going to bed. First, I destroyed the identification cards that video shops require when renting tapes. Second, I wrote a letter to my wife, confessing my failure and asking her to pray for my spiritual recovery. Third, I confessed my sin to the Lord and appropriated His cleansing. Fourth, I made a decision before God to stay out of video shops. . . .
>
> I'm writing this not to provide a catharsis for my soul, for I'm assured of God's forgiveness (1 John 1:9), but to warn other Christians. No Christian is immune to the temptations of video seduction.[1]

"A study by University of Maryland professor Mark Levy shows that almost all the prerecorded tapes watched by 10th graders are R-rated films."[2] Practically speaking, children are free to rent just about anything that they are tall enough to reach, and the viewing habits of Christian teens are no better than their non-Christian friends. When you combine cable TV viewings with video viewings and theater attendance, "Christian teens . . . average the same *fifty* R-rated films per year as their secular counterparts."[3] The vast majority of secular video-store clerks do not even try to enforce the rating system set up in the late 1960s by the Motion Picture Association of America. To do so undermines the primary reason for their existence—profit! Once again, it is the responsibility of parents to train and monitor their children. The entrepreneur squeaking a living out of his neighborhood video-rental franchise is not likely to do it for us.

SO WHY OWN A VCR?

Kids love videos! An adult usually tires of a show after seeing it two or three times, but children will watch a video dozens of times. Today's children run around the house hugging videos the way their parents used to hug their favorite dolls or teddy bears. The VCR is definitely reshaping the way that children of all ages watch television. In the United States, "VCRs are used an average of seven hours a week, with half of the time used to play rented or purchased tapes. Children spend 50 percent more time watching VCRs than their parents."[4]

The captivating nature of video has been expertly manipulated to teach humanistic values through a wide variety of shows, which, at first glance, appear to be of a generally wholesome nature. However, a wonderful selection of high-quality, Christ-centered, or genuinely wholesome videos are now available. The entire final section of this book is devoted to evaluating over two hundred of the best or most widely marketed Christian and family-friendly videos.

No longer is it necessary for your loved ones to be brainwashed with spiritually harmful messages when all they want is a short period of visual entertainment.

Parents, especially, can rest in the realization that there *are* programs available that they don't have to be on guard against. You can experience the thrill of allowing your children to watch dramas and cartoons that are carefully written to convey Bible-

based truths through entertainment. You can enjoy a refreshing sense of success in your attempts to wean the kids away from the customary diet of inane, violent, and magic/occult-oriented "children's shows."

Seeing Christian principles and biblical stories acted out on the TV screen goes a long way in helping to impress them in young, pliable minds. Additionally, seeing an animated or dramatized version of a well-researched Bible story gives the viewer an even greater feeling of confidence in the Bible's reality. (But be careful, there are also many *poorly* researched Bible story tapes out there. Refer to our video reviews at the end of this book to help avoid getting "burnt.")

How refreshing it is to finally watch people on your television screen that actually accept the presupposition of a God who is in control! What a wonderful reassurance to your children that their parents are not "weird" and that yours is not the only Christian family on the face of the earth.

We recommend that you call around to the Christian bookstores and video shops in your area to find out which ones have a good selection of family-oriented and Christian videos for rent. By getting videos from Christian bookstores (or by limiting your selections at secular video stores to those carrying the "Dove" seal of approval), you can avoid many of the temptations and frustrations that were revealed by the author of the article quoted earlier in this chapter. Also, the more we rent from these family-oriented sources, the more they will be financially able to invest in additional titles to broaden their selection. (For a comprehensive list of videos that carry the "Dove" approved seal, contact the Dove Foundation in Grand Rapids, Michigan, or at their site on the Internet's worldwide web.)

If you own a VCR, become familiar with its operation so that you can quickly set the automatic timer to record programs scheduled for broadcast at an hour that is otherwise inconvenient for you. This "time shifting" is vastly underutilized by most VCR owners. Never again should you feel that you have to miss a church service or eat dinner in front of the TV set because a show that you simply "must see" is going to be aired at the same time.

Videos can be a very positive alternative to normal network and cable-TV fare, but viewing even the best videos should not be seen as an alternative to family or personal times of other, non-TV activities. When carefully used, the videocassette player can be a tremendous tool for family and spiritual enrichment.

Once a person decides to try to at least partially close the door to negative influences by initiating new TV and movie-viewing standards, he finds himself desperately searching for viable alternatives. Without other enjoyable activities in which to invest your time, your good intentions may amount to only that.

It is to meet this very real need that Karen has designed the next section. The following alternatives to TV viewing and other forms of electronic entertainment are a key component to this book. In fact, they are key in your attempt to change ingrained media habits and restructure your prime time.

I'll be waiting for you in chapter 12!

Part IV

151 Fantastic TV Substitutes

10

Creating New Habits
Can Be Fun and Games!

Dale and I know from experience that old habits are hard to change. As of this writing, we are determined to shed a few pounds by changing some eating habits.

I do want to lose some weight, be healthier, and look better; but I still find myself magnetically drawn into the kitchen. There I stand scouring the refrigerator shelves in search of some forbidden snack. I am about to succumb to a culinary evil until my eyes fall upon a little bowl of carrot sticks. They wait humbly on the shelf, carefully prepared for just such a moment of temptation. I pick up the healthy alternative and enjoy one more small victory over an old habit.

Changing television consumption is, in some ways, like changing old eating habits. We know that too much TV isn't good for us. We want to have better communication and new abilities. We want our children to do more than beg for junk-food TV. But we are doomed to failure unless we plan ahead for those moments of temptation.

This section is an easy-to-use catalog of ideas of things to do other than watch television. Whether you are a burnt-out parent, a childless couple, or single, this section is your resource for the moments of weakness. Use it to retrain yourself and anyone else who will join you in the arts of recreation, work, communication, togetherness, crafts, and service to others. Although many of the ideas are innovative, I unapologetically include suggestions for *ordinary* activities because, sometimes, the things that should be the most painfully obvious are not.

It was important for our family to actually make a list of TV alternatives for those times when it seemed impossible to recall even the simplest ideas.

Like most mothers, I, too, have those days when creativity is far from

> *Becoming an excellent TV manager will pave the way to personal spiritual revival, and a much happier family!*

me. The baby is clinging to my leg, screaming at the top of her little lungs as I drag her around the kitchen desperately trying to work on dinner preparations. As I glance over my shoulder, I see my two-year-old finger painting in the flour she has just spilled all over the counter. I know that my husband will be walking through the front door any minute with that wearied look that says, "I'm going to die of starvation in five minutes! What's for dinner?" And then my eldest whines, "Can we watch TV, Mommy?" At times like this, a strange thing happens. My mind becomes a blank fog. Except for the word *television,* nothing else comes through clearly on my mental screen. (We call this Mason-family phenomenon "television tunnel vision.")

How can it be, I wonder, *that a college graduate, an experienced school teacher, cannot think of one activity for her children besides watching TV?* This uncanny loss of memory is what motivated me to compile a list of TV Alternatives as an easy reference and planning guide for such moments of temptation . . . and desperation. And I know that if you want to remember specific points, it helps to begin each one with the same letter. So here are six guidelines that I *guarantee* will change a lifetime of TV habits:

1. Pray for God's help.
2. Plunge in.
3. Personalize this book.
4. Place this book on your TV.
5. Plan ahead.
6. Put a priority on people.

1. PRAY FOR GOD'S HELP

God is deeply concerned about the thoughts and images with which we fill our minds. If you have been carelessly allowing various kinds of pollutants to enter the gates of your eyes and ears, confess poor viewing habits to the Lord.

In myriad homes and churches, shoddy TV management has become the main roadblock to spiritual vitality. Dale and I are convinced—from personal experience and from numerous testimonies that have been shared with us—that becoming an excellent TV manager will pave the way to personal spiritual revival, and a much happier family!

If you or someone you love is ensnared by TV's bewitching charm, pray. Whatever you do, don't scold or nag. Pray instead. Let God do the convicting. Remember, too, that our loving God has the days of our lives numbered. Ask yourself: *Do I want to use that limited, God-given time as I have been, or do my TV habits need to change?*

2. PLUNGE IN

Plunge right in and acquaint yourself with the following suggestions, and think of your own TV alternatives too. Open your mind. Pour in heavy doses of activity ideas that can be recalled when your TV seems to whine for attention.

3. PERSONALIZE THIS BOOK

Make the list your own by highlighting the activities that are most appealing to you or someone in your family. There is no doubt that once you have broken the old pattern of automatic TV viewing, you will begin thinking of hundreds of new ways to spend your time. Jot down your ideas in this book. Include ways to adapt the activities to better fit your family's needs.

In some sections, blanks have been provided for you to fill in information such as phone numbers and hours of operation at skating rinks and swimming pools. The "Indoor Games" and "Outdoor Games" sections have a place reserved for your personal game inventory. The more you personalize this book, the sharper it will become as a weapon against old habits of TV viewing.

4. PLACE THIS BOOK ON YOUR TV

After you have read and highlighted the alternatives list, you may be wondering how you will ever remember the ideas when you need them. I suggest that you help your memory as well as your self-discipline by leaving this book in plain view on top of your television set. In those moments of temptation, before you flip on the TV, flip through the following TV alternatives and find an activity that interests you.

5. PLAN AHEAD

Most of the activities listed can be done on the spur of the moment. However, some require a little forethought and preparation. Don't let this scare you. Preparation in itself can be an alternative to TV. When I sit down to make my to-do list, I've learned to include a few fun activities that I want to prepare during the week. This may mean gathering supplies for a craft, writing up 3-by-5 cards for a verse memory game, or phoning some friends and inviting them to join our family on a particular evening. Sometimes a few minutes of forethought is just what you need to make nontelevision activities more attractive than Hollywood's allure.

6. PUT A PRIORITY ON PEOPLE

It is amazing how the simple addition of a few guests turns an ordinary activity into a special event. I remember an evening several years ago when Dale was out of town on a business trip. My children and I had enjoyed a lot of togetherness that day, but by evening I felt that I had honestly endured all the preschool conversation that one adult could handle. I was determined not to turn on the television, but the evening walk I had planned as an alternative didn't hold much appeal either; that is, until I thought about asking my neighbor to join us. She happily accepted my impromptu invitation, tucked her little ones into a stroller, and we were off. As the wheels began to roll, so did our conversation. Since that evening we have enjoyed many neighborly strolls together. I lost my sense of frustration while gaining a trusted friend.

At our house we have one more rule regarding people and TV: *people take priority over television.* In most circumstances, we insist that the TV goes off when company comes in. Giving our full attention to others is one of the best ways we can show them that they are valuable. Honor others by showing them that they are more important than even your favorite TV show.

11

TV-Free Activities

—FAMILY NIGHT—

Show your family that you enjoy spending time with them by declaring a weekly or even a monthly "Family Night." I define Family Night as an evening reserved exclusively for doing fun things with the immediate family. It is a great way to demonstrate that you value their company as well as a perfect opportunity to model what families can do other than watch television.

Ideas listed in this first section are particularly well suited to Family Night activities, but consider scanning the alternatives listed under other headings for greater variety.

1.   Plan a Cultural Dinner

Plan an evening where your menu, dress, and conversation all focus on a specific foreign country. Check at the library for music recordings, videos, recipes, and interesting trivia about the culture you have chosen. Plan one of the country's popular children's games. Pray for the leaders and Christians of the land. An excellent resource book to guide you is P. J. Johnstone's *Operation World* (available from any Christian bookstore). It lists statistics and prayer requests for every nation in the world.

2. Assemble a Missionary "Care Package"

Boost the morale of your missionary friends on the front lines of spiritual service by mailing them some items that they need or would just enjoy. Some ideas might be:

- Greeting cards and envelopes
- Special-occasion paper napkins and tablecloths
- Birthday candles
- Chocolate chips
- Christian music tapes
- Christian and educational magazines (Send your own recent copies or buy some at your Christian bookstore.)

An extra note: In some countries, missionaries have to pay duties of 100 percent or more of an item's value just to accept the package. Ask your missionary or missions board what you can do to avoid these expenses to your overseas friend. For instance, it has been suggested that one should send used rather than new books and mark the package accordingly.

3. Read Stories with a Message

For entertaining and inspirational reading, borrow books and magazines from your friends or church library, or make a family outing to your local Christian bookstore. Select stories from the following categories:

- Bible, children's Bible, or Bible storybooks
- Novels that emphasize biblical principles
- Biographies of great Christians
- Missionary stories—from books, magazines, and mission newsletters such as *In Other Words*, published by Wycliffe Bible Translators, P.O. Box 2727, Huntington Beach, CA 92647

To "jazz up" a story: Either have one reader read expressively to the whole family or take turns reading to each other. For a dramatic touch, have the reader dress up as the main story character, or the whole family could act out the story as it is narrated.

Older listeners can draw illustrations for the book being read while younger ones color them. Big brother and sister can also have fun illustrating the story for the little ones in the family with puppets or flannelgraph figures. (I either buy our figures at the educational or Christian bookstore or make them from our girls' coloring books and Sunday school papers. Our board was easily made by attaching flannel to a rectangular piece of cardboard.)

4.   Modernize and Dramatize a Familiar Bible Story

Look at an old, familiar story in a fresh, new light by placing yourself in the modern equivalent of Bible-time challenges. For instance, consider what modern obstacles Daniel might have faced if he had lived in today's society. Make a lasting memory of your skit by videotaping it. Here are some suggested stories for you to dramatize.

Bible characters:
- Noah (Gen. 6–9)
- Mary and Joseph (Luke 1–2)
- Jonah (Jonah)
- Daniel in the Lion's Den (Dan. 6)
- Zacchaeus (Luke 19:1–9)

Parables:
- The Lost Sheep (Matt. 18:10–14)
- The Unmerciful Servant (Matt. 18:21–35)
- The Workers in the Vineyard (Matt. 20:1–16)

5.   Produce Your Own Puppet Show

A simple impromptu show can be wonderful, creative entertainment. Begin by making your own puppets out of paper bags, paper plates, popsicle sticks, socks, cardboard tubes, dolls, or stuffed animals. Then convert a cardboard box or just a cloth-covered table into a puppet stage. Now you can perform your own version of a nursery rhyme, children's story, Bible story, or your family's one-of-a-kind original script. If your family is really good, volunteer to perform in children's church. Leaders are always looking for a fresh way to relate a lesson.

6.   Record an Audio or Videotape for a Friend or Relative

Send that missed loved one a special message that he or she will never forget. Let your whole family individually share their news, sing a song, or even show off a little; and you will have a unique "letter" that will leave the listener with the feeling that he has practically been with you. Below are some ideas for making your tapes more interesting.

Don't feel compelled to fill the entire tape; simply stop when you are done.

- Enhance your audiotape with humorous sound effects.
- Record your video in more than one location.
- Make family members magically appear by photographing first an empty sofa, then pause the camera; have one member sit down on the couch and start the camera again. Repeat these steps until each member seems to have miraculously appeared on the sofa.
- Have children (or adults!) perform short stunts like turning cartwheels, swinging from a tree, playing a segment of a piano piece, making a great football pass, or belting out a cheer routine.
- Cover up lens to record sounds, uncover to reveal their sources (for instance, blowing nose, sucking on a straw, crumpling paper, . . .)

7.   Talk about and Record Memories

If you never seem to get around to writing down your family history or those especially comical experiences, making a tape may be the easy way for you to record those precious moments. Invite an older relative to join you and share stories from earlier years. Remember that youngsters can also contribute and will immensely enjoy reviewing the tape in years to come. Begin your family's memory tape by selecting a topic from below.

- What are some funny things the kids did when they were little?
- Who made the greatest impact on your life and why? Describe them.
- How and where did you become engaged?
- What were the events surrounding your salvation?
- What were some of the highlights of your school years?
- What did you do during the war (for older relatives)?
- How would you describe one of your favorite times with Grandpa (or another relative)?
- What was your favorite Christmas or birthday? Why does it stand out in your memory?

Now just turn on the recorder and give each person an opportunity to respond to the question. When you have exhausted a subject, label the tape and store it for your next recording session.

8. Take Fun Pictures of Your Family

Are the years slipping by without a visual record for your family's memory? Take the time now to photograph the people who are most important to you. Be silly; be creative. Photograph family members holding their most cherished possessions. Have your young children model in adult clothes. Think of a theme such as your favorite vacation spot, either one you've been to or one you'd like to visit. Have everyone dress for that vacation. Take pictures of individuals such as Dad repairing a bike in the workroom. (I wish that I had a photograph of my childhood home, the kitchen, my bedroom, our spacious attic. There is so much that we forget, and photographs renew our slipping memories.)

9. Look at Old Photos

Every once in a while a family should pull down the photo albums, home videos, slides, or movies and relive some of their family history.

10. Sing Together

Sing for fun, and don't worry if you don't sound perfect. A hymnbook will aid your impromptu concerts. Let your children teach you some new songs from the youth group or children's choir. You may even want to select a number to practice for a performance at a family gathering or church. If no one plays an instrument at your house, either sing a cappella as we do, or sing along to an instrumental tape.

- Sing before a nightly story or devotional time.
- Sing while taking a hike in the woods.
- Sing while riding together in the car. (We sing on the way to church. It calms us after the rush of getting ready and reminds us that the day belongs to the Lord.)
- Sing before you give thanks at the evening meal. (In our home, this is a tradition that focuses our attention and sets a positive tone for the evening.)

11. Watch a Wholesome Video

Transform your video night into an "evening of entertainment" for your family and a few guests. Let the kids set up and run a concession stand. Turn off all the lights to enhance the atmosphere, and have a child use a flashlight to usher "patrons" into the darkened room. Here are some good video choices:

- Christian videos: The video review section of this book has lots of great suggestions.
- Family shows: Musicals, classics, animated stories, and comedies are usually good choices. Many of these can be pre-recorded from the TV for use on your special evening.
- Home videos, movies, and slides: These can be as much fun as any commercial production.

12. Scripture Memory Games

Make up your own Scripture memory games or try these. They're fun as well as educational.

Scramble

1. Write each word of the Bible verse on a separate 3-by-5 card.
2. Mix up the cards.
3. Try to put the cards back in the correct order.
4. For stiffer competition, time how long each person takes to put the cards in order.

Tick-Tack-Toe

1. Write the Bible verse references on cards.
2. Place cards face down on the table.
3. Teams take turns drawing a card and reciting a verse.
4. Members who recite the verse correctly may place an X or an O in the tick-tack-toe square.
5. Make the game easier by putting the first word in the verse along with the reference.

Match up

1. Write verses on 3-by-5 cards and spread the cards out face up on a table.
2. Write the references to the verses on other 3-by-5 cards and place them face down in a stack on the table.

3. Players take turns drawing reference cards and matching with verse cards.

4. Player keeps verse cards for each correct match.

5. Winner is the player with the most cards at the end of game.

13. Mail Bible Portions to Foreign Countries

Put your love for God's Word into action by mailing Bibles to some of the four billion people who have never owned one. Organizations such as Bibles for the World will provide you with the Bibles, packaging, and labels. Even young children can participate in this simple yet rewarding project. All you do is wrap, mail, and pay for the postage. To request a free multipak introductory Bible kit, call Bibles for the World at (800) 323–2609. In Illinois, (312) 668–7733.

14. Picnic: Breakfast, Lunch, or Supper in the Park

Picnics are a tried and true winner with people everywhere. Consider these variations on an old theme.

- Serve the meal on china complete with goblets of sparkling grape juice.
- Pick a theme like "Hillbilly Picnic." Wear clothes and play games that fit the part.
- Plan a breakfast picnic. Bicycle to a park on a Saturday morning and enjoy breakfast in your favorite spot. Include a devotional reading and prayer time. (Some of my favorite childhood memories were made in this very fashion.)

15. Camp Out in the Backyard

Set up a tent; pull out the sleeping bags, a lantern, and a big bag of popcorn. After "camp" is set up, fire up the barbecue grill and cook a "hobo" dinner for each camper. (Hobo dinners consist of sliced potatoes, carrots, onions, and a ground beef pattie broiled in an aluminum foil pouch on red-hot coals, either on a grill, or a campfire.)

Finally, settle down for a family time of singing, storytelling, and stargazing. This TV alternative—which works especially well with *young* children—is one that your family, and your neighbors, will remember for years to come!

— GOING AND DOING —

Here are some activities that will get you out of the house. The new surroundings may be just what you need for a fresh attitude and a relaxed feeling. Under several of the headings, space has been provided for you to write the names, phone numbers, admission fees, and business hours of local attractions. These quick reference helps will make scheduling your outings fast and convenient.

16. Take a Bike Ride

Each year is filled with gorgeous days that we simply let slip by. Don't let another one pass. Try a devotional cruise for just you and the Lord. Recite familiar Scriptures, or spend your time talking to God. Plan to stop at a friend's house for a short hello. Bring an extra smile with cookies or flowers from your garden as a gift of friendship.

Kids only:

- Races: Invite your friends to join you for speed races in a deserted parking lot. Try slow races too.
- Follow the Leader: Play "Follow the Leader" on bikes. Pretend that you are biking on a safari or in a foreign country.
- Bike Parade: Have your friends join you in decorating your bikes outlandishly. Weave streamers through the spokes of your bike. Create a motorized sound by clothespinning a playing card to the spokes. Maybe you will want to go all out and disguise your bike with big pieces of cardboard to look like a car, a carriage, or even a dinosaur.

17. Feed the Ducks

An outing as simple as a trip to the park can be the backdrop for a precious memory. Call an elderly neighbor and invite him or her to join you in spreading a feast for hungry birds. Pack up your stale bread, popcorn, and cereal. Don't forget the camera so you can capture the outing on film.

18. Explore Your Library

Make this trip to the library an adventure. Scan the magazines your library offers. There are magazines about parenting, cooking, cars, photography, sports, writing, teaching, business, antiques, dogs, cats, fish, films, four-wheeling, skydiving, and almost every other special interest imaginable. Let your second discovery be the audiovisual department and its array of records, audiotapes, videocassettes, and films.

19.   Take a Hike

Get in touch with nature in your favorite state park or national forest. Before you go, check out books from the library on native state plants and animals. Pack a lunch, water, a can of insect repellent, and some Band-Aids for your trek. Select your clothes with the weather in mind. Take your camera. Park officials can point out landmarks and provide you with maps. Consider joining one of the park's planned hikes. As you hike, look for things that reflect the Creator and share these thoughts with each other.

20.   Go Roller Skating

Whether you choose street or rink roller skating, it is a great way to exercise and have fun too! Outdoor basketball courts are a great place to skate, but my personal favorite is a big, deserted parking lot. I used to get my exercise by rising early to skate around the mall parking lot before the stores opened. If you are skating with a friend, play tag. See if you can dribble a ball while skating. Bring along a tape player and skate to music.

Call your closest rink to find out what nights they play Christian music. Then get on the phone and invite friends to join you. You might plan a clothing theme like "crazy ties" or "silly socks." Be friendly and decide that everyone has to meet at least one person who is not with your group before the evening is over. You can have fun turning a few heads by agreeing that when one person calls out "crazy ties!" everyone converges in the center of the rink, shakes hands, and then returns to nonchalantly skating around the rink as before.

Quick reference information:

Name of rink _____
Address _____
Phone #_____
Cost _____
Hours _____
 _____

21. Go Ice Skating

During the cold months, you can take advantage of rinks and frozen ponds. Always check the depth of the pond ice and bring along a rope or pole for emergencies. Some ideas: Play hockey with brooms and a homemade puck made from a butter tub filled with gravel and secured shut with strapping tape; or perform your own mock "ice capades." Don't forget about ice skating in the summer, either. Spending an afternoon at an indoor rink is a great way to beat the heat!

Quick reference information:

Name of rink _____

Address _____

Phone # _____

Cost _____

Hours _____

22. Attend a Concert

Enjoying a great concert doesn't have to cost a lot of money. Check your newspaper for city- or church-activity listings. Frequently, these concerts are free and very good. Sometime, though, you might want to go all out, purchase tickets, and dress up for an evening at the symphony.

23. Eat Salad and Dessert at an Exclusive Restaurant

Dress up for a "meal" out at an exclusive restaurant without killing your budget. Eat a larger-than-usual lunch at home, and then simply order salad and dessert. Chances are you will probably get a nice basket of bakery rolls too. It can be a quiet date for two or an opportunity to invite another couple to join you. Parents can make this a date with a child.

24. Visit a Museum or Planetarium

This is a fun as well as an educational activity that will give you a new appreciation for art, history, science, or nature. If the museum has a current special exhibit, read up on it a bit before you make your visit. Keep in mind that secular museums and planetariums are steeped in evolution, which they present as a proven fact rather than a theory.

Quick reference information:

Name of museum (or planetarium) _____
Address _____
Phone #_____
Cost _____
Hours _____

25. Go Bowling

Relax a little and make the evening fun. See how many heads you can turn with some ridiculously elaborate windups performed with stoic expression. Once the game gets rolling, you might enjoy a little friendly competition by declaring a "booby prize" for the losers such as opening all the doors for the winning team that evening.

Quick reference information:

Name of bowling alley _____
Address _____
Phone # _____
Hours _____
Cost: per game _____ Shoe rental_____

26. Visit the Zoo

Revive this old favorite by giving each person in your group a list of things to look for in the zoo, such as: a nocturnal creature, an animal that lives in your state, a waterbird, an animal from Australia, an animal from India, etc. The first to find all the answers gets a snow cone (or some other treat). On another day at the zoo bring along your camera and take comical pictures of your friends or family imitating the animals in their cages. When the photos are developed, you can make up an album called "Bizarre and Unusual Creatures."

Quick reference information:

Zoo name _____
Address _____
Phone #_____
Cost _____
Hours _____
_____

27. Go for a Sunset Drive

Take a relaxing drive to a scenic spot and watch the sun set. Then stop for a soda on your way home.

28. Go Swimming

Splashing in the water is a great way to cool off in the summer heat. Whether you swim in a wading pool or the ocean, water games will make the day even more fun.

Water games:

- Retrieve a coin from the floor of the pool or lake.
- Play tag.
- Play catch or keep away.
- Stand on your hands on pool bottom.
- Play water volleyball or basketball.
- See who can make the biggest splash.
- Have your group stand in a circle and toss a beach ball back and forth, always trying to keep it in the air.
- Have swimming races or running-in-the-water races.

Keep your swimming safe by following these important rules:

1. Never leave a child unsupervised by the water.
2. Don't dive where the water is shallow or there are any obstructions.
3. Insist on a buddy system for a large group.

Quick reference information:

Public pool name _____

Address _____

Phone # _____

Cost _____ Hours _____

29. Go Horseback Riding

A special trip to the stables is definitely on the memory-maker list. Be sure to bring the camera and record this fun outing for family memory night.

Quick reference information:

Stable name _____

Address _____

Phone # _____

Cost _____ Hours _____

_____

30. Go Out for a Frozen Dessert

This mini-outing is a favorite at our house. More than once we have been seen pulling our little red wagon loaded with kids up to the corner yogurt shop. The evening stroll and after-dinner treat are the perfect opportunity to hold hands and talk, something I never get enough of.

31. Go on a Weekend Campout

Get completely away from the everyday routine with a weekend campout. Adequate planning will prevent most frustrations. Joining a family of veteran campers might be helpful for your first trip out. Decide ahead of time your route, destination, supplies, and schedule. Then determine to be flexible. As you pack your camping gear, include these items: a ball, Frisbee, board games, pencil and paper, bags for collecting woodsy treasures, a magnifying glass, a Bible, songbooks, and a camera.

(In their excellent book *The Blessing,* Gary Smalley and John Trent printed the response of people in numerous seminars and counseling sessions to the question, "What is one specific way you knew that you had received your parents' blessing?" It was interesting to read that one of the answers that they received most often was, "We went camping as a family.")

32. Leave an Anonymous Gift at a Friend's Door

Take some time to brighten a friend's day with an anonymous gift. You could give a favorite dessert, a cartoon book, or a restaurant gift certificate. Deliver the gift to their front doorstep, ring the doorbell, and watch the surprise from behind the bushes.

33. Visit Your Local Chamber of Commerce

Your local Chamber of Commerce may have more ideas of local places of interest or ways to become involved in your community.

Street address _____

Phone # _____

Hours _____

_____

34. Sit in on a City Council Meeting, Visit a Courtroom in Session or Your State Legislature

Judicial and governmental proceedings are interesting and educational activities for all members of the family.

City council meets _____

Street address _____

Time _____

Trial or session time _____

State legislature meets _____

Our local representative is _____

35. List the Attractions Available in Your Area

List attractions in your area that you would like to visit some-day. Then, when you don't know what to do, you can quickly scan your list for appropriate activities.

— INDOOR GAMES —

These are some reminders of what you can play inside the house, just for the fun of it. The ideas listed cover a wide range of ages. Most of them can be enjoyed by anyone who is young at heart. We encourage parents to take some time to play with their children, but kids can use this list to make their own fun too.

36. Hide and Seek

In the original game, one seeker hunts several hidden children. Try reversing this by choosing one hider and several seekers. Make it even more fun by declaring that a seeker who finds the hider joins him in his hiding spot until all are discovered by the last seeker.

Another variation of the game is to hide an object. Give the seeker clues by saying, "You are getting hot," or "You are getting cold." Finding their hidden toys is a delight for small children, and they are anxious to play again and again.

37. Board Games and Card Games

Take an inventory of your family's games and write them here for quick reference in the future. Then, you may want to make a trip to a toy store, department store, or educational store to pick out a few additional games that your family would enjoy. Don't forget to watch garage sales for bargains on games. Or you might swap games with a friend for a month.

Table games we have: Table games to buy:

_____   _____
_____   _____
_____   _____
_____   _____
_____   _____
_____   _____
_____   _____
_____   _____
_____   _____

Here are a few suggestions for your consideration:
- Password
- Jacks
- Pictionary
- Darts
- Concentration
- Pick-up sticks
- Ring Toss
- Matching games for colors, letters, or pictures
- Dominoes (look for variations like animal and alphabet dominoes)
- Bingo (look for educational versions that emphasize math or language skills)

38.   Jigsaw Puzzles

Jigsaw puzzles can be lots of fun alone or in groups. The giant puzzles may take days to complete, so assemble them on a board, card table, or some other surface that can be easily moved out of the way when not in use. (For a group activity, buy identical puzzles for each group of five people, then give a set amount of time to complete as much of the puzzle as they can. The team that has the fewest unattached pieces wins!)

39.   Crossword Puzzles

You can develop your vocabulary and have fun at the same time by completing crossword puzzles. Find puzzles in books, the daily newspaper, and children's Sunday school papers. Clip puzzles out of papers whenever you see them and store in a shoebox for a TV alternative some night. However, you might find that you can have just as much fun challenging others with your own homemade puzzles.

40. Explore Kids' Sites on the Internet

With a little bit of parental involvement, kids can now find wonderful entertainment, great activities, and positive education sites on the worldwide web. We strongly recommend that you start at "Kids' Quest," a subsection of the huge "Christian Answers Network" site. The on-line "address" (URL) for Kids' Quest is: http://www.ChristianAnswers.Net. You'll also find more of our video reviews there, and you can send us EMAIL as well!

41. Forgotten Toys

Select a few toys that seem to have lost their appeal and store them out of sight for a few months. Later, pull them out to be played with. You might be surprised at your children's interest in these "old" toys. Occasionally, it will be necessary to sort out the toys your children have outgrown. Suggest that your children select several of these toys to be given to friends or organizations that will appreciate them. Take your children with you so they can give the toys to others themselves.

42. Building a Block City

People of all ages enjoy building. Just vary your techniques and your building materials and you have an activity suited to any ability level. Some of the materials you can use are: wooden blocks, Legos, Tinker Toys, Lincoln Logs, cardboard tubes, boxes, and even sheets of paper, which can be folded, taped, and colored.

An unlimited number of structures that can be built are available. Here are some ideas to get your young engineers and architects started:

- airport
- church
- dog house
- doll house and furniture

- farm
- Ferris wheel
- lawn mower
- skyscraper
- space station
- submarine
- train
- _____

43. Ping-Pong

Challenge your friends to a game of Ping-Pong or begin a whole tournament. Maybe you will want to create your own games or enjoy an old variation like Around the World (also known as Round Robin).

44. Domino Trails

Line up dominoes on end and in trails or patterns across the floor. When you're finished, hit the leading domino and watch them fall. You can make forks in the path that set off two or three other paths. Make bridges of books or blocks. Go under tables and around chair legs. Time how long it takes for your trails to collapse. Compete with yourself for longer collapsing times. Before you set off your most spectacular trails, pull out the camera or video camera.

45. Balloon Games

Here are some silly ideas for playing with balloons.

- *Balloon bombs:* This is an active game for one person or a whole crowd. Blow up four or five balloons. The object of the game is to keep the balloons in the air at all times. Pretend that if they touch the ground or the furniture, they explode.
- *Clinging balloons:* Rub balloons on your hair to create static electricity. Find out what your balloon will cling to. Look at yourself in the mirror. Is your hair sticking up?
- *Balloon squash:* Race other players to see who can sit on and break the most balloons.
- *Balloon toss:* How far can you toss a balloon? Compete for distance.

- *Balloon people:* Draw faces on balloons. Cut noses, ears, hats, and mouths out of paper and tape to balloon faces. Create balloon portraits of your family.

Caution: When playing with balloons, remember that broken balloon pieces can be swallowed and choked on by little ones. Be alert and pick up all broken pieces.

46. Water-Glass Concert

Create your own "percussion instrument" by filling drinking glasses with varying amounts of water. A water glass is "played" by gently tapping the side with a spoon. "Wind instruments" are made by filling narrow-necked bottles with varying amounts of water. Play these by blowing across the top of the bottle opening. Experiment with different water amounts until you can perform your own unique concert.

47. Make and Fly Paper Airplanes

Let your creativity fly with paper airplanes. Experiment with various designs and sizes as you compete for flight distance. There are some great library books on how to make paper airplanes and other things that fly. Look under the Dewey decimal call number 745.592. I recommend these two books: *Air Crafts: Playthings to Make and Fly,* by Leslie Linsley and Jon Aron; and *Easy-to Make Spaceships That Really Fly,* by Mary and Dewey Blocksma.

48. Rhyming Words

The starting player chooses a good short word for rhyming, such as *hat, can,* or *night.* Then, everyone gets sixty seconds to write down words that rhyme with the starting word. The player who has the most correct rhyming words wins the game.

49. Block Bowling

Yes, you can go bowling right in your family room! It is just a matter of playing with old toys in a new way. Set up tall building blocks on end in a triangular pattern. Station players across the room and roll a ball at the blocks. Give points for the number of "pins" knocked down on each roll.

50. Charades

This time-tested game is always good for a few laughs. Silently act out your clues so other players can guess the book, movie, or song title that you are dramatizing. Give younger children different categories: ordinary activities (like sweeping or brushing teeth), animals (a monkey, an alligator), Bible stories (like Jesus calming the sea), or familiar children's book titles.

51. Tent Hideouts

Create tent hideouts by draping sheets and blankets over tables and chairs. Secure the sheets in place with pins and heavy books or by closing the sheet corners in drawers. If provided with a few sheets and a friend or two to help, children entertain themselves for hours by making their own forts and hideouts.

52. Aroma Bag

Choose an item with a distinct smell, such as an apple, onion, or a perfumed hanky, and put it in a paper bag. Blindfolded children then take a whiff through the opening of the bag and make a guess at what is inside.

53. Twenty Questions

This game for two or more can be played anytime, anywhere. To begin, the first player thinks of a person, place, or thing. Then the other players ask him questions to determine what he is thinking about. Only questions that can be answered with a yes or a no may be asked. Continue gathering clues with up to twenty questions until the secret identity is unveiled.

54. Name that Sound

These are simple guessing games for identifying sounds.

- *Game one:* Tape record various noises throughout the house, such as running water, the clatter of dishes being put away in the cupboard, or the padding of footsteps. Then play back the tape for others to hear and name the sounds. This can also be expanded by taping other sounds throughout your locale, such as a train, cows mooing, traffic in a tunnel, and so on.
- *Game two:* Play only the beginning notes of a familiar song. See if others can identify the tune.

55.   Pretend

When you pretend, you can go anywhere, be anything, and do everything! Parents can teach as well as learn a lot about their children by watching or, better yet, participating in their children's pretend play. Below are examples of the endless possibilities for pretend play. Add your own. Make up stories; act out the adventures. Have fun!

Adventures:

- underwater treasure hunt
- jungle safari
- space exploration
- shipwrecked on a desert island
- _____

Feelings:

- winning or losing a contest
- meeting a new friend; losing an old one
- getting a new baby
- moving to a new place
- _____

Occupations:

- ballerina
- doctor
- fire fighter
- Indian chief
- lawyer
- missionary
- _____
- _____

— OUTDOOR GAMES —

One of the best things about outdoor games is that they combine fun with the exercise that we know we should be getting. They also help us to let off steam and get some fresh air at the same time. Many of these games can be enjoyed by all ages right in your own backyard.

56. Frisbee

There are lots of ways to play with a Frisbee. You can play fetch with the dog. You can have a good time playing a simple game of catch or keep away with your friends, or you can try a few of the games described here.

- *Frisbee football:* Substitute the Frisbee for the football and a toss for football's kickoff and then play by basically the same rules as regular football.

- *Frisbee golf:* Poles replace the holes in golf as you try to hit the mark. Keep track of the number of tosses it takes to complete the course. The lowest score wins.

- *Target practice:* Aim at trees, fences, or even tin cans to improve your accuracy.

Check out a book from the library on the subject of Frisbee games. I recommend *Frisbee: More Than a Game of Catch*, by Judy Horowitz, women's world Frisbee champion.

57. Play Ball

Whether you play the full game or just practice your dribbling, passing, and throwing, this is a fun way to get your exercise. Don't forget these old favorites:

- Basketball
- Catch
- Football
- Four-Square
- Handball
- Kickball
- Softball
- Volleyball

58. Water-Balloon Toss

To play this game you need at least four people (two teams of two). Each team begins by tossing a water balloon to one partner. After each successful catch, each of you should take a step backward and throw again. If the balloon bursts, your team is eliminated. The last two players left in the game are the winners.

59. Kick-the-Can

Kick-the-can is played by two or more kids using only their feet to kick or steal an empty tin can in an active game of keep away.

60. Tug-of-War

A familiar game in which the center of a sturdy rope is marked and teams take their places at opposite ends. On "Go!" each team pulls and tugs on the rope in an effort to make their opponent cross the center line. You can add some extra excitement to the game by placing a wading pool or even a mud puddle between the two teams. In this case, the losers will be obvious!

61. Yard Games that Use Special Equipment

Below are a few good yard games, which, if you don't already own, you might consider buying. Use the blanks to make a list of your own family's yard games for future reminders.

- Badminton
- Croquet
- Horseshoes
- Tetherball
- _____
- _____
- _____
- _____

62. Hopscotch

An old-fashioned game that today's high-tech kids may not know very well. All you need is a piece of chalk to draw your hopscotch outline on the driveway and a stone for each player. Begin the game by tossing your rock onto the square numbered 1. Then hop on one foot in each square except the one that has a rock in it. When you get to the end, turn around and start hopping back. When you reach the square with your rock, pick it up and hop on out. The game continues as you roll your rock to box two, three, four. You lose a turn if you step on a line, step on a square with a rock in it, put two feet in one square, your rock rolls into the wrong square. The winner is the first person to move their stone all the way to number eight.

63.   Sledding, Sculptures, and Snow Forts

If you live in the right part of the country at the right time of the year, there is no end to the possibilities for snow play. You can sled with the side of a refrigerator box, design a park bench in the snow, sculpt a snow zoo in your front yard, or even build a snow house. Then, prepare for snowball attacks by building a walled fortress.

64.   Fly a Kite

Here is an ever-popular pastime. All you need is an inexpensive kite, some string, and a breeze. (Buy the kite at your local department store, or enlarge this idea into *several* TV alternatives by going to the library and checking out a book about kite making; then spend an evening or two building the kite, and, finally, go to a park some Saturday morning and actually fly your new creation!) Invite a friend and have contests to see who can fly their kite the highest or get their kite to do the most creative swoops and dives.

65.   Good Shepherd

Toddlers are more successful at this variation of "Simon Says" called, "Good Shepherd, Bad Shepherd." We tell our kids, "The Good Shepherd says, 'Scratch the back of the person next to you.' The Bad Shepherd says, 'Make a mean face.'" The goal is to be a good listener and only do what the Good Shepherd says and never what the Bad Shepherd commands. It's a good reminder for us to listen for the voice of our one, true Good Shepherd.

66.   London Bridge

As you probably remember, this game is played when two children clasp hands and hold up their arms to form a "bridge," under which the other children walk single file. Instead of the traditional song "London Bridge," try new words such as:

> "Jesus Christ loves you and me,
>   you and me, you and me.
> Jesus Christ loves you and me.
>   And we love you too."

At this point the arms of the bridge collapse capturing whoever was walking under it. Then:

"We'll give you a hug and kiss,
hug and kiss, hug and kiss.
We'll give you a hug and kiss,
because we love you so."

After receiving a hug and a kiss, the child is released and the game continues as before.

67. Blow Bubbles

Enjoy the wonderful colors and sizes of these floating, exploding delights. To make your own bubble solution, mix four parts water and one part liquid dishwashing soap. You can also add a drop of food coloring for new colors. Many items around your house make great bubble wands, such as drinking straws, pint-sized plastic fruit crates, or tin cans with the tops and bottoms removed.

— IN THE KITCHEN —

It has been said that the kitchen is the heart of the home. Welcome your friends and family members into your kitchen and your heart with creative, taste-tempting treats. Whether you are doing dishes or preparing some special treat together, time in the kitchen might be just the right ingredient for stirring up the best conversations and warmest memories. The TV alternatives listed here will start you cooking with fun activities that will get you out of the TV room and into the kitchen!

68. Make Caramel Corn

Make popcorn and put it in a roaster pan along with the peanuts.

16	cups	(4 quarts) of popped corn
2	cups	salted peanuts

In a saucepan stir together:

¼	cup	white corn syrup
½	cup	margarine or butter
1	cup	brown sugar
½	tsp.	salt

Bring these ingredients to a boil and cook five minutes. Remove from heat.

Stir in:

     ¼ tsp.   baking soda

Pour the mixture over the popcorn and peanuts. Stir it well. Bake uncovered at 250 degrees for one hour. Stir the baking mixture at 15-minute intervals. Cool and break apart the caramel corn on cookie sheets. Munch your homemade caramel corn now, freeze some for later, or bag it up as gifts for your friends.

69.   Make Pretzels

In a big bowl, mix together:

1	pkg.	yeast
1	tbsp.	sugar
1½	cups	warm water
1	tsp.	salt

Stir in:

    4 cups   flour

Knead the dough until it is smooth and then shape into traditional pretzel-shaped ropes, or be creative and make pretzel elephants, flowers, and people. Brush your creations with beaten egg and sprinkle with salt. Bake at 450 degrees until browned, about 15 minutes.

70.   Make Caramel Apples

At our house, this is Dad's specialty. Once or twice a year, he and the children spend the evening preparing and enjoying their special treat together.

All you need is five apples, caramel pieces, popsicle sticks, and a little water. Most packages of caramels contain the sticks for your apples and have a recipe printed on the package as well. Insert sticks into the top of the washed apples and dip into the caramel sauce to coat. Place on greased wax paper to cool in the refrigerator.

71.   Make Gelatin Shapes

An easy treat is gelatin. Cut it into squares or holiday shapes you can pick up with your fingers to eat. You will need:

4	envelopes	unflavored gelatin
4	cups	cold fruit juice (apple, cranberry, orange drink, or lemon-lime)

In a medium-size saucepan, sprinkle unflavored gelatin over 1 cup juice; let stand 1 minute. Stir over low heat until gelatin is completely dissolved, about 3 minutes. Stir in remaining 3 cups juice. Pour into 9-inch square baking pan; chill until firm, about 3 hours. To serve, cut into 2-inch squares or press cookie-cutter shapes into pan. Remove carefully with thin, flexible spatula. Makes about 9 treats.

72. Bake and Decorate Cookies

Here is a surefire way to generate a few big smiles around your house! Any cookbook has dozens of cookie recipes. Make a list of your favorites and make two special events out of this one. One would be a trip to the store to buy the ingredients; the other is the evening you bake—and *eat!*

73. Kids: Plan and Prepare a Meal

Arrange a night once a month to be Kid's Night in the kitchen. Kids may need some guidance initially, but eventually should be able to plan and prepare a meal for the whole family. Here are some guidelines that will help the event run more smoothly:

1. Include at least one food item from each of these categories: protein, green vegetable, starch, and fruit.
2. Give your grocery list to the family shopper at least two days prior to the meal.
3. Clean up the kitchen after the meal.

Make the evening more fun by using some of these creative ideas: Write and decorate a card that lists "Tonight's Menu" for your "guests." Play background music and decorate the table with candles and flowers. Wear a chef's hat and apron. Be creative as well as responsible, and Kid's Night is sure to become a favorite of the whole family.

— READING AND WRITING —

If you are struggling to overcome the TV temptation, prepare for success by placing your favorite reading material, paper, and pen next to your easy chair. Promise yourself that you will not turn on the tube until you have read or written at least a page.

Reading and writing possibilities are limitless. However, this list is intended to give you a few specific ideas.

74. Read One of Your Dad's Favorite Books

Sit down with a book that your dad once read and loved. You may learn something about him as well as honor him by showing an interest in a book he enjoys. And who knows? It may become one of your favorites too.

75. Write a Love Letter

Include specific qualities that you appreciate about your spouse or friend. Make your writing sincere. Use imagery from creation or everyday life to paint word pictures that will give your message more meaning and beauty. The very fact that you took the time to write about your love or friendship for her (or him) will be a real encouragement. Mail your letter to the office, or hide it under the pillow.

76. Read to Your Family or Friends

Share a good story with someone else, even if it just means reading the paper to your wife while she is cooking dinner in the kitchen. Children can take turns reading out loud to brothers and sisters. Enjoy the story over several weeks by reading only a chapter a night. My husband and I began our attack on the TV habit by reading Christian novels to each other. It's a great way to pass a cold winter's night in front of the fireplace too.

77. Cut and Paste a Funny Letter to a Friend

Do you have a pile of old newspapers and magazines sitting around somewhere? Pull them out along with scissors, glue, and a piece of paper. Snip and paste phrases and words to create your own zany messages. If you can't find the right word you want, cut out a picture to represent it and include it in your sentence. Your creation is bound to be as much fun in the making as in the reading. Sign your name, or only hint at your identity. Then mail your letter to a friend who has a sense of humor.

78. Write Letters to Your Elected Officials

Pen a note of encouragement to your federal or state representatives, your local school superintendent, or city councilperson. Praise them for positive voting records or even a street improvement if appropriate. Let your voice be heard on issues such as abortion, pornography, evolution taught in schools, or some other issue of importance. Officials will be much more able to meet the needs of the people if they know what those needs are.

79. Encourage Your Pastor with a Note

As shepherd of the flock, your pastor probably receives many divisive, disturbing comments and "suggestions." It is difficult to be watched constantly and evaluated by others. Take a moment to minister encouragement to him or his family by writing a short letter of praise and assurance of your prayers for them. Sign it from both yourself and your spouse, if applicable.

80. Write a Poem or a "Rap" About Your Children or Parents

Make up a fun rhyme that describes each of your children, friends, or parents and expresses your feelings for them. Repeat it often, and it will become a sweet and silly reminder of your love for them. Here is a "rap" that I wrote for one of our daughters:

> My little Sunshine Girl
> is sweet Kristin Marie.
> She can make her dress twirl
> and she loves her Mommy.
> We know she likes to tease
> to laugh and run and play.
> I will give her a squeeze
> and love her every day!

81. Write a Comical Message for a Phone Answering Machine

If you have an answering machine, have the family gather around the kitchen table and get each member to write out a message for the recorder. After each has designed his or her personalized message, keep them. Change your recording each week as each family member records the message. Or you may want to make a family message by entertaining callers with accents, sound effects, or special themes (English mansion, space ship, Old West, etc.). Be creative and have fun. Don't be surprised if your friends begin calling just to hear your messages!

82. Write a Short Story for Publication

Try out your writing skills by preparing a short story, article, or filler for publication. You may have some experiences or knowledge that others can benefit from. Submit your story or article to your favorite magazines or Sunday school take-home papers. *The Writer's Market* by Writer's Digest Books, updated and published annually by F & W Publications, Cincinnati, Ohio, can be found in most libraries. It is available from most libraries and provides information on where and how to get your work published.

I want to write a _____ for_____ market.

83. Write to a Prisoner

Prison Fellowship Ministry, founded by Chuck Colson, offers volunteers an opportunity to write encouraging letters to inmates. Volunteers must be twenty-one years of age or have parental consent. To receive an application used to match you with an appropriate inmate, write: Prison Fellowship Ministry, Pen Pal Program, P.O. Box 17500, Washington, DC 20041.

84. Just for Kids: Write and Illustrate Your Own Book

Make up an adventure about someone like yourself and write it down. This is the "rough draft" of your story. Read it over and make changes to improve it. Sketch some picture ideas for each page of your book. Now you are ready to neatly copy your story and pictures onto construction paper. Make a cover for your book from paper, cardboard, or cloth. Staple, sew, or glue the back edge together, and you have your very own originally written and illustrated masterpiece. Make one for Mom, Dad, or grandparents; and they will cherish it for a long time.

— LISTENING AND LEARNING —

The nice thing about just listening as opposed to the listening and viewing that TV requires is that our eyes and hands are free to engage in some other activity while we listen. If we spent more time listening, we would also probably learn more. Focus your mind on some of those things that you have always wanted to know, because when we stop learning, we stop growing. You are never too young or too old to listen and learn.

85. Listen to Inspiring Messages

Use your Christian radio program guide to find out when your favorite speakers can be heard, and plan to listen to them the way you would plan to watch a TV program. You can also check out tapes from your church library. (If your church doesn't have a tape library, consider organizing one.) Listen while you work in the kitchen or the garage. Listen while driving or doing yardwork or stretching out on the couch.

86. Listen to Music

Christian music is a good way to fill our minds with whatever is true, pure, and lovely. The Holy Spirit can use godly words to encourage, admonish, or strengthen us. Make a special event out of listening to a tape or CD. Give it your full attention, as you would at a concert. Dim the lights, make a fire in the fireplace, light some candles, pull up a comforter, and snuggle up close to your beloved spouse!

87. Take a "Talk Walk"

Invite a friend, child, spouse, parent, or neighbor to take a "talk walk." As you walk around the neighborhood, consider yourself a student of your loved one. How well do you really know him or her? Here are some question/conversation possibilities:

Light and Easy

- What is your favorite dinner? Dessert? Breakfast?
- What are some of the funnest things you have ever done?
- Describe how you proposed to (or were proposed to by) your spouse.
- What were/are your favorite subjects in school? Why?

Stop and Think

- Tell me about two of your most embarrassing moments.
- What would you do with $10,000?
- What is the best and worst thing that happened to you this week?
- What is the first thing you remember from your childhood?
- What are two or three of your best childhood memories?
- What is the best thing we have ever done together?

- Who are your closest friends? What do you like about them?
- If you knew you only had one week to live, what would you do? Who would you talk to? What unanswered questions would you seek to satisfy?
- What do you think you are pretty good at doing? What are your talents or abilities (even those you enjoy but haven't used a great deal)?
- Is there anything you deeply regret?
- What would you like your life to be like in ten years?

88. Research Your Family Tree

Begin with a trip to the library for a genealogy-tracing book. Start corresponding with near and distant relatives and share your findings. Use maps to identify the places your ancestors lived. Check out some books on the ethnic background and culture of your family. Find out when the gospel was first brought to your national group. Are there many believers in that culture now? Remember that we can all claim Noah and his wife as our ancestors, and in the pre-Flood world, Adam and Eve also. If you have a personal computer with CD-ROM drive, consider purchasing one of the excellent programs that aid you in compiling all of your information in a very organized fashion. The better ones, like *Family Tree Maker* from Banner Blue Software, even allow you to scan in family photos, maps, audio messages, and video clips.

89. Find an Old Friend and Call Her

Have you ever wondered what happened to your old childhood friend? You used to have great times together, but you haven't heard from her in years. Call any mutual friends for information on her whereabouts, then call her. Find out what she is up to; reminisce about old times. She will be honored by your detective work, and you will have a great time sharing each other's news.

90. Take a Bible Correspondence Course

Replace the light of the TV with the light of the Word. Enroll in a correspondence course offered by a radio ministry or a Bible institute. Moody Bible Institute's correspondence school has a wide offering of courses from New Testament studies to "Exposing Cults" to "Keys to Happy Family Living." Write for their catalog at: Moody Correspondence School, 820 North LaSalle, Chicago, IL 60610

91. Enroll in a Class

Look through the local college catalog for classes that will improve your abilities or that just sound interesting. You can audit the class or take it for credit whether you are interested in American history, gourmet cooking, or calligraphy. Many arts or crafts classes are offered by the city parks and recreation department, or consider forming a crafts group of friends. Taking classes is a natural avenue for meeting unchurched friends with whom you can share Christ.

92. Teach Yourself to Use Your Personal Computer

Those who have personal computers usually are not using them to their full capabilities, simply because they have never taken the time to sit down and work through it step-by-step. The Internet, on-line services, and CD-ROM software can be wonderful for education and edification, but, like the TV, they must be monitored and carefully utilized. As you gain confidence and speed, your PC will become a valuable tool that you will use regularly and confidently.

93. Help Children with Homework

Parents as well as older siblings have a wonderful opportunity to review academics while helping the younger ones in the family. Whatever the homework is, be available to answer questions and explain new concepts. Your children will gain confidence in their ability and in your interest in them.

94. Explore Your Globe

Improve your knowledge of geography as you study a globe or map. How many countries are in the world? How many can you name? What islands are in the Pacific Ocean? How many oceans, continents, and seas can you name? Have fun imagining faraway places as you explore your globe. Consult an encyclopedia, use the Global Pursuit game by the National Geographic Society, or study a copy of P. J. Johnstones's excellent book, *Operation World*, for interesting facts.

95.   Collect and Label Leaves

You may be surprised at just how excited a young child can get at this kind of an activity if Mom or Dad is involved! This is an excellent way to get time one-on-one with your child and have a common goal in mind at the same time.

You will need a book about leaves from the library, 3-by-5 cards, a pen, a book for pressing leaves between pages, and a photo album. As you collect the leaves, look them up in your book and write their names on 3-by-5 cards. Place the leaf and the card together in between the pages of a book. You may even want to make crayon rubbings of the tree bark, and you might include a photograph of each tree in your leaf album. At home, place your book of fresh leaves under a stack of heavy books. In a few days, take the leaves out of the book and place them in the photo album along with their names and any other information you have gathered.

Keep your leaf book out on the coffee table for others to admire and learn from. Use it to quiz your own knowledge. The same idea can be used with a rock collection. Identifying and displaying rocks as well as keeping a journal of where you found them can be a lifelong interest.

96.   Study Bugs and Plants with a Magnifying Glass

Explore the tiny wonders in your own backyard with the aid of a magnifying glass. Answer these questions:
- How many legs does a ladybug have?
- Do any of your plants have hairy surfaces?
- What does pollen look like?
- How does a spider spin its web?
- Are there any bugs in the bark of your tree?
- Are there bugs on your roses? What kinds?
- What is crawling around out in your lawn?

97.   Start a New Hobby

You can study and collect stamps, coins, model airplanes, or almost anything else as a family activity, one that will interest everyone. Or try one just for you. If you already have a collection, get it out and take another look at it. Chances are, you will soon have a curious onlooker or two, and a lively conversation about the collection will result!

I want to start developing a hobby or collection of: _____

_____

— THINGS TO MAKE —

Young and old alike enjoy the tangible benefits of making things. Activities in this part are not only entertaining but productive as well. Additionally, several of the items suggested will make heartwarming gifts for those you care about.

98. Make a Coupon Book

Think of some things that you can do with or for friends or family members. Ask yourself, *What help do they need?* Or, *What would they think is fun?* Give them these gifts of your time in coupon form. Coupons from an adult to a child might include:

- "This coupon is redeemable for two games of 'Chutes and Ladders' with me."
- "The bearer of this coupon is entitled to thirty adventurous minutes of indoor fort building with me."
- "This coupon is redeemable for two hours of roller skating with a friend this Saturday night."
- "The bearer of this coupon is entitled to a Sunday afternoon at the park with your family and a guest."

A child might give a parent services such as mowing the lawn, washing the car, dishwashing for a week, or organizing the junk drawer. Adults can give adults coupons for baby-sitting, a pizza delivery, a batch of their favorite homemade cookies, or a date of their choice on Friday night. Cut a piece of 8½-by-11 paper into four strips. Write and maybe illustrate each coupon. Add a cover and a back to your coupon book, then staple them together at one end, and you have a great gift!

I want to make a coupon book(s) for: _____

_____

_____

_____

_____

_____

99. Create a Birthday Card

Make a birthday really special for someone by taking the time now to design your very own card. Write an honest verse about why you appreciate him or her. Using high-quality paper, design the cover. Consider stenciling a design, or attach a photograph of the birthday person. Try out your painting or drawing skills for the cover, or cut pieces from used store cards to be combined on your new, original one.

100. Make a Memory Album

This can be a precious gift for an anniversary or a special birthday. Begin at least two months in advance by secretly asking friends of the honored person to write a short note expressing some trait they appreciate or some experience they remember about the special person. Ask them to include a photograph of themselves for the album. Display the letters and the photographs in a photo album with magnetic pages. (Remember that letters can be reduced on a photocopier to enable you to fit them in the album.) Spruce up each page with flowers or other designs cut from old greeting cards. Use photographs of the honored person (or couple) to illustrate a brief history of their life (lives) to this point. Include captions with dates and important details. Your special person will treasure his or her memory album for years to come.

101. Make "A Day in the Life of . . ." Book

Take pictures of your child, spouse, or friends brushing their teeth in the morning, making their beds, playing in the yard, reading, running with friends, or whatever other things they do in a day. Combine the photos in a book to create a story, complete with a narrative you have written. This will make a fun book to read again and again.

102. Make Christmas Presents

Anyone who has crammed on December 23rd to finish Christmas presents knows that April is not too soon to begin making Christmas gifts. Brainstorm for ideas by thumbing through hobby and craft magazines. Once you have made your list and gathered your supplies, you will be set until December with productive ideas.

Name of Person: Gift Idea(s):

_____   _____

_____   _____

_____   _____

_____   _____

103. Make Doll Clothes

Every little girl is delighted by homemade doll clothes. Lay the doll or an old doll dress on a piece of paper and trace it to design your own patterns. Choose a fabric and style that is similar to the little girl's own dress. This is a great way to make use of your fabric scraps. Even if you don't have any little girls of your own, hospital children's wards, your church benevolent collection, an orphanage, or homeless children's shelters will be thrilled with your gifts.

104. Redecorate the Kitchen Bulletin Board

Replace the outdated phone numbers and messages on your bulletin board with some seasonal borders or decorations. Be sure to attach a fresh pad of paper and a pencil.

105. Paint a Picture

Could it be that you are one of those people who says, "I'd like to try my hand at oil or watercolor painting someday?" Well, maybe now is your big moment. Gather your equipment and plunge in. Allow yourself plenty of practice and enjoy learning through doing. Store your painting supplies in one convenient location where they will be easy to get to the next time you are in the mood to paint.

106. Make Patio Furniture

Check out your favorite do-it-yourself book for instructions on cutting and assembling a planter for the patio or maybe a porch swing or lawn chair. Your creative efforts will be admired and appreciated by many.

107. Make Shelves for Your Closets

Do you feel like you are running out of storage space? The answer may be simpler than moving to a new house. Chances are, you could use your closet space much more efficiently by adding a few more shelves. Once you have taken measurements and obtained your supplies, the project can probably be completed in one evening. If you prefer (or if you are an apartment dweller) you can have the shelving fiberboard cut to the proper lengths at the lumber department of most large home-improvement stores. Then all you have to do is bring it home and nail or screw it together.

108. Revive Old Furniture with a Fresh Coat of Paint

Dig out an old stool, chair, table, or bookcase. You might find just the thing one of your rooms has been needing. Give the item a fresh coat of paint, and then enhance it further with a stencil design or a contrasting color of trim. You may create a cherished new item for your home.

109. Make an Educational Board Game

Create an original, homemade board game for the kids or the whole family. You can make reviewing academics as much fun as developing strategy.

- *Board:* A game board can be made from a piece of poster board, a rectangle cut from a cardboard box, or a flattened file folder. For the most basic game, begin by writing "start" in an upper corner and make a trail of boxes that wind around the board, finally reaching the bottom, opposite corner of the board, and the word *end.* Intersperse the trail with phrases such as: "Sorry, move back two spaces," or "Hooray! Move ahead four spaces."

- *Cards:* Use 3-by-5 cards for question cards. On each one, write a question. If you are practicing geography, ask questions about capitols and country locations. If you need to review math facts, use flash cards for your question cards. Just about any subject can adapt to this format including history, literature, music, reading, and science. Write answers on the backs of the cards or on an answer sheet.

- *Place markers and dice:* Plastic milk-carton caps with colored stickers or buttons make good place markers. Use a die or a game spinner to determine how many spaces each player may advance.
- *How to play:* Two or more players begin by choosing who will go first. The first player places his cap on "start" and selects a question card without looking at the back of the card. If he answers correctly, he may roll the die and advance accordingly. Each player in turn selects a card, tosses, and moves. The winner is the first player to reach the end box.
- *Variation:* Pick a theme for your game board such as "Space Flight" or "Marathon" or "The Circus" and decorate the board with pictures that reflect the theme. Change "start" and "end" to "takeoff" and "touchdown," "starting line" and "finish line," or "ticket booth" and "grand finale." Be creative and imaginative, capturing your family's specific interests.

110. Make Puppets

- *Popsicle-stick puppets:* Cut people and animals out of coloring books or Sunday school papers. Glue them to a heavier paper backing and then attach a Popsicle stick with glue or tape.
- *Sock puppets:* Put your hand in the foot of an old sock. Determine where the mouth, eyes, and hair should be. Cut these out of felt and yarn to be glued or stitched in place. These puppets are some of the best because they can move their mouths.
- *Finger puppets:* Draw a face on your fingertip with a pen. Make clothes for your puppet by taping tissue paper skirts and pants onto your fingers.
- *Glove puppets:* Glue felt pieces and pompons onto the fingers of a pair of white gloves. Add facial features and you have ten wiggly puppets ready to tell a story.
- *Paperbag puppets:* Cut faces out of construction paper and glue to a small paper bag. The folded bottom of the bag forms the mouth.
- *Paper-plate puppets:* Staple two paper plates together around the edges, leaving an opening at the bottom for inserting

your hand. Draw a face on the front. Attach ribbon or yarn for hair.

Now, make up a story and act it out for the family using your very own puppets. A theater stage can be made from cardboard boxes. Let imaginations really soar for this performance.

111. Create a Papier-Mâché Masterpiece

Papier-mâché crafts are created by wrapping pasty strips of newspaper around boxes and wads of newspaper to make a new shape or figure.

- *Flour and water paste:* Homemade paste can be made by mixing together one cup of flour with one-half cup of cold water until smooth. Pour two cups of boiling water over the mixture and stir until it becomes transparent. Dilute with water until it is the consistency of heavy cream. Tear or cut newspaper into ½-inch strips. Pour some of the paste into a shallow dish. Pull the strips of paper through the paste and wrap around the form. (Wire forms of many designs can be purchased at craft stores.) Continue layering the strips, placing each new layer at right angles to the layer beneath it until it is about ¼-inch thick. Let dry; sand and paint.

- *To make a piggy bank:* Tape or tie toilet-paper rolls as legs to a cylindrical oatmeal box, which is the pig's body. A ball of wadded newspaper with a stubby snout can be the pig's head. When the pasty strips are attached, ears and other details can be added. Cut a slit in the top for the coins to slip through and a hole in the bottom for a cork stopper. When the paste is completely dry, sand down the rough spots. Give the bank a coat of paint and a happy pig face, then cover it with a shiny coat of shellac.

Use this same method to make masks, helmets, contour maps, or other interesting creations.

112. Make Bookmarks

Cut a piece of felt into a strip ten inches long and two inches wide. Cut 1½-inch slits into the top and bottom of the felt strip to create a fringed appearance. Decorate the bookmark by gluing or sewing on strips of embroidered ribbon or lace. Children can make these for special friends or family members and use as birthday or Christmas gifts.

113. Make Paperweights

Gather smooth stones for your paperweights. Paint them to look like ladybugs or faces, or paint pretty flowers and designs on the stones. Cover with a coat of shellac. These also make creative and personal gifts for children to give.

114. Make Something Fun from a Big Cardboard Box

With a good imagination, some paint, crayons, and maybe even scissors, you can transform a big box into a motor home or a boat or a house or an airplane. Draw in wheels and gauges. Cut out windows and doors. If you make a boat, bounce around in it a bit as you pretend you are sailing through turbulent waters. If you make a house, pillows and blankets can become chairs and carpets. Tape paper-towel curtains at the windows and invite friends over. Serve cookies!

115. Make a Bird Feeder

- *Pie tin bird feeder:* You will need a disposable pie tin and four pipe cleaners. Poke four evenly spaced holes around the rim of the tin. Insert the pipe cleaners and bend the ends to secure. Twist the pipe cleaners together at the top where they meet and attach a loop. Hang it from a tree branch. Fill with birdseed or crumbs and have fun bird watching.

- *Pinecone feeder:* Attach a loop to the top of a large pine cone. Smear peanut butter all over the pinecone being sure to fill all the undersides. Now roll it in birdseed and hang it in a tree for some hungry little birds.

— OUTREACH ACTIVITIES —

"Love one another" is one of Scripture's primary commands, yet we sometimes have difficulty expressing that love. A plaque I admired in the home of a missionary read: "Love is an action word." How true! We need action if the world is ever going to believe that God loves them. Reach out to those in need physically, emotionally, and spiritually.

As we begin to get our TV time into line, we can look outside our four walls for ways to show Christ's love. Giving your time to another person is about the best way we can say "I love you." In fact, getting involved in people's lives is one of the best ways to ensure that we will continue to watch less TV. Look through the alternatives that follow and find something that can help you put your love into action.

116. Do Repairs for Someone in Need

Is there something that you can do for a neighbor, friend, or church member? Think of those you know who are sick, elderly, handicapped, just had a baby, experienced a recent death or divorce in the family, or are facing some other crisis. Don't forget the single parents who are trying to meet the responsibilities of both mom and dad in the home. If you can't think of anyone in need, call your church office for some suggestions.

Then, give your friend a call and tell her that you are planning on doing a few chores or repairs for her. Where would she like you to start? If it is a big project like replacing the roof, invite other friends to join the team. Here are just a few suggestions for ways you can help:

- baby-sit
- change the car oil
- clean out the gutters
- mend clothes
- mow the lawn
- rake the leaves
- repair a leaky faucet
- run errands
- shovel the walk
- wash the car
- wash second-story windows
- weed the garden

117. Walk and Talk with Neighbors

Take a walk with the intention of stopping to talk to any of your neighbors you happen to see outside along the way. Or begin by inviting a neighbor to join you for a walk. Eventually, you may get the privilege of sharing Jesus with him or her. (See idea number 86, "Take a Talk Walk," for a list of conversation-starter ideas.)

118. Visit an Elderly Person

Some of the loneliest people in the world may live on your street or attend your church. Elderly people often know the pain of seeing their best friends or spouses die, and they are starving for companionship; yet they're striving not to be a "burden" to anyone. Visiting the elderly is for kids and adults alike. If you don't already know some older person you can visit, call the local nursing home and ask them to direct you to someone who would appreciate regular visits. You can:

- spend an hour or two just listening and talking.
- invite them over for dinner.
- take them out for a ride in the car.
- send them notes in the mail.
- read to them.

119. Host a Neighborhood Children's Carnival

This event will be great fun for the children on your block as well as provide a great opportunity for the neighbors to work together and get to know each other. Ask each family or pairs of families to prepare a carnival booth or table with some game or activity for attendees to enjoy, such as:

- a cakewalk
- a dunk tank
- a fishing booth where simple prizes are hooked
- a popcorn and lemonade stand
- basketball free throws
- ringtoss game
- face painting
- guess how many jelly beans are in the jar
- soapbox derby
- throw the Frisbee through the hoop

Encourage children to do a large part of the planning and running of the carnival day. Hold your carnival in a large back-yard, or arrange for the police to barricade the street for the evening so that you can set up in the street. Have a potluck dinner and then show a Christian movie outdoors after dark. Maybe you can borrow your church's projector and screen.

120. Plan a Neighborhood Ice Cream Social

A fairly easy neighborhood party to plan is an ice cream social. Schedule it for a Sunday afternoon, and ask everyone to bring a half gallon of ice cream, a scoop, and at least one topping to share. You arrange for the tables and chairs, paper bowls, cups, and plastic spoons. Provide water or some beverage for thirsty ice cream eaters. You might ask the police to set up barricades for the event and have your party right in the middle of the street. Plan some simple get-acquainted games and relay races to get people interacting. Use the party to strengthen friendships and as a jumping-off point for inviting neighbors into your home at some other time.

121. Host a Backyard Bible Club

If you have ever wondered how to reach the kids on your block with the good news of God's love, beginning a kid's Bible club may be just the thing for you. There are lots of materials out there to aid you; some are designed specifically for neighborhood clubs. Start by making a trip to your local Christian bookstore or by contacting your own pastor for curriculum ideas. Your club could run for an hour everyday for five days, or six weeks, or even nine months. Or maybe an evangelistic party club that meets once a month or just for holidays might be more appropriate for your neighborhood and your situation. A meeting schedule could include singing, Bible lessons, verse memorization, games, and handicrafts. If it seems like an overwhelming task to complete on your own, why not invite a friend to join you in this ministry?

122. Hostess a Girls' Tea Party

Girls will have fun planning and decorating for this special little event all by themselves. They can send out homemade invitations. Decorate the table and arrange for snacks. You can serve tea or any other beverage children enjoy but be sure to pour it from a teapot into pretty teacups. Remember to include some special treat that you don't usually serve, such as mints or cut-out cookies that the children decorate. The young hostess can learn the joy of sharing the good news with her guests by reading a gospel story from a book or telling it with flannelgraph figures. Another possibility is to show a Christian children's video after tea time. Check the video reviews in this book for suggestions.

123. Host a Boys' Root-Beer-Float Party

Boys can prepare for an afternoon root-beer-float party by inviting a few friends and asking them to bring their favorite or most unique mug or glass. Serve the floats in the boys' mugs. After the snack, the boy host can share the gospel with his friends by reading an exciting Christian story or showing a Christian video. You may want to continue your meetings together and form a kind of "club" that gets together to snack, play, and read a boys' Christian adventure series.

124. Take Care of a Homebound Person for a Day

Give the parent of a handicapped child or the child of an aging parent a day out of the house. Arrange to learn their responsibilities and allow them some much needed time away from their constant responsibilities of caregiving. You will gain new understanding and compassion for the handicapped as well as their caretakers. Contact your church or local health agency to put you in touch with someone who would appreciate your help.

125. Walk Someone's Pet

Kids can offer to help a neighbor, have fun, and get exercise all at the same time. Take their dog for a run around the block. They are likely to make two new friends.

126. Organize a Church Workday

There are many projects around the church that never seem to get accomplished until members join forces. Many hands make light work as well as good company. You can be a real blessing to your pastor and church staff by coordinating a workday for your church. Get or make a list of projects that need to be accomplished. Gather the necessary supplies. Set a date for your workday and promote it well. As workers arrive, assign them tasks in small groups and watch how quickly the jobs can be accomplished. Arrange for a lunch to be provided for workers, or have everyone bring a sack lunch.

127. Volunteer at a Non-profit Ministry

Make a list of the ministries in your area. Select the ones that you are most interested in helping. Give them a call. Tell them you would like to volunteer two hours or so a week. Ask if there is anything that they would like you to do. You may find yourself answering phones, counseling unwed mothers, stuffing envelopes, sweeping floors, typing, filing, or visiting patients. The possibilities are endless. You may not be able to contribute financially, but you will be contributing a great deal when you give dependably of your time.

128. Help in Children's Ministries at Your Church

It is surprising that there appears to be a shortage of children's workers in our churches. There are plenty of opportunities for everyone. Let your church know that you would like to help out. You are needed, whether your abilities lie in storytelling, song leading, piano playing, game leading, listening, praying, being a friend, driving cars, preparing food, or organizing records.

129. Serve a Meal at a Rescue Mission

Volunteer to help in the kitchen of a rescue mission or ministry that provides meals for the homeless. Your church, Sunday school class, or family can take responsibility for preparing and serving one meal a month. Put your Christianity into action; call up your local mission or shelter to learn what you can do.

Quick reference information:

Shelter name _____
Address _____
Phone #_____
Needs _____
_____

130. Volunteer

Some Christians never get out of their Christian circle of friends to rub shoulders with people who need to know Christ. One way to solve this problem may be to volunteer your services at the public library, a local hospital, or in your child's school classroom. You will help your community as well as make new friends with whom you may someday share Christ.

— FORGOTTEN WORK PROJECTS —

Every household has jobs that tend to be forgotten or neglected. These are usually the maintenance items that only require monthly or even annual attention. This is a list of projects that are typically forgotten or put off. At the end of the list is space where you can jot down your own personal job reminders. Before you flip on the TV, why not complete some of these projects? You will enjoy a sense of accomplishment when you finish tasks that never seem to get done.

131. Clean Out Your Junk Drawer, Tool Chest, Closet, Attic, or Garage

Do you have difficulty finding a place to put things? Do you have trouble finding the items you are looking for? If so, it is time to clean out and organize your junk drawers, tool chest, closet, attic, or garage.

A simple project like organizing drawers can be done by declaring a drawer-organizing night when everyone in the family works on the same project. On the other hand, a project like cleaning the garage may take the whole family's efforts one Saturday or over several evenings until little by little the whole garage is neat and organized.

132. Organize Your Photos into an Album

Are the photos you have taken piling up? Organizing them into photo albums can be fun. The whole family can be involved as they look at pictures of themselves and relive happy memories. (This is a project that I try to do at least once each year. My family is especially appreciative of my labors when I include funny and descriptive notes on the same pages that the pictures appear.)

133. Simple Home Repairs

Every household has a few irritating maintenance needs that could be easily repaired if someone just took the time to fix them. Begin by making a list of needs throughout the week. The next time you are tempted to watch TV out of habit rather than conscious choice, pull out the list and choose one of the items to repair.

134. Clean Out Your Files

Filing cabinets have a way of accumulating vast quantities of paper that are never seen or retrieved again. Periodically, everyone needs to flip through their files to reacquaint themselves with the contents as well as clear out unnecessary items.

135. Mend Clothes

Gather together all the clothes that are in need of repair. Sew on buttons, restitch seams, repair pockets, adjust hems, and fix zippers. In a few hours you dispose of a bundle of little annoyances as well as revitalize a whole wardrobe.

136. Shine Shoes

Instead of running out the door with scuffy looking shoes, take a few minutes now to shine them. The next time you are dashing around getting ready for a dressy occasion, you will thank yourself for a pair of ready-to-go, clean, and polished shoes.

137. Wash Windows

Get out the window cleaner and some rags and wash the windows. Maybe you can entice a friend into washing the insides while you clean the outside. The fresh, clear panes will give you a brighter outlook on the world.

138. Wash the Car

Whether you drive a jalopy or a Corvette, a good clean-up job improves one's pride of ownership. After you have washed, vacuumed, scrubbed, rinsed, dried (and maybe waxed!), treat yourself to a scenic drive with your sweetheart.

139. Clean Out the Gutters

Choose a pleasant day and a surefooted ladder to clear your gutters of the debris that accumulates through the season.

140. Clean the Barbecue Grill

This is everybody's least-favorite job, so do the family a favor and scrub that grungy barbecue grill. When your mouth is watering for some delicious hamburgers, the last thing you want is to put them on a dirty grill. Get this chore out of the way, and you will be ready to enjoy your next barbecue.

141. Wash the Dog

With the right attitude, this job can be a fun one. Suds and rinse Fido until he looks and smells as lovely as a rose again. You will appreciate his fresh appearance and Fido will enjoy the attention he receives. (Our Bichon Frise, Bubbles, is not a big fan of baths, but she sure is fun to watch after the bath is through! She goes crazy running around the house, jubilant that the ordeal is over!)

142. List Your Own Work Projects

_____

_____

_____

_____

_____

_____

— PLAN-AHEAD ACTIVITIES —

Activities in this category take a little time and planning. Some people find the planning as much fun as the doing. At any rate, pull out a piece of paper and jot down your creative ideas for these plan-ahead activities.

143. Secretly Plan an Extra-special Date

What do you think your beloved would most enjoy on this extra-special date? Does he like baseball? Plan on taking in a game on your special day. Does she enjoy art galleries? Include it as part of your date. Maybe you will want to arrange for some unusual transportation like a horse and buggy or a limousine. Consider making it a day-long event beginning with breakfast, then outdoor fun, and dinner at an elegant restaurant. Married couples could consider an overnight stay at a local resort.

For many zany date ideas, read _Creative Dating_ by Doug Fields and Todd Temple. It's available at Christian and secular bookstores and many libraries. However you personalize your date, make it an extraspecial evening that your beloved will cherish for a long time.

144. Plan a Fun Date with One of Your Children

Kids are delighted in knowing that you planned a special date just for them! Send your child an invitation in the mail for a "Fun date with Dad (or Mom) on Saturday." The added suspense and anticipation can make the event even more exciting. Maybe you will want to make it a yearly event celebrated on each child's half-birthday (a day six months from his or her real birthday). Cater the date's activities to things the child enjoys. Start conversations that give him or her an opportunity to express their feelings. Be vulnerable yourself and share some of your feelings. Express some of the qualities that you appreciate about your son or daughter.

145. Plan a Vacation

Give your vacation plans some time to form this year by planning far in advance of your departure date. Begin by taking an informal survey of what each person in the family thinks makes a good vacation. Jot down the different ideas and try to incorporate at least some of their desires into your plans. Determine your dates and budget. Check out a travel book from the library such as Reader's Digest's *America from the Road* or *Off the Beaten Path*.

Be careful not to plan so much travel that your time is spent solely on interstate highways. Plan where you will stay, what sights you want to include, how much money you can allot to each day's activities, and how you can make the travel time fun and relaxing. Highlight the sights you will be seeing on the map. Include older children by allowing one teenager to be in charge of the daily finances and another to be in charge of in-car entertainment and morale. Have fun making your plans, but determine to be flexible when things don't go the way you planned.

146. Design and Build a Tree House

It may be that you have always wanted to build a tree house, but you have never gotten around to it. Make your evenings more entertaining by pulling out paper and pencil and coming up with a realistic sketch and plan for what you want the tree house or playhouse to be. Get a book from the library or hardware store that suggests building plans. Include your children as you purchase supplies and begin building. Even if they are too young to hammer, they will be thrilled to hand you the nails and help with painting and sanding. When a child feels like she is an important part of a project, she will have more appreciation and respect for it.

147. Organize a Neighborhood Craft or Garage Sale

Set a date and a location and invite your friends and neighbors to contribute their homemade or used items. Come up with a plan for managing the money, manning the sale, advertising, displaying items, and redistributing profits and unsold goods. Call a casual meeting in your home to inform your neighbors and ask for their help with specific tasks. Many problems can be avoided if everyone is properly informed. The sale may be just the vehicle you've been looking for to develop friendships and make a little extra money as well.

148. Draft a Will

If drafting a will is something you have been putting off, now is the time to plan for the future. Seek out a lawyer and take care of it. For most families, it is a simple matter that can be settled with one visit to the lawyer's office. Prior to your meeting with the lawyer you will want to consider these items:

- Who will you name as the preferred guardian for your children should you both die?
- Who will be the estate executor/executrix?
- Do you want to establish a living will?
- Do you want specific possessions to be willed to specific people?
- Will you leave a portion of your estate to a church or ministry?
- Would a living trust be a better way to distribute your estate? Consider involving adolescent and older children in these discussions, in generalized terms, so it is less threatening or uncertain for them. Consider their wishes for guardians and other matters too.

149. Plan a Treasure Hunt

Write and hide clues that will lead your treasure-seeking guests to one hidden clue after another until at last they are given the final clue that should lead them to the "treasure." Your treasure can be a box of foil-covered chocolates, a book, or a Christian video. To play in teams, make up two equally difficult sets of clues that lead to the same treasure. The team that reaches the treasure first is the winner.

150. Develop a Family Budget

Many families find themselves in a position where their expenses exceed their income. If yours is one of those families, you need to sit down with pencil and paper and determine where your money is going as well as where you would like it to go. Set a realistic budget and learn to live within your means again.

For materials dealing with financial management, we suggest you call or write to the organization founded by author and radio speaker Larry Burkett: Christian Financial Concepts, 601 Broad St. SE, Gainsville, GA 30501, phone: 1-800-722-1976.

Good books on the subject are Amy Ross Mumford's *It Only Hurts Between Paydays* and various books by Christian financial counselor Ron Blue. By involving all family members, the children will begin to understand financial responsibility as well as why they can't have everything they want. Help them become responsible stewards too.

151. A Special Idea Just Your Own

Write out the basics of a custom-made special event for you or your family.

_____

_____

_____

_____

_____

_____

_____

Part V

202 Video Reviews You Can Trust

12

Finding the Best Family-Friendly Videos

The owner of a flourishing video rental store found himself in quite a quandary. Having recently dedicated his life to Christ, he was increasingly troubled by the type of videos that he was renting and selling. His shelves were laden with more than 1,600 different titles, but among them were very few that he felt good about. In fact, he stated that "if the Lord Jesus walked into [my] video shop and asked for a decent video, out of the 1,600 on the shelves I could probably only scrape together twelve!"[1]

That realization hounded his conscience. Even though he had invested thousands of hours in the hard work of building his business, and even though he would face a large financial setback, he knew that he had to get out of the business. And he has.

Most video movies portray an even coarser level of the same types of offensive behavior that we try to avoid on TV. It's the same old story: free to choose but nothing to choose from. The National Coalition on Television Violence has documented "a steady deterioration in Hollywood films since the birth of the MPAA rating

There is a gross lack of morally commendable movies being released today. But that doesn't excuse us from our responsibility to live in a way that is faithful to the beliefs we espouse.

system. The MPAA now gives PG and PG-13 to films that would have been rated X (NC-17) in 1970. G-rated films, which in 1970 made up 30 percent of all films, have all but disappeared."[2]

In the 1990s, almost 70 percent of the movies being released carry an R-rating,[3] most of them brimming with sex and gore. In an Associated Press survey, 82 percent of those polled said there is too much violence in films; 80 percent said there is too much profanity; and 72 percent said there is too much nudity.[4]

It is probably safe to assume that most Christian viewers would agree that the majority of Hollywood productions are not worth viewing, yet the films are feverishly consumed anyway. Why? Because *all of us* want to sit back and be entertained from time to time.

Sadly, the majority of us simply show too little discretion when it comes to our personal viewing choices. We *talk* about the importance of "family values." We endorse the picketing of large corporations that sponsor overtly violent and sensual TV programs—which can be very effective; don't stop!—but when our doors are shut and our curtains pulled, do we live out the values that we so emphatically advocate?

It is undeniable that there is a glaring lack of morally commendable movies being released today. But that doesn't excuse us from our responsibility to live in a way that is faithful to God's plan for our lives.

Ironically, some of the best and most captivating films available are also some of the best-kept video secrets. The majority of Christians simply don't know how to find Hollywood's small but excellent selection of family-friendly videos. And most of us are almost totally unaware of the wonderful Christian and other family-friendly videos that have become available in recent years.

You will note that the following VideoGuide showcases a sampling both of recent productions and those that we consider to be the most valuable of the classics. Primarily, however, the VideoGuide is unique in that it candidly introduces you to the best and most popular of the *Christian* dramas, documentaries, and children's programs that are available on video. (For information about services that provide up-to-the-minute reviews of the newest Hollywood films and videos, from a biblical perspective, see the endnotes for this chapter.[5])

The Importance of the Fine Print

Whether serious drama or fun children's tapes, carefully selected videos can provide a natural, friendly way to communicate our faith, or to question society's standards; but there are important rights and restrictions connected to all copyrighted videotapes.

We encourage all Christian families—especially those with preschool and grade school-aged children—to begin building a collection of Christ-centered videos from among those described in the following pages. Or you can sponsor them for your church's lending library so that lots of families can have easy access to them.

But be careful not to dishonor God by ignoring or disobeying the copyright owner's showing license. A declaration of usage rights and limitations is usually printed on the back of the video package or on the label on the videotape.

Usage Rights

If you intend to use a tape somewhere other than a private home setting, be *sure* that you clearly understand whether the videos you are considering are licensed for "public use" (i.e, church services, Sunday school classes, VBS, youth-group meetings, etc.) or if they include only the standard private "home-use" rights. Like their Hollywood counterparts, all professionally produced Christian videos are automatically copyrighted and thereby restricted to use in homes, with your family, and normal social acquaintances only.

> Today, almost 70 percent of the movies being released are R-rated.

Unless you have *specific* authorization from the producer (or his legal agent), tapes licensed for "private exhibition" or "home use only" cannot legally be exhibited at or to church groups, no matter how small your group may be, and no matter what the salesperson may tell you!

Why?

As you probably know, secular producers derive profits from the national theater system, domestic cable and network television, international theatrical release and television, ancillary product licensing (you know, stuff like T-shirts, lunch boxes, and toys), plus domestic and international video sales—all of which help them to recoup their production and distribution costs relatively quickly. That's why secular filmmakers usually don't monitor whether *Old Yeller* or *Bambi* are used for a church function or not. Simply stated, the church isn't important to the secular producer.

However, the only "theater" usually available to a struggling *Christian* producer is the church itself. If local churches don't pay the required public-exhibition fees, it won't be very long before film producers who make Bible-based films and videos are forced to find another line of work. (Unfortunately, many already have.) Producers of high-quality Christian dramas cannot survive without the financial and ethical support of the Christian community.

How to Obtain Public-Use Showing Rights

Only the copyright owner, or his legally authorized agent, can grant permission for public-use showings of copyrighted videotapes. Contact the distributor listed on the video package, or call the phone number shown alongside many of our VideoGuide reviews to inquire about how much extra it might cost to show your video publicly (in a church setting). Then, ask that the company with whom you have spoken send you their permission in written form. According to international copyright law, *every* professionally produced video is *automatically* copyrighted. As such, it is limited to in-home showings only and protected by law from unauthorized public showings, no matter how small the audience, unless additional rights are specifically granted.

Christians must come to grips with the fact that, while the gospel message is free, putting it into an entertaining format by using paid scriptwriters, directors, actors, sound technicians, set designers, lighting technicians, and makeup artists, is not. These expenses easily run into the hundreds of thousands of dollars, and most Christian producers (I know several dozen personally) operate on an extremely tight budget.

Don't Compromise

We heartily agree with respected copyright authority Dr. Jerome Miller who says, "I find it unsettling to hear pastors and church workers say copyright infringement is necessary to advance the work of the Lord. To put it simply, copyright infringement, regardless of the purpose, is stealing."[6]

God's command is clear, "Do not steal" (Rom. 13:8–9). "For we are taking pains to do what is right, not only in the eyes of the Lord but also in the eyes of men" (2 Cor. 8:21). Illegally copying or exhibiting a tape in public-use settings (without paying for the right to do so) that is licensed only for home use pulls the financial rug right out from under the struggling producer's feet.

Please, let's be very careful not to make it any harder for the God-fearing film producers to make more movies!

HOW THE VIDEOGUIDE WORKS

The following VideoGuide provides a standard for considering the relative value of videos before buying or renting them. Even those individuals who have seen only one or two of the listed films can gauge the quality of other shows simply by comparing the rating of the titles they have seen to those that they have not.

Rating

A rating of up to five stars has been assigned to each production in each of two areas: "Content" and "Technical Quality." The definition of each rating is generally described as follows:

★★★★★	Excellent!
★★★★	Very Good
★★★	Good
★★	Fair
★	Poor (*Don't waste your money!*)

Content

This category deals with the video's *message*. While technical aspects are often the most noticeably excellent or horrible parts of a program, they are not the most important. Secular producers have created thousands of *technically* excellent movies. However, only a handful have contained a message truly worthy of the viewers' time. In assigning a rating of one to five stars for each production, we have posed and answered the following questions:

- Does the program have a wholesome, family-friendly message with morally commendable qualities?
- If the production claims to be based on a Bible story, how true to the scriptural account is it? If it adds to the story, are its embellishments logical and probable in light of the historical, scientific, and/or cultural knowledge that is available?
- Is this video appropriate for the intended age group?

Of overriding concern in this category, especially when evaluating children's videos, is question number two. If the production claims to be based on a Bible story but presents material not in keeping with scriptural, historical, and cultural knowledge, the production could not score highly in this category even if the production was wholesome, and entertainment aspects were excellent.

Technical Quality

Again using the one-to-five-star rating system, each show was evaluated with regard to its technical considerations. Those considerations include such aspects as the quality of the screenplay, acting, lighting, cinematography, editing, soundtrack, and animation.

Primary Audience

The age group listed is that which we feel would derive the greatest benefit from viewing the show. This is not to imply that a wider age range would not also enjoy the production.

Distributor

Most of the productions listed in our VideoGuide can be purchased from any Christian bookstore or Christian film/video dealer. In case you do not live near one of these retail outlets, we have also listed the name and phone number of each video's producer or a knowledgeable distributor, if they are willing to sell directly to the public. The company listed should be able to answer any questions you may have about content, usage rights, prices, and ordering information.

Our Comments

The comments that we have included with each video evaluation are designed to cut through the marketing hype often written by those who are trying to sell the tapes. We give a brief summary of the topic, story, or message communicated, as well as an honest appraisal of the overall value of each production.

It is our sincere hope that our evaluations will open your imagination to some of the many uses possible for the broad range of Christian and family-friendly videos that are now available. Whether you want to enjoy a bowl of buttery popcorn while relaxing in front of an inspiring family drama, trim your waistline by doing aerobic exercises to Christian music, learn about how dinosaurs fit into the Bible, teach your youngster about wholesome sex by watching and discussing a Bible-based video on the subject, or invite a friend over to watch an evangelistic video, there is a wonderful array of valuable productions out there to meet your needs.

It's really true! The TV *can* be an instrument for happiness and improved communication in your family. *When managed right,* TV is a wonderful tool. But whether that tool is used in a constructive or a detrimental manner is ultimately up to you. It is our desire that—with the help of this book—yours will soon be an even more "fine-tuned" family.

God bless you!

Authors' Choice

ABSENT MINDED PROFESSOR, THE

CONTENT: ★★★★½   TECHNICAL QUALITY: ★★★★

PRIMARY AUDIENCE:	Family (Ages 4+)
DIRECTOR:	Robert Stevenson
STYLE:	Drama (Colorized)
DISTRIBUTOR:	Walt Disney Home Video
LENGTH:	1 hr., 36 min.
FEATURING:	Fred MacMurray, Nancy Olson, Keenan Wynn
MPAA RATING:	G

The Absent Minded Professor is great "unwinding medicine" for anyone looking for a short escape from the cares of life. Here an inventor/college professor gets himself into one hilarious situation after another as he strives to persuade his fiancée, his school, and even the Pentagon that both he and his discovery—an antigravity force called "Flubber"—are credible. Kids will love the flying car, the high-jumping basketball team, and many other stunts and special effects. Contains one proevolution statement (by the professor's housekeeper) and one short car-chase scene where a man fires a pistol (but hits no one). No profanity or sexual overtones. ©1961

ACTS: Volume 1

CONTENT: ★★★★   TECHNICAL QUALITY: ★★ ½

PRIMARY AUDIENCE:	Ages 5–Adult
DIRECTOR:	Keith R. Neely
STYLE:	Filmation
DISTRIBUTOR:	Biblevision (209)825-5645
LENGTH:	38 min.

This video covers Acts 1–7 with integrity and scriptural purity. This series of four tapes combines a word-for-word dramatized version of the NIV translation of the entire Book of Acts (including sound effects and music) with pans, zooms, and dissolves of nicely detailed paintings. The illustrated characters are realistic, not cartoonish. An optional Teacher's Guide and Video Game Book includes suggested questions to help review every segment plus age-graded game ideas to benefit viewers beginning at about eight years. Well suited to small-group Bible studies and family devotions. The panoramic overview of Jewish history by Stephen in Acts 7 (just prior to his stoning) is a highlight of this tape. This series should be in every church video library. These tapes are great tools for dads who need help to initiate or revitalize family devotions. ©1986

A.D.

CONTENT: ★★★   TECHNICAL QUALITY: ★★★★★

PRIMARY AUDIENCE:	High School–Adult
DIRECTOR:	Stuart Cooper
STYLE:	Live-Action Drama
DISTRIBUTOR:	Gospel Films Video (800)253-0413, (616)773-3361
LENGTH:	6 hours

This multimillion-dollar production was filmed on location in Tunisia, Pompeii, Herculeneum, and Rome and originally broadcast in the USA as a network miniseries in the mid-1980s. This version, which has been abridged for wider use in churches, covers the years from 30–69 A.D. and focuses on the confrontation between the mighty Roman empire, Jewish zealots, and the early Christians. Mixes historic facts, biblical narrative, and the result of years of research into customs and conditions in the first century. While it is not scripturally precise, it is close enough that—if used in conjunction with the study guide provided—carefully led discussion times following each of the twelve segments can reveal and correct most of the important misrepresentations. The soap-opera-type storyline includes fictional characters, romance, violence, and killing. WARNING! Last half of third tape is *very* gruesome. ©1984

ADVENTURES OF CHARLIE WANDERMOUSE

Tape 1: "FORGIVENESS and FRIENDSHIP"

CONTENT: ★★½   TECHNICAL QUALITY: ★★★

PRIMARY AUDIENCE:	Ages 3–8
DIRECTOR:	Dan Peeler (animation)
STYLE:	Animated Puppetry
DISTRIBUTOR:	Brownlow Publishing Co. (800)433-7610, (817)831-3831
LENGTH:	29 min.

This tape contains two stories. Each retells a Bible parable but with a contemporary flare. Both stories are led into and summarized by a short discussion between three puppet characters, with the story itself presented in colorful animation. This first tape in the Charlie Wandermouse series introduces the star, Charlie Wandermouse (a mouse character that is described as "a world-famous musician, traveler, and explorer") and his writer/friend, Professor Scribbler. The two stories on this tape are "Learning about God's Forgiveness" (a takeoff on the parable of the prodigal son of Luke 15, which encourages viewers to say they are sorry when they do something that disappoints their parents) and "Learning How to Be a Real Friend" (similar to the Luke 10 story of the good Samaritan, which challenges viewers to be a friend to people who are in need). Quality of animation is superior to the short puppetry sequences. ©1989

ADVENTURES OF MILO and OTIS

CONTENT: ★★★★   TECHNICAL QUALITY: ★★★★

PRIMARY AUDIENCE: Family (ages 4+)
DIRECTOR: Masanori Hata
STYLE: Live-Action Drama
DISTRIBUTOR: RCA/Columbia Pictures
LENGTH: 1 hr., 16 min.
FEATURING: Narration by Dudley Moore
MPAA RATING: G

Delightful, funny, and heartwarming! Those three words best describe this unique film where the two on-screen stars are a curious kitten (Milo) and a so-ugly-he's-cute pug-nose puppy (Otis). Plus, all of the "supporting actors" are farm animals, wild animals, and an occasional insect. Though no human ever appears on-screen, Dudley Moore (the star of *Arthur* and other not-so-family-friendly Hollywood movies) lends his humorous style and British accent in the role of an unseen narrator. Combined with great music and sound effects, Moore keeps viewers of all ages laughing while Milo and Otis tumble from one misadventure to the next in their barnyard world and beyond. Never before have two small farm pets provided so much wholesome viewing pleasure. An excellent video to add to your home video library, especially in homes with pre-adolescents. Nothing objectionable. ©1989

AMAZING BIBLE (series)

Tape 1: "The Amazing Book"

CONTENT: ★★★★★   TECHNICAL QUALITY: ★★★★★

PRIMARY AUDIENCE: Ages 3–10
DIRECTOR: Tony Salerno
STYLE: Animation
DISTRIBUTOR: Bridgestone Multimedia (800)523-0988, (602)940-5777
LENGTH: 25 min.

When it comes to assembling a home video library, this one is an essential. Excellent quality animation *and* message (a combination not found often enough in children's videos). This is a spellbinder that should mesmerize every child over and over again. Instills a genuine interest in and hunger to know the Bible. Includes six sing-a-long songs that get even Mom and Dad tapping their feet. Deals with how we got the Bible, interesting stories in the Bible, memorizing the books of the Bible, Bible trivia, famous men who loved the Bible, and the timelessness and applicability of the Bible. Uses animated mice characters (Revver and Doc Dickory) and a mole (Dewey Decimole) to move into each subject and song. ©1988

Tape 2: "The Amazing Children"

CONTENT: ★★★   TECHNICAL QUALITY: ★★★ ½

PRIMARY AUDIENCE: Ages 3–8
DIRECTOR: Marija Miletic-Dail
STYLE: Animation
DISTRIBUTOR: Bridgestone Multimedia (800)523-0988, (602)940-5777
LENGTH: 25 min.

While both the story and the technical aspects of "Amazing Children" are good, neither matches the excellence of its predecessor, "Amazing Book." In this episode a couple of young mice wish they could grow up quickly because they don't think kids count for much. However, after several short Bible stories about children from the grandfatherly Doc Dickory, and then a backyard battle with a big mean cat, the youngsters discover that being a kid has its advantages. In fact, it is one of the best things you can be. ©1990

AMERICA'S GODLY HERITAGE

CONTENT: ★★★★★   TECHNICAL QUALITY: ★★

PRIMARY AUDIENCE: Adults, Teens
DIRECTOR: Unknown
STYLE: Embellished Lecture
DISTRIBUTOR: Wallbuilders (817)441-6044
LENGTH: 59 min.

This highly enlightening video should be seen by every adult and every student in America. Using a simple set and cutaways to scores of illustrations, photographs, and charts, American history authority David Barton reveals the true beliefs of many of America's famous Founding Fathers regarding the foundational importance of Christianity to law and government. Of particular interest are the facts and alarming true stories concerning the recent false doctrine of "separation of church and state" and the apparently direct relationship between removal of biblical references and sanctioned prayer from public-school classrooms in the early 1960s with the immediate rise in social ills and the decline in the academic competence of American students. This video is unique. As such, you will probably want to watch it several times and share it with friends and relatives. ©1990

AN AMERICAN TAIL

CONTENT: ★★★   TECHNICAL QUALITY: ★★★★★

PRIMARY AUDIENCE: Family (Ages 4+)
DIRECTOR: Don Bluth
STYLE: Animation

DISTRIBUTOR:	MCA Universal Home Video
LENGTH:	1 hr., 21 min.
FEATURING:	Voices of: Dom De Luise, Madeline Kahn, Christopher Plummer
MPAA RATING:	G

The year is 1895. In an attempt to escape "cat persecution" in his native Russia, a young mouse (Fievel) and his family stow away on a steamship bound for the fabled land of no cats—America. However, during a careless act of disobedience, Fievel is swept overboard and lost at sea. Though he is assumed dead by his heartbroken parents, Fievel floats into New York harbor inside a bottle. He has to face many dangerous and exciting obstacles in his determined attempt to find his family. This heartwarming animated drama contains several nice songs, but may be scary at times for young preschoolers. Shows mice characters drinking alcohol but not in a favorable light. The climactic reunion of the dejected Fievel with his Papa and family provides an emotionally satisfying ending. Adults can use this film to emphasize the importance of obeying parents' instruction and to show what *could* happen when children do something that they know Mom or Dad would not want them to. ©1986

ANCIENT SECRETS OF THE BIBLE (series)

Episode: "Shroud of Turin"

CONTENT: ★★★★   TECHNICAL QUALITY: ★★★★

PRIMARY AUDIENCE:	Adults, Teens
DIRECTORS:	Dave Balsiger & D. Campbell
STYLE:	Documentary
DISTRIBUTOR:	Group Productions (800)541-5200, (303)669-3836
LENGTH:	35 min. (approx.)

The *Ancient Secrets of the Bible* series is not a model of outstanding research or always trustworthy Bible storytelling. However, some of the episodes in this thirteen-part video collection do appear to be solid enough to merit use in discussing with unbelievers the veracity of the events addressed. This episode—dealing with whether the image on the Shroud of Turin is a medieval artist's fraud or the result of radiation energy that left an accurate image of Christ at the moment of His resurrection—leans significantly on the side of the latter ("The preponderance of evidence favors authenticity.") On-screen interviews with various experts, including scientists, historians, an attorney, even a coroner who postulates that the image on the intensively studied artifact is that of a 5-foot, 11-inch Caucasian male weighing about 170 pounds. You will probably find yourself eager to view all episodes, but heed this warning: Do so with a healthy measure of careful skepticism because there is a tendency to explain the miraculous by the natural, and because not all "experts" and evidences are as reliable or as well documented as the producers would have you believe. ©1994

ANIMATED STORIES FROM THE BIBLE

ABOUT THE SERIES: In this beautifully animated series of Old Testament Bible stories attention to scriptural detail is good overall, but there are discrepan-

---

cies in some episodes (most of which are very minor). Always compare a video Bible story to the actual Bible account and point out any differences, especially to younger viewers. Bible knowledge should be based on the infallible Word of God, not on a video producer's screenplay of a biblical account.

Volume 1: "ABRAHAM AND ISAAC"

CONTENT: ★★★★   TECHNICAL QUALITY: ★★★★★

PRIMARY AUDIENCE:	Family (Ages 4+)
DIRECTOR:	Richard Rich
STYLE:	Animation
DISTRIBUTOR:	Family Entertainment / Nest (800)551-1799, (214)402-7100
LENGTH:	24 min.

The story of Abraham and Isaac (and Sarah, Hagar, and Ishmael) is uncomfortable for most parents to recount to their children. This is one of those stories that most adults would rather not spend too much time discussing with youngsters. But that fact is exactly what makes this top-quality video so valuable. By combining high-quality animation with a logically enhanced depiction of Genesis 16, 17, 18, and 21, this emotion-packed video delicately shows how the barren Sarah may have justified sending her servant Hagar to Abraham to bear Ishmael. It also depicts the stark contrast between the selfish heart of Ishmael and his younger half brother, Isaac. Most important, it effectively communicates the devastating task that confronted Abraham—to offer his beloved son Isaac as a blood sacrifice to God. This true story emphasizes the importance of unwavering obedience to God. Includes an excellent soundtrack! ©1992

ANIMATED STORIES FROM THE NEW TESTAMENT

ABOUT THE SERIES: This is a beautifully animated, wonderfully scored series of Bible-based children's videos. In fact, it is probably the best example of technical professionalism and scriptural purity produced to date.

Volume 1: "THE KING IS BORN"

CONTENT: ★★ ½   TECHNICAL QUALITY: ★★★★★

PRIMARY AUDIENCE:	Family (Ages 4+)
DIRECTOR:	Richard Rich
STYLE:	Animation
DISTRIBUTOR:	Family Entertainment / Nest (800)551-1799, (214)402-7100
LENGTH:	26 min.

This is an animated retelling of the birth of the baby Jesus. Unlike Hanna-Barbera's widely distributed "Greatest Adventure" series, (also reviewed in this book), no modern characters travel backwards in time and interfere with the Bible story. However, the scriptwriters of this high-quality production have trouble accurately representing some very straightforward scriptural details. Here are two examples: Only one angel is shown at the announcement to the shepherds of Jesus' birth; no reference to the Matthew 1:19–25 account of Joseph's intention to "divorce Mary quietly" before an angel came to him and assured him of Mary's favor with the Lord. Animation, editing, sound effects, music, and all other technical details are top quality, but viewers should have their Bibles handy to recognize script versus Scripture discrepancies and to point them out to younger viewers. ©1988

Volume 2: "HE IS RISEN"

CONTENT: ★★★   TECHNICAL QUALITY: ★★★★★

PRIMARY AUDIENCE: Family (Ages 4+)
DIRECTOR: Richard Rich
STYLE: Animation
DISTRIBUTOR: Family Entertainment (800)551-1799,
                      (214)402-7100
LENGTH: 29 min.

This technically superb video sensitively portrays the emotions of the Resurrection story. Depicts the fear and remorse of the disciples after Jesus' death. Gives an account of the angel's appearance to the Roman guard at Jesus' tomb and then of Jesus' appearances to all of His disciples during the weeks prior to His ascension. Regretfully, the *writers* of this video were not as attentive to details as were the skilled animators and musicians. Some Easter-story Scriptures contradicted here include John 20:5–7; 21:4, 12; Matthew 28:11. The basic story of Christ's death and resurrection is communicated well and in a very entertaining manner, but keep a Bible handy to point out the minor inaccuracies. ©1988

Volume 3: "THE PRODIGAL SON"

CONTENT: ★★★★   TECHNICAL QUALITY: ★★★★★

PRIMARY AUDIENCE: Family (Ages 4+)
DIRECTOR: Richard Rich
STYLE: Animation
DISTRIBUTOR: Family Entertainment / Nest (800)551-1799, (214)402-7100
LENGTH: 27 min.

The whole family will enjoy this highly but logically embellished version of the story of the prodigal son (from Luke 15:11–32). In this parable a young man asks for his share of his father's estate prior to his father's death, goes to the big city where he squanders everything, returns destitute, and is lovingly welcomed back by his very concerned father. The Disneylike animation is excellent—bright, colorful, and with good attention to detail. The soundtrack includes an excellent theme song. The story itself is well written, emotion charged, and includes several statements and actions that are not specifically recorded in Luke but are in keeping with the tone of the scriptural account. We noticed only one statement contrary to the Luke account, but that was minor. (Upon the return of the son, and his father's joyous welcome, the frustrated older brother jealously refers to the roasting of a *lamb* rather than a *goat*, as is recorded in Luke 15:29.) Worthy of many repeated viewings! ©1988

Volume 4: "THE GOOD SAMARITAN"

CONTENT: ★★★ ½   TECHNICAL QUALITY: ★★★★★

PRIMARY AUDIENCE: Family (Ages 4+)
DIRECTOR: Richard Rich
STYLE: Animation
DISTRIBUTOR: Family Entertainment / Nest (800)551-1799, (214)402-7100
LENGTH: 27 min.

Based on the familiar, emotionally touching story of the good Samaritan found in Luke 10: 25–37, this beautifully animated video is very well written and benefits from an excellent soundtrack. Includes lots of logical extrabiblical embellishments, but there are also some that hinder rather than aid in communicating this important story. (The two thief characters are funny but too unrealistic. They detract slightly from this otherwise believable account.) A few minor details of the Luke 10 account were altered (shows Samaritan riding a horse rather than a donkey, doesn't allude to the robbed man's clothes being stolen, and the Bible says the Samaritan gave the innkeeper only two coins.) but nothing of great spiritual or doctrinal significance. With its Disney-like qualities, this video succeeds in communicating our responsibility to reach out in love to those in need. ©1989

ANNE OF GREEN GABLES

CONTENT: ★★★★★   TECHNICAL QUALITY: ★★★★★

PRIMARY AUDIENCE: Family (Ages 4+)
DIRECTOR: Kevin Sullivan
STYLE: Live-Action Drama
DISTRIBUTOR: Wonderworks (Walt Disney)
LENGTH: 3 hr., 17 min.
FEATURING: Megan Follows, Colleen Dewhurst, Richard Farnsworth,
                    S. Grant
MPAA RATING: Not Rated

This refreshing, family-friendly drama benefits from a superbly written story, rich, colorful Canadian scenery, and an absolutely delightful combination of characters. Set in the early 1900s on Prince Edward Island, an elderly bachelor (Matthew Cuthbert) and his firm, old-maid sister (Marilla) place an "order" for an orphan boy. They are looking for help with chores on the farm; but, by a misunderstanding, the orphanage sends Anne Shirley—a red-haired dreamer—instead. The free-spirited thirteen-year-old is eager to please and brings both trials and joy to Green Gables. As she matures to young womanhood, Anne learns to funnel her ambition and overwhelming creativity. And Matthew and Marilla find fulfilling joy in the love and freshness that Anne brings into their stale old ways. But Anne is not perfect. She must also learn to forgive and love, especially one particular young man who adores her and desires her affection. There is no objectionable content, but *lots* that is pure and delightful. (See also the sequel, *Anne of Avonlea*). ©1985

BEAR, THE

CONTENT: ★★★   TECHNICAL QUALITY: ★★★★

PRIMARY AUDIENCE:	Ages 12+
DIRECTOR:	Jean-Jacques Annaud
STYLE:	Live-Action Drama
DISTRIBUTOR:	RCA/Columbia
LENGTH:	1 hr., 32 min.
FEATURING:	Youk (the bear cub), Jack Wallace, Tcheky Karyo
MPAA RATING:	PG

This not-quite-family-night video is both intense and sometimes humorous. Set in 1885, it engenders respect for wildlife and an appreciation for the majestic beauty of the Canadian mountain wilderness. The star of this film, an adorable Kodiak bear cub, is orphaned when his mother is crushed by a rock avalanche as she pillages a honey-rich bee hive that is buried in the side of a mountain. After days on its own, the cub finally wins the friendship and protection of a wounded adult bear. Together, the powerful adult and the naive cub struggle to avoid being killed by two "ruthless hunters." Very intense in places, including animals killing animals. A segment with implied "lovemaking" between two moaning, groaning bears could be embarrassing and hard to explain to children. Five profanities. ©1989

BEAR HUGS (series)

Volume 2: "BEARING FRUIT" and "BEAR BUDDIES"

CONTENT: ★★★   TECHNICAL QUALITY: ★★★

PRIMARY AUDIENCE:	Ages 2–7
DIRECTOR:	Dan Peeler (animation)
STYLE:	Animation and Live Action
DISTRIBUTOR:	Brownlow Publishing Company (800)433-7610, (817)831-3831
LENGTH:	25 min.

This animated children's video contains two stories. Each is taken from the *Bear Hugs* book series. In the first segment, "Bearing Fruit," a short, live action dramatic sequence between a father and his son and daughter discussing their fresh basket of fruit leads into an animated story that uses teddy-bear-type cartoon characters to introduce children to the concept of the fruit of the Spirit (Gal. 5:22–23). Symbolism of the fruit in this first story is probably above the comprehension level of most children in the intended age group, however. The second segment, "Bear Buddies," uses the same style to develop a story based on Proverbs 17:17. Very understandable for intended audience. Reinforces parent's admonitions for children to share their belongings and to treat others kindly. Helps children understand how to make and keep friends. The quality of animation is very basic. Characters move, but only slightly. Most "movement" is simple dissolves between pictures. Good narrator and lively background music. ©1987

BEAUTY AND THE BEAST

CONTENT: ★★★   **TECHNICAL QUALITY:** ★★★★★

PRIMARY AUDIENCE:	Family (Ages 6+)
DIRECTORS:	Gary Trousdale and Kirk Wise
STYLE:	Animation
DISTRIBUTOR:	Walt Disney Home Video
LENGTH:	1 hr., 24 min.
FEATURING:	Voices of: Paige O'Hara, Robby Benson, Richard White
MPAA RATING:	G

Romantic? Yes. Predictable? Yes. But this story carries an important message all too infrequently related by modern media—true beauty springs from the heart, not outward appearance. *Beauty and the Beast* contrasts the inner qualities of three characters: Belle, the heroine, is not only beautiful on the outside but she shows a heart of compassion, bravery, and love. Gaston, the suitor, is a conceited, handsome bully much admired by the local townspeople who are impressed by his strength and good looks. The beast, separated from the rest of the world in his dark castle, was once a handsome prince. But his own cold, selfish ways caused a spell to be cast on him, changing his form to that of an ugly, fearsome beast (better personifying his inner character). As viewers might imagine, through the beast's love for Belle, his heart is softened; and he learns to sacrifice himself for others. Yes, he must defend himself against Gaston; but with his dying breath, Belle reveals her love for him and the spell is broken. The beast magically returns to his human form, and they live "happily ever after." There is much to be admired in this fairy tale (Belle's devotion to her father, her desire not to simply marry a handsome and popular man, etc.); but we must admit that we are not comfortable with Belle's falling in love with an animal, especially since she has no clue that the beast is really a man under a spell. Finally, Disney's continuing emphasis on revealing/tight-fitting dresses and suggestively "bolstered breasts" in children's animated cartoons is one trend that we hope will be reversed. (You may wish to consider *The Swan Princess* as an alternative to this title.) ©1991

BEN-HUR

CONTENT: ★★★★ ½   **TECHNICAL QUALITY:** ★★★★★

PRIMARY AUDIENCE:	Ages 12+
DIRECTOR:	William Wyler
STYLE:	Live-Action Drama
DISTRIBUTOR:	MGM/UA Home Video
LENGTH:	3 hr., 31 min.

It is almost unbelievable that Hollywood once produced this dynamic drama, which so beautifully communicates both close family love and the love and message of Jesus Christ. Though he is offered power and even greater material wealth, the fictional Prince Judah Ben-Hur, a contemporary of Jesus Christ, refuses to abandon his loyalty to God and his fellow Jews by becoming an informant to the Romans. As a result, Ben-Hur is sentenced for a crime he did not commit and sent to the inhuman conditions of the rowing galleys of Roman war vessels. Eventually attaining freedom, Ben-Hur finds revenge in the masterfully re-created (and somewhat violent) Roman chariot races. However, he also learns a horrifying secret about his mother and sister whom he had been told were dead. The immense scope of this epic-length film ends with the broken, hateful Ben-Hur finding the ability to forgive and the strength—through Jesus Christ—to love again. This is a wonderful film, but parents should be aware that younger children will find several scenes of agony and violence too intense. *Ben-Hur* is an emotion-packed production, which, in this reviewer's opinion, is the best of the Bible-inspired dramas that Hollywood has created. Even if you've seen *Ben-Hur* before, reserve another uninterrupted evening for this inspiring Academy Award winner! ©1959

BERENSTAIN BEARS (series)

Episode: "LEARN ABOUT STRANGERS" and "THE DISAPPEARING HONEY"

CONTENT: ★ ½   TECHNICAL QUALITY: ★★★ ½

PRIMARY AUDIENCE: Ages 3–7
DIRECTOR: Buzz Potamkin
STYLE: Animation
DISTRIBUTOR: Random House Video
LENGTH: 23 min.

If your children enjoy the popular illustrated books about this family of bears by Stan and Jan Berenstain, they are sure to enjoy these videos as well. But be forewarned, Mom and Dad. With the books you could "edit" out or verbally change certain aspects to better mirror the values and beliefs that you are striving to instill. With the videos this is much harder to consistently do. The video version still contains those same "I wish they hadn't said that" elements, but there is no practical way to "fix" the message. This double-feature tape, for example, contains evolution-based statements in "Learn About Strangers" and a crystal-ball-reading clairvoyant (Grandma Bear) in "The Disappearing Honey." Additionally, the Papa Bear character gives poor advice, wrong information, and is emotional and illogical more often than not. He is the brunt of jokes rather than a good family leader. To their credit, the stories are fun and always have a good "moral" overall. In "Learn About Strangers," Sister Bear is initially too friendly with complete strangers but then becomes paranoid of them after a talk with Papa. In the end she sees better the need to be careful but not to be unnecessarily afraid. Also includes a good definition of what a "tattletale" is and is not. In "The Disappearing Honey," Papa Bear falsely accuses several townspeople of stealing his boysen-

---

berry honey, only to find out later that it was he who "stole" the sweet treat during nightly sleepwalks. ©1982, 1983

BEYOND THE NEXT MOUNTAIN

CONTENT: ★★★★★   TECHNICAL QUALITY: ★★★★

PRIMARY AUDIENCE: Jr. High–Adult
DIRECTORS: R. Forsberg and James Collier
STYLE: Docudrama
DISTRIBUTOR: Bibles for the World (800)323-2609, (708)668-7733
LENGTH: 1 hr., 37 min.

In 1905 a twenty-two-year-old chemist ventured into the dangerous mountain jungles of an Indian tribe of headhunters. He lived among them, learned their language, and shared the gospel message with them. Soon, however, a political situation forced him to (very unwillingly) return to his native Canada. He felt that his efforts were for naught. But God's purpose had been accomplished. The seeds that this young man had faithfully sown made possible a tremendous harvest of souls. This challenging, heartwarming film follows the life and spiritual growth of Rochunga Pudaite, the son of one of the Canadian missionary's few Indian converts. It dramatically shows how Rochunga leaned on God to overcome tremendous hardships to educate himself so that he could translate the entire New Testament into the language of his people (a language that had never even been written down before!). Rochunga's attitudes and actions are an inspiration to all who seek to follow Jesus Christ. Technical aspects of this production, including the excellent photography and authentic costumes and sets, provide a good feel for India's culture and customs. View this on video with your family, or better yet, get your church to rent the film version and show it on the big screen to your entire congregation! (Also available on 16mm film.) ©1981

BLACK STALLION, THE

CONTENT: ★★★★   TECHNICAL QUALITY: ★★★★★

PRIMARY AUDIENCE: Family (Ages 6+)
DIRECTOR: Carrol Ballard
STYLE: Live-Action Drama
DISTRIBUTOR: MGM/UA Home Video
LENGTH: 1 hr., 57 min.
FEATURING: Mickey Rooney, Teri Garr, Kelly Reno, Hoyt Axton
MPAA RATING: G

Here is a great film that probably every member of the family will enjoy. Based on the novel by Walter Farley and set in the 1940s, *The Black Stallion* is a story of love and the building of trust between a young boy (Alek) and a beau-

---

tiful Arabian stallion (the Black). In a fierce ocean storm, Alek and the Black are shipwrecked together but eventually rescued. A special bond develops between the boy and the wild-spirited horse. At last Alek convinces his mother to allow him to jockey the horse in an exciting race. Music, sound effects, and special effects—as opposed to a lot of dialogue—are the language of this emotionally appealing and visually rich film. Includes one profanity. Be prepared to comfort young children (especially preschoolers), who may want to climb up on an adult's lap during one of several short but intense segments. ©1979

BLUE YONDER, THE

CONTENT: ★★★★   TECHNICAL QUALITY: ★★★★★

PRIMARY AUDIENCE:	Family (Ages 6+)
DIRECTOR:	Mark Rosman
STYLE:	Live-ActionDrama
DISTRIBUTOR:	Walt Disney Home Video
LENGTH:	1 hr., 29 min.
FEATURING:	Peter Coyote, Huckleberry Fox, Dennis Lipscomb, Art Carney
MPAA RATING:	Not Rated

The Blue Yonder is the touching story of a young boy's deep love and admiration for his aviator grandfather, a man that he never knew. In this made-for-TV movie, eleven-year-old Jonathan dares to travel backward in time (with the help of a time-traveling machine) to the year 1927. He desperately wants to stop his grandfather from embarking on the solo trans-Atlantic flight in which he was originally killed. Can Jonathan change history? This high-quality Disney drama is both entertaining and inspiring and contains no cursing or sexual innuendo. Great for the entire family and possibly nostalgic for grandparents, but a bit tense at times for preschool-aged children. (Be sure to emphasize to young kids that time-travel machines don't really exist. This is simply fun fantasy.) ©1985

BORN AGAIN

CONTENT: ★★★ ½   TECHNICAL QUALITY: ★★★★

PRIMARY AUDIENCE:	Jr. High–Adult
DIRECTOR:	Irving Rapper
STYLE:	Docudrama
DISTRIBUTOR:	Sultan Entertainment (310)285-6000
LENGTH:	1 hr., 50 min.

During Richard Nixon's last two years as president, Charles Colson was best known for his involvement in the Watergate break-in and ensuing cover-up. In Born Again, Dean Jones plays the role of Colson and is joined by other top-quality actors to reenact the circumstances that led to Colson's salvation, his subsequent jail term, and his experiences while in prison (which inspired him to later found Prison Fellowship). Shows the corruptive influence of unbridled power and reveals how, while in prison, Colson desperately struggled with unanswered prayer. Upon his release, he recognized that God had, in fact, heard his prayers and that all things do work together for good to those who love God and are called according to His purpose. The realism and warmth of this story add a nice touch to the technical excellence with which it was produced. Too bad that it is so frequently peppered with profanity (though realistic, twenty-five instances is a bit much). ©1978

BUTTERCREAM GANG, THE

CONTENT: ★★★★   TECHNICAL QUALITY: ★★★★

PRIMARY AUDIENCE: Family (Ages 6+)
DIRECTOR: Bruce Neibaur
STYLE: Live-Action Drama
DISTRIBUTOR: Feature Films for Families (800)347-2833
LENGTH: 1 hr., 33 min.

You probably won't find this limited-release video on store shelves, but its technical quality, positive values, and affordable price make it well worth ordering. Set in small town Elk Ridge, the ButterCream "gang" is an extraordinary club of boys who meet in a special tree house and help fulfill the needs of others. When one of their members (Pete) temporarily moves to a big city, he falls in with a law-breaking gang of fighting teens. Upon his return to Elk Ridge, he continues his bullying ways. Scott, the fourteen-year-old leader of the Butter-Creamers, is especially singled out by Pete. But this excellent role model lovingly endures Pete's harsh treatment. Though frustrated, he controls his own anger and desire for revenge. Eventually, "traditional" values (there is no mention of the Bible as the foundation of these values) and persistent, self-sacrificing love win out in this dramatic struggle. In the emotional close, Pete finally learns to accept himself and to once again serve others. Some adults may not appreciate the "puppy love" subplot—a young girl asks a boy to a school dance and later kisses him on the cheek—but these scenes are portrayed in a very sweet and wholesome way. No profanity. No on-screen violence. ©1992

CATHOLICISM: Crisis of Faith

CONTENT: ★★★★   TECHNICAL QUALITY: ★★★

PRIMARY AUDIENCE: Adults
DIRECTOR: James G. McCarthy
STYLE: Documentary
DISTRIBUTOR: Lumen Productions (510)613-8310
LENGTH: 54 min.

Have you ever wished that you better understood the Catholic faith? Or do you know a Catholic who is somewhat open to accepting Jesus Christ as Savior but still has nagging doubts that he or she can actually be saved from hell simply through faith, apart from works? If so, view this video. The history, essential tenets and works-oriented doctrines of the Catholic religion are carefully and lovingly explored here. This documentary-style production discusses the

Catholic mass, use of statues, belief in the immaculate conception and assumption of Mary, the seven essential sacraments, purgatory, belief in salvation by good works, and other Catholic doctrines. Produced by former Catholics, this video includes many interviews with former Catholics and approaches the subject with care and sensitivity. A great and sure-to-be-used resource for every church lending library. ©1991

CAUGHT

CONTENT: ★★★★   TECHNICAL QUALITY: ★★★★

PRIMARY AUDIENCE:	High school–Adult
DIRECTOR:	James F. Collier
STYLE:	Live-Action Drama
DISTRIBUTOR:	Broadman & Holman (800)251-3225, (615)251-2721
LENGTH:	1 hr., 55 min.

In this exciting, high-energy drama, eighteen-year-old Tim Devon accidentally learns that his birth was the result of a premarital college affair. Angry at his mother and desperate to learn more about his true father, Tim goes to the Netherlands to search. With only an old yearbook picture and a name, he soon runs out of leads and becomes trapped in a life of selling drugs, stealing, and male prostitution to earn money. Into Tim's hellish life walks the refreshing Rajam. Rajam is a naive, tenderhearted, itinerant evangelist from India. He repeatedly shows exemplary Christian love to the very unlovely Tim. The cold, worldly reality of Tim's circumstances contrast sharply with the warmth of Rajam's deeply committed life. Scenes of harsh violence and clear allusions to male prostitution earned this show a PG-13 rating. Not recommended for preteens, but a fine motion picture with a good gospel presentation and challenge to Christians to pursue non-Christians for the glory of God. You will be impressed by the power of one person caring deeply about another. (Also available on 16mm film.) ©1987

CHARACTER BUILDER STORYBOOK (series)

Volume: "OBEDIENCE & SELF CONTROL"

CONTENT: ★★★★ ½   TECHNICAL QUALITY: ★★ ½

PRIMARY AUDIENCE:	Ages 2–7
DIRECTOR:	Tony Salerno
STYLE:	Filmation
DISTRIBUTOR:	Bridgestone Multimedia (800)523-0988, (602)940-5777
LENGTH:	23 min.

Using the simple animation technique known as "Filmation" (pans and zooms of nonmoving pictures) the entire *Character Builder* series is just the right pacing for the young viewers for whom it is intended. The screen is usually uncluttered, helping the colorful characters to capture children's attention—and the excellent stories hold it. There are two episodes on this tape: "More Trouble with Tuffy" shows that being obedient to adult's rules is really much better than trying to do things your own way. (When Tuffy disregards his teacher's instructions and wanders away from his class, a day at the zoo becomes anything but fun.) The second episode, "Benny and the Birthday Berries," teaches the value of exercising self-control. On his way to a birthday party, Benny Bear eats the fiddleberries he was taking as a gift. With the help of his caterpillar friend, Scooter, Benny learns the value of stopping yourself when it is best for you and others. ©1988

CHARIOTS OF FIRE

CONTENT: ★★★★ ½   TECHNICAL QUALITY: ★★★★ ½

PRIMARY AUDIENCE:	Ages 13+
DIRECTOR:	Hugh Hudson
STYLE:	Docudrama
DISTRIBUTOR:	Warner Home Video
LENGTH:	2 hr., 4 min.
FEATURING:	Ben Cross, Ian Charleson, Nigel Havers, Alice Krige
MPAA RATING:	PG

Set in the United Kingdom during the early 1920s, this Academy Award winning drama is an inspiring true story of athletic competition and spiritual commitment. A devoted Scottish Christian (Eric Liddell), an intensely competitive Jewish Englishman (Howard Abrams), and other track stars of the 1924 Olympics share a common desire to win medals and bring honor to their homelands. But Liddell's longing to honor God supersedes his opportunity for personal and national recognition. Liddell sees Sunday as sacred and refuses to compromise his conviction that to run in an Olympic race on Sunday would be against God's law. What is especially beautiful about this film is that it also shows that "he who honors God, God will honor" when Liddell runs in a different race later in the week. Though mildly impaired by the sometimes hard to understand European accents, *Chariots of Fire* inspires viewers to define and press toward good goals by using the gifts that God has entrusted to them, but to live by His rules. PG rating due to four profanities. ©1981

CHILDREN'S VIDEO BIBLE (series)

Volume 1: "THE BEGINNING"

CONTENT: ★★ ½   TECHNICAL QUALITY: ★★ ½

PRIMARY AUDIENCE:	Ages 4–7
DIRECTOR:	Terry Page
STYLE:	Filmation
DISTRIBUTOR:	Bridgestone Multimedia (800)523-0988, (602)940-5777
LENGTH:	50 min.

The Beginning is the first of five watercolor-illustration-based videos in the *Children's Video Bible* series. Contains short Bible stories that are each about five minutes in length and are taken directly from Lion Publishing's popular children's book *The Lion Story Bible.* While neither the book nor video are designed to present a thorough account of each Bible story, most of the important highlights are included. The stories are presented in chronological order, providing children with a better understanding of the sequence and interrelationship of various events of Old Testament history. Although the brevity of each story provides a good overview of Scripture, it is also a hindrance. Five minutes per story is not enough time to include or develop some very important specifics. Also, while the illustrated characters are good and generally lifelike, they do not actually move. Rather, an illusion of movement is created by the camera's pans and zooms. ©1988

CHINA CRY

CONTENT: ★★★   TECHNICAL QUALITY: ★★★★ ½

PRIMARY AUDIENCE: Adults
DIRECTOR: James F. Collier
STYLE: Live-Action Drama
DISTRIBUTOR: Nora Lam Ministries (408)629-5000
LENGTH: 1 hr. 43 min.

China Cry is the (supposedly) true story of the early life of evangelist Mrs. Nora Lam. The main story of this well-produced drama is set in China in the 1950s and depicts the unjust actions of the repressive China state against Lam (Chinese name is Sung Neng Lee), her first husband, and others whom the state identifies as Christians or Christian sympathizers. This film received a PG-13 rating due to multiple violent scenes plus inferred premarital sex. *China Cry* has a moving romantic subplot, and it may stir some viewers to a deeper commitment to Christ. However, it should be noted that some Christian periodicals have carried stories disputing the veracity of Lam's miracle claims and the circumstances leading to her eventual divorce from the man depicted in this film. These and other concerns cause this reviewer to seriously question whether some of the most important parts of this film are fact, as promoted, or fabrication. ©1990

CHRISTMAS IS

CONTENT: ★★★   TECHNICAL QUALITY: ★★★★

PRIMARY AUDIENCE: Ages 3–10
DIRECTOR: Unknown
STYLE: Animation
DISTRIBUTOR: Family Films / Concordia (800)325-3040, (314)664-7000
LENGTH: 18 min.

In this fully animated children's drama, a young boy, Benji, is frustrated. For the second year in a row, he has been given the "unimportant" role of the second shepherd in his school's Christmas play. While reading through his script at home, Benji imagines that he and his dog, Waldo, are present at the birth of

---

Jesus two thousand years ago. After speaking with the "real" second shepherd, Benji decides that his part in the play is important after all. Benji ends up playing his part with enthusiasm. Entertaining. No scriptural inaccuracies. A good teaching tool or discussion starter for family devotions. Also great for children's Sunday school and youth group, since it is cleared for these types of public-use settings. ©1974

CHRISTY (series)

Volume 1: TV PREMIER

CONTENT: ★★★★   TECHNICAL QUALITY: ★★★★ ½

PRIMARY AUDIENCE:	Family (Ages 6+)
DIRECTOR:	Michael Rhodes
STYLE:	Live-Action Drama
DISTRIBUTOR:	Broadman & Holman (800)251-3225, (615)251-2721
LENGTH:	90 min. (approx.)
FEATURING:	Kellie Martin, Tyne Daly, Tess Harper, Randall Batinkoff
MPAA RATING:	Not Rated

One can hardly view this wonderful film without feeling both pity and thankfulness. Pity for the "backward" people represented, and thankfulness for the dedicated Christians who worked so hard to help improve the physical and spiritual condition of the families secluded deep in the Tennessee Smokies during the early 1900s. This pilot for the *Christy* television series is based on characters from the novel by Catharine Marshall and introduces a young woman (late teens) who feels led of God to invest herself as teacher to a needy group of children. But her expectations of appreciation from the parents are crushed again and again by their pride, superstitions, feuding, and lack of acceptance. A "city girl," Christy discovers that life in tiny Cutter Gap is much more harsh than expected. The school in which she is to teach has almost no textbooks, its walls are unfinished, and smelly pigs live under the floor. Her students have no shoes, dirty, tattered clothes, and empty stomachs. This look back at an American subculture provides insights into our nation's history that modern children might not otherwise be aware of. Includes a romantic subplot and an excellent example of dedication that all viewers can be inspired by. Unfortunately, it also includes two profanities. ©1994

Volume 2: "THE SWEETEST GIFT"

CONTENT: ★★★ ½   TECHNICAL QUALITY: ★★★★ ½

PRIMARY AUDIENCE:	Family (Ages 6+)
DIRECTOR:	Michael Rhodes
STYLE:	Live-Action Drama
DISTRIBUTOR:	Broadman & Holman (800)251-3225, (615)251-2721
LENGTH:	90 min. (approx.)

FEATURING:	Kellie Martin, Randall Batinkoff, Tyne Daly, Robert Foxworth
MPAA RATING:	Not Rated

The mountain families of Cutter Gap face the prospect of great hunger during the coming winter, due to the poor harvest of the fall. Through a combination of hard work (consistent hunting for wild game) and God's provision (the discovery of a large grove of fruit trees following a dream that led to them), the people of this remote Smoky Mountains community are sufficiently provisioned for the cold months to come. But much transpires in the simultaneous story subplots. (Christy's father arrives for a brief visit but suffers a stroke while there, forcing Christy to prepare to leave her work at the mission school to assist in the care of her father; the gifted local physician must prove himself as more than just a "backwoods doctor"; a young boy must learn to overcome his prejudice against Indians; the mission pastor receives an answer to his prayers, through the very people that he has selflessly served, and more.) This episode contains no swearing, sexual innuendo, or violence, but it still manages to hold the attention of all ages by revealing interesting situations and believable characters of depth. This Thanksgiving-themed episode is good entertainment with some commendable Christian content. Watch it *with* your children and be sure to discuss together the issues of Indian spiritism, prejudice, and commitment. ©1994

CHRONICLES OF NARNIA, THE (series)

ABOUT THE SERIES: From the pen of British author C. S. Lewis came many tales of exciting fantasy, but perhaps none so wonderful as his *Chronicles of Narnia* series. While you would benefit by first reading the genius of Lewis in his books, don't miss these videos. Also, try not to let the "epic" length of this series discourage you. We recommend that families watch about thirty minutes per night, discussing the symbolism so that it won't be missed by younger children. This series can be a fun, exciting, and spiritually enriching multievening "family time" event!

Volume 1: "THE LION, THE WITCH, AND THE WARDROBE"

CONTENT: ★★★★ ½   TECHNICAL QUALITY: ★★★★

PRIMARY AUDIENCE:	Ages 7+
DIRECTOR:	Marilyn Fox
STYLE:	Live-Action Drama
DISTRIBUTOR:	Bridgestone Multimedia (800)523-0988, (602)940-5777
LENGTH:	2 hr., 45 min. (approx.)

In this first volume, set in rural England during World War II, four children step into an old wardrobe but find themselves transported to the magical kingdom of Narnia. They enter a land where animals speak and fanciful creatures roam. Lucy, Peter, Susan, and Edmund soon meet the evil White Witch who has kept Narnia in never-ending winter and turned all her enemies to stone. Aslan, the powerful lion-king (beautifully symbolic of Christ), leads and wins the fight against her darkness. One of the most positive aspects of these adventures is that the viewer will emerge with a better understanding of the character of Christ through Aslan the lion. (Note: Also consider the fully animated version of this volume, which is perhaps less intense and therefore more appropriate for

---

younger children. See *The Lion, the Witch, and the Wardrobe* reviewed separately in this book.) ©1988

Volume 2: "PRINCE CASPIAN AND THE VOYAGE OF THE DAWN TREADER"

CONTENT: ★★★★   TECHNICAL QUALITY: ★★★★

PRIMARY AUDIENCE:	Ages 7+
DIRECTOR:	Alex Kirby
STYLE:	Live-Action Drama
DISTRIBUTOR:	Bridgestone Multimedia (800)523-0988, (602)940-5777
LENGTH:	2 hr., 45 min. (approx.)

Many years have passed in the magical land of Narnia since the close of the first volume. Narnia is now ruled by the corrupt King Miraz. His nephew, Prince Caspian, beckons Lucy, Peter, Susan, and Edmund to help him defeat King Miraz and restore Narnia to its former glory. Their battle against Miraz is, of course, successful. Years later (Narnia time) an older King Caspian, plus the still young Lucy, Edmund, and their obnoxious cousin, Eustace, set sail on an adventure to rescue six lords who were banished by Caspian's evil uncle. The young people's adventures lead them to a lake that turns everything to gold (and attitudes to greed), a sea serpent, a fierce dragon, and, finally, the "edge" of the world. Good, but Lewis' excellent story is not as captivating in this film version. ©1988

Volume 3: THE SILVER CHAIR

CONTENT: ★★★   TECHNICAL QUALITY: ★★★★

PRIMARY AUDIENCE:	Ages 7+
DIRECTOR:	Alex Kirby
STYLE:	Live-Action Drama
DISTRIBUTOR:	Bridgestone Multimedia (800)523-0988, (602)940-5777
LENGTH:	2 hr., 45 min. (approx.)

This third volume in the *Chronicles of Narnia* series is probably the poorest-written screenplay of the three books thus far adapted by the British Broadcasting Company (BBC) for film. Unless you are a very deep thinker, don't expect to find meaningful allegorical similarities between this film and the Bible. For the most part this is simply an entertaining fantasy. Aslan the lion charges Eustace, and his new friend, Jill, with the job of locating old King Caspian's adult son, Prince Rilian. They are to bring Rilian home to be crowned king before the frail Caspian dies. Eustace and Jill meet up with an interesting character while on their journey, and the three of them almost become dinner for a castle full of giants; they narrowly escape by entering a secret underground world. It is there that Eustace and Jill find Prince Rilian. It is also there that a scene that is very scary for younger, more impressionable children takes place. (The White Witch changes into a green serpent, which is killed by Prince Rilian's repeated thrusting of his sword into the serpent's neck.) ©1988

CIRCLE SQUARE GANG (series)

Volume 12: "BROKEN MIRRORS"

CONTENT: ★★★   TECHNICAL QUALITY: ★★

PRIMARY AUDIENCE:	Family (ages 4+)
DIRECTOR:	John Spalding
STYLE:	Educational Live Action
DISTRIBUTOR:	Tyndale Christian Video (800)323-9400, (708)668-8300
LENGTH:	45 min.

Subtitled *I Only Feel Handicapped When You Treat Me that Way,* this cassette has two programs on one tape. One is about respecting the handicapped, and the other is about the importance of being prepared to use CPR. The program about CPR in itself makes the tape well worth viewing and should be seen by the whole family several times. The main program (treating the handicapped normally) is an encouragement to strive to be the best you can be. Shows a group of leg and arm amputees learning how to snow ski and to overcome their handicaps. ©1985

CITY OF THE BEES

CONTENT: ★★★★★   TECHNICAL QUALITY: ★★★★

PRIMARY AUDIENCE:	Family (ages 4+)
DIRECTOR:	Unknown
STYLE:	Documentary
DISTRIBUTOR:	Moody Institute of Science (800)621-5111, (312)329-2190
LENGTH:	28 min.

This classic film contains information that all age groups will enjoy. Using very appealing and educational close-up photography, *City of the Bees* reveals how bees guard their hives from intruders, how a queen bee is selected, how bees communicate by using sounds and dances, how many bee miles and bee hours it takes to build a honeycomb, and other fascinating facts. Features narration and a short closing "sermon" by the late Dr. Irwin Moon. Dated only by 1960s model automobiles and a few other insignificant items, but not to the detriment of the excellent content in any way. Children will be fascinated by this production, and Mom and Dad will be very happy to allow the kids to see it again and again. ©1962

CITY THAT FORGOT ABOUT CHRISTMAS, THE

CONTENT: ★★★   TECHNICAL QUALITY: ★★★ ½

PRIMARY AUDIENCE:	Ages 4–12
DIRECTOR:	Unknown
STYLE:	Animation
DISTRIBUTOR:	Family Films / Concordia (800)325-3040, (314)664-7000
LENGTH:	28 min.

The City that Forgot about Christmas teaches that "it isn't the decorations and celebrations that make Christmas important, but the love of God, who sent the baby Jesus." A real-life modern grandfather shares with his grandson the story of a gloomy city that did not celebrate Christmas any longer. Animation then carries viewers back in time to the streets of that city. The people of the town didn't realize the joy they were missing until Matthew the carpenter came to live there. Matthew wins the townsfolk's friendship and finally shares with them that the birth of Jesus is the whole reason for the celebration of Christmas. Regretfully, the writers of this otherwise very good story do not even touch on the reason *why* Jesus' human birth was necessary. Parents should be sure to point out to children that the whole reason why the Son of God took on human form was to provide a way for people to be saved. Jesus' divine humanity is nice, but also pointless when salvation's important fact is overlooked. ©1974

COACH

CONTENT: ★★★★   TECHNICAL QUALITY: ★★ ½

PRIMARY AUDIENCE: Jr. High–Adult
DIRECTOR: John Taylor
STYLE: Live-Action Drama
DISTRIBUTOR: Russ Doughten/Mark IV (800)247-3456, (515)278-4737
LENGTH: 1 hr., 18 min.

Coach is the story of a young science teacher (Stewart Linley) who reluctantly accepts the responsibility of coaching a very undisciplined basketball team at the Christian high school where he teaches. The team is the laughing stock of their conference, having won only two games in the last three years. Coach Linley is dedicated to the task of teaching this ragtag group to strive toward excellence for God's glory. His love and dedication pay off as the individual players learn to control their tempers and cooperate on the court. Coach Linley also emphasizes the applicability of God's Word to everyday life. While the movie gets off to a slow start and contains a couple of mediocre actors, it is very good overall and is built upon an excellent story sure to have a positive impact on its viewers. ©1982

COMMON CENTS: TRAINING YOUR CHILDREN TO MANAGE MONEY

CONTENT: ★★★★   TECHNICAL QUALITY: ★★★

PRIMARY AUDIENCE: Parents
DIRECTORS: Stephen Stiles and R. Vernon
STYLE: Lecture
DISTRIBUTOR: Focus on the Family Films (800)232-6459, (719)531-3400
LENGTH: 56 min.

In this unique, easy-to-watch educational video, financial counselor Ron Blue speaks to a small studio audience about how to impart important money-management skills to children. The video opens with a short animated cartoon and utilizes several colorful still-cartoon illustrations, plus video graphics, to help illustrate the facts and principles that Ron—and wife, Judy—shares. Explains and endorses the use of an "envelope system" for each family member to budget his or her money. This is a parenting skill video that probably every mom and dad—especially those who parent young children up through junior high school—would benefit from seeing. ©1990

THE CRASH: THE COMING FINANCIAL COLLAPSE OF AMERICA

CONTENT: ★★★★ ½   TECHNICAL QUALITY: ★★★ ½

PRIMARY AUDIENCE: Adults, Teens
DIRECTOR: Pat Matrisciana
STYLE: Documentary
DISTRIBUTOR: Jeremiah Films (800)828-2290, (909)925-6460
LENGTH: 39 min.

While some may deride this video as "alarmist," its clear presentation of facts and fiscal trends is both compelling and disquieting at the same time. *The Crash* combines historic news footage (for instance, the infamous stock-market crash of 1929, the ensuing Great Depression of the 1930s, and Ronald Reagan's "Grace Commission") and colorful charts and graphs with interviews of present-day experts from both government and the private financial community. It also reveals the uncomfortable realities of our federal bureaucracy's lack of willingness to deal decisively with America's now-irreversible decline into national indebtedness. According to those interviewed, this will soon lead to national bankruptcy or, more likely, hyperinflation resulting from large-scale printing of unbacked dollars. While at least one of the experts predicts anarchy in America's near future, the tape goes beyond pessimism by providing the average family with solid advice on how to be prepared for the tough times to come. Includes appearances by former Attorney General Edwin Meese, Congressman Bill Dannemeyer, author Larry Burkett, Senator Trent Lott, and others. ©1993

CREATION CELEBRATION (Series)

CONTENT: ★★★★   TECHNICAL QUALITY: ★★★★

PRIMARY AUDIENCE: Ages 5–12
DIRECTOR: Ladd Allen
STYLE: Live Action and Nature
DISTRIBUTOR: FFC/Eden Communications (800)332-2261, (602)894-1300
LENGTH: 35 min.

Titillating *edutainment!* A merging of exciting educational segments with humorous entertainment and very nice kids' songs yields this award-winning video. The third in Moody/Maranatha!'s *Creation Celebration* series, "Countdown to Adventure," continues the series' formula of using an eccentric-but-lovable traveling professor, an easily flustered housekeeper, and various animal "guest stars" (in this case an elephant, a monkey, and a large seal). Subjects touched upon include: water organisms, gravity and weightlessness (the professor is on-board the space shuttle!), and the importance of recycling to help conserve the environment. Includes beautiful nature scenes and some sensational NASA footage of fun-loving, weightless astronauts. ©1991

CROSS AND THE SWITCHBLADE, THE

CONTENT: ★★★★   **TECHNICAL QUALITY: ★★★★**

PRIMARY AUDIENCE:	Jr. High–Adult
DIRECTOR:	Don Murray
STYLE:	Docudrama
DISTRIBUTOR:	Vision Video (800)523-0226, (215)584-1893
LENGTH:	1 hr., 45 min.

This film was made several years before most of the young people who now view it were even born. However, it exposes a drug culture and inner-city racial conflict similar in many respects to the situation of the present. Rated PG for language, violence, and drugs. *The Cross and the Switchblade* is based on a true story and stars Pat Boone (as David Wilkerson) and Erik Estrada (as Nicky Cruz). While some of the scenes of gang warfare go on longer than necessary, and though there are six instances of cursing, it is a realistic representation of the depravity and hardness of the heart of man. It is also an encouraging and challenging enactment of how God can use willing servants in His plan to renew lives that the rest of society has written off as worthless and "beyond saving." Excellent in acting and in all technical aspects. A great film to view with neighbors or non-Christian friend in the proper age category. (Also available on 16mm film.) ©1970

CRY FOR FREEDOM, A

CONTENT: ★★★★★   **TECHNICAL QUALITY: ★★★★**

PRIMARY AUDIENCE:	Jr. High–Adult
DIRECTOR:	Bill Myers
STYLE:	Documentary
DISTRIBUTOR:	Gospel Films Video (800)253-0413, (616)773-3361
LENGTH:	40 min.

This award-winning documentary takes an honest and sometimes startling look at the drug problem facing youth from virtually all social and economic segments of society. Focuses on cocaine and crack. Moderated by a college-aged young man, *A Cry for Freedom* is fast-paced, challenging, and eye opening. Especially well suited for teenage to young-adult audiences, the film was produced in association with David Wilkerson's tremendously successful drug-rehabilitation ministry, Teen Challenge. Includes interviews with the Harlem Globetrotters' Meadowlark Lemon, the Beach Boys' Mike Love, a Hollywood stuntman, a model, and various medical doctors. Current and past drug users describe both the "positive" and negative sides of using cocaine and its hybrid, crack. Addictive and other detrimental effects are described in no uncertain terms. Closes with several short testimonies from past cocaine users. This production should be available as a resource tool in every church's library. (Also available on 16mm film.) ©1987

CRY FROM THE MOUNTAIN

CONTENT: ★★★★ ½   TECHNICAL QUALITY: ★★★★ ½

PRIMARY AUDIENCE:	Family (ages 6+)
DIRECTOR:	James F. Collier
STYLE:	Live-Action Drama
DISTRIBUTOR:	Broadman & Holman (800)251-3225, (615)251-2721
LENGTH:	1 hr., 16 min.

In this action-packed drama, a father (Larry) and son (Cal) fly deep into the Alaskan wilderness to share a special kayak trip together. Early on the trip Cal learns that his father and pregnant mother are planning a divorce, due chiefly to his father's infidelity. The next day Larry is seriously injured while he and young Cal attempt to navigate some rapids. With the help of a hot-tempered mountain man, Larry is rushed out of the wilderness by rescue helicopter to a hospital. There he asks his wife, Carolyn, to reconsider her decision to divorce. He promises his deepest love to her. (Carolyn had been strongly considering aborting their unborn child while Larry and Cal were gone.) Through a well-scripted turn of events, Carolyn, young Cal, and the mountain man all end up attending a Billy Graham evangelistic crusade where they each receive Christ as Savior. A beautiful scene of Carolyn's acceptance of Christ and His love is portrayed as she returns to Larry's hospital room and tearfully tells her unconscious husband that she now has new hope—in Christ—for their marriage. Excellent in all aspects. Rich music and beautiful wilderness photography. Great viewing for the entire family. (Also on 16mm film.) ©1985

C. S. LEWIS: THROUGH THE SHADOWLANDS

CONTENT: ★★★★   TECHNICAL QUALITY: ★★★★

PRIMARY AUDIENCE:	High School–Adult
DIRECTOR:	Norman Stone
STYLE:	Docudrama
DISTRIBUTOR:	Vision Video (800)523-0226, (215)584-1893
LENGTH:	1 hr., 13 min.
FEATURING:	Joss Ackland, Claire Bloom

C. S. Lewis's writings are some of the most popular and enjoyable works of Christian fiction ever published. But many Lewis fans probably are not aware of the near faith-shattering experience that he faced after most of his works had already been released. In this wonderful drama, produced by the BBC, we meet Joy, the divorced woman who had become a Christian through her reading of Lewis's books. Lewis eventually marries Joy in a secret "technical" wedding that is never consummated. (The purpose of the marriage is simply to provide Joy and her two young sons with English citizenship.) However, their relationship blossoms. When it is discovered that Joy has cancer, Lewis marries her again, this time in her hospital room "before God." Painfully grief stricken by her eventual death, this famous man of God seriously questions his basic Christian beliefs. He questions God's love and exhibits anger at Him. Eventually, however, Lewis regains faith in his own oft-used statement that this earthly life is but a "shadowlands" of what is to come. Especially meaningful to (and potentially hard on) anyone who has ever lost a loved one to an extended illness. (Note: This film was produced prior to and should not be confused with the 1993 release, *Shadowlands*.) ©1985

DANGEROUS JOURNEY

CONTENT: ★★★★★   TECHNICAL QUALITY: ★★★ ½

PRIMARY AUDIENCE: Ages 8–Adult
DIRECTOR: John Marsden
STYLE: Filmation
DISTRIBUTOR: Vision Video (800)523-0226, (215)584-1893
LENGTH: Nine 15-min. segments

An animated version of John Bunyan's immortal classic, *Pilgrim's Progress*, this is an excellent series to use for family devotions or small-group study. A very well-written story with tremendous spiritual symbolism, *Dangerous Journey* introduces viewers to basic themes of the Christian life. Uses allegory, animation, and a compelling soundtrack to depict many of the challenges of a life committed to Jesus Christ. Animation is simple—pans and zooms of excellent illustrations and no movement of characters whatsoever. The narrator does almost all character voices, but he is very good. This series should be seen and discussed by every Christian family. Sponsor this one for your church's video lending library. (Also available on 16mm film.) ©1986

DAVEY AND GOLIATH (series)

Episode: "HALLOWEEN WHO-DUN IT"

CONTENT: ★★★ ½   TECHNICAL QUALITY: ★★★★

PRIMARY AUDIENCE: Ages 4–10
DIRECTOR: Raymond Peck
STYLE: Claymation
DISTRIBUTOR: Gospel Films Video (800)253-0413, (616)773-3361
LENGTH: 29 min.

The *Davey and Goliath* series can be counted on to include Christian values without sounding preachy. This episode is no exception. Davey, sister Sally, and Goliath (the talking dog) all dress up for a Halloween costume contest and then for trick-or-treating. Davey becomes very secure in thinking that he can be mischievous without being found out because no adults are able to tell who he is when he is dressed up in his homemade "Man from Mars" outfit. He even ends up destroying a beehive that is owned by one of his adult friends. The next morning Davey feels remorseful and realizes that God knows who destroyed the hive even if the owner does not. He ends up confessing and apologizing to the owner. The story is dated by the fact that young children are freely allowed to trick-or-treat after 10:00 P.M. without an adult chaperone. ©1967

Episode: "HAPPY EASTER"

CONTENT: ★★★   TECHNICAL QUALITY: ★★★★

PRIMARY AUDIENCE:	Ages 4–10
DIRECTORS:	Art Clokey and Raymond Peck
STYLE:	Claymation
DISTRIBUTOR:	Gospel Films Video (800)253-0413, (616)773-3361
LENGTH:	30 min.

This "special" episode in the series deals with the death of a loved one and the promise of resurrection for those who are in Christ. Davey has a special affection for his grandmother, a unique woman who lets him help her bake cakes, practices baseball with him, and doesn't get angry when he accidentally breaks an attic window. ("Don't worry Davey; we'll fix it together.") To everyone's surprise, grandmother dies unexpectedly. Davey is heartbroken, but later becomes happy for his grandma when he is reminded while watching the rehearsal of an Easter pageant that he will be with her again one day, thanks to Jesus' death and resurrection. The pastor's comforting words at graveside service that "where He is all of us will be" assumes that all viewers are already Christians, since there is no mention anywhere in the film of the need for repentance from sin and acceptance of Jesus as Savior to receive the free gift of salvation. Mid-1960s

---

DECORATION DAY

CONTENT: ★★★★   TECHNICAL QUALITY: ★★★★★

PRIMARY AUDIENCE:	Adults, Older Teens
DIRECTOR:	Robert Markowitz
STYLE:	Live-Action Drama
DISTRIBUTOR:	Republic Pictures
LENGTH:	1 hr., 39 min.
FEATURING:	James Garner, Judith Ivey, Bill Cobbs, Larry Fishburne
MPAA RATING:	PG

This *Hallmark* made-for-TV movie is built on a superbly crafted script that contains several unexpected turns. The multifaceted story revolves around the relationships of Albert Finch, a retired judge (played by James Garner). The recently widowed judge is convinced by an overzealous Washington bureaucrat to attempt to discover why Finch's boyhood friend, now an elderly black man, steadfastly refuses to accept a long overdue World War II Congressional Medal of Honor. At the same time, Finch learns that his married godson has been seeing a local legal secretary. But things are not as they seem, so don't make the mistake of turning the VCR off until the very end. This engaging drama masterfully blends mystery with romance. Though it contains one profanity and mature subject matter dealing with such issues as prejudice, cancer, and an older man dating a younger woman, *Decoration Day* is a film that adults can feel good about seeing and have fun discussing. However, not recommended for children or young teens. ©1990

DESTRUCTIVE DAVID

CONTENT: ★★★ ½   TECHNICAL QUALITY: ★★★★

PRIMARY AUDIENCE: Ages 3–10
DIRECTOR: Bob Singleton
STYLE: Animation
DISTRIBUTOR: Family Films/Concordia (800)325-3040, (314)664-7000
LENGTH: 25 min.

If you are in the process of trying to guide an active young boy through the "seek and destroy" stage of childhood, you will certainly appreciate this animated story. David squashes daisies, maliciously stomps through ant hills, and destroys beautifully woven spider webs. It is through a visit with a talking peacock statue at an outdoor art fair that David learns why he should care about such "useless" things. The message is good: we should appreciate and care for God's creative beauty and recognize His love in sending His Son. Music and songs complement the story well. Worth replaying often even if just to sing along with the songs. Don't pigeonhole this tape as one only for terrorizing little boys. It is also great to use as preventive medicine in those families who enjoy the presence of "little angels" too! ©1988

DISTANT THUNDER, A

CONTENT: ★★★★   TECHNICAL QUALITY: ★★★ ½

PRIMARY AUDIENCE: Jr. High–Adult
DIRECTOR: Donald Thompson
STYLE: Live-Action Drama
DISTRIBUTOR: Russ Doughten/Mark IV (800)247-3456, (515)278-4737
LENGTH: 1 hr., 17 min.

This drama, the second in a four-part "series," begins where its predecessor (*A Thief in the Night*) ended. An extremely challenging production, both emotionally and spiritually. Acting and technical aspects are generally good, only infrequently distracting from the well-written story of Patty, a young woman living in the "end times" of the Great Tribulation referred to in biblical prophecy. She and two friends live as fugitives, relentlessly pursued and finally captured by the evil forces of UNITE. Inevitably, they must choose between taking "the mark of the Beast" or facing a terrifying death. This entire series brings up strongly debated theological interpretations regarding a pretribulation rapture, the Tribulation, and end times. While the viewer may not agree with all points raised, the film is extremely stimulating—challenging both Christians and non-Christians to explore God's Word for a deeper understanding of Scripture on this important topic. Also challenges the believer to live righteously and share the gospel message with others. Not recommended for pre-junior high ages due to level of intensity. (Also available on 16mm film.) ©1977

Authors' Choice

DISTINCTIVELY HUMAN

CONTENT: ★★★★★   TECHNICAL QUALITY: ★★★★★

PRIMARY AUDIENCE: Ages 10–Adult
DIRECTOR: Unknown
STYLE: Documentary
DISTRIBUTOR: Moody Institute of Science (800)621-5111, (312)329-2190
LENGTH: 58 min.

From the attention-grabbing introduction straight through to its mild evangelistic conclusion, this documentary is a joy to watch! By combining mind-boggling statistics and information with excellent visual footage, *Distinctively Human* reveals how every cell, every nerve, every bone in the human body points unmistakably toward the Master Craftsman who created us all. Subjects covered include: footage showing the growth of a baby beginning only minutes after conception, X rays of men and women performing different activities, film of the inside of a functioning human heart, and unique animation depicting the complexity of the human brain. This award-winning production deserves a place in every home, church, and school video library. (Also available on 16mm film.) ©1987

DONUT MAN (series)

Episode: "THE DONUT ALL STARS"

CONTENT: ★★★   TECHNICAL QUALITY: ★★★

PRIMARY AUDIENCE: Ages 2–7
DIRECTOR: Annie Biggs
STYLE: Live-Action Musical Drama
DISTRIBUTOR: Integrity Music, Inc. (800)240-9000
LENGTH: 27 min.

Young children love this series because it combines the fun and compassionate Rob Evans (the "Donut Man") with a simple plot, fun-to-sing songs, puppets with wit, and a small group of children who confront some of the same struggles that the viewing audience also faces. In this episode, the Donut Man and his young followers (the "Donut Repair Club") find themselves in need of a good deal of practice to prepare for their upcoming softball game against last year's champions, the Warriors. All the while sporting his trademark overalls, the Donut Man leads the boys and girls from discouraged disorganization to a new positive attitude that, when combined with plenty of practice, equips them for the important game to come. While the sing-along songs and funny puppets are more responsible than the simple storyline for holding viewers' attention, the video does include a subplot about the fear of rejection and low self-confidence of a young boy whose parents have recently divorced. Bottom line message:

encourage each other and have a good mental attitude, because these things are almost equal in importance to practice. ©1995

DRIVING MISS DAISY

CONTENT: ★★★★   TECHNICAL QUALITY: ★★★★★

PRIMARY AUDIENCE:	Ages 12+
DIRECTOR:	Bruce Beresford
STYLE:	Live-Action Drama
DISTRIBUTOR:	Warner Home Video
LENGTH:	1 hr., 39 min.
FEATURING:	Morgan Freeman, Jessica Tandy, Dan Akroyd, Patti Lupone
MPAA RATING:	PG

This Academy Award winner inspires thoughtful consideration of prejudice, aging, and the importance of appreciating those who reach out to us with a loving hand of friendship. It is the humorous and heartwarming story of a headstrong Jewish widow (Miss Daisy) and Hoke Colburn, the ever-patient black man who chauffeurs this reluctant passenger. As the rich old woman ages, she slowly realizes that she is much more prejudiced than she ever thought herself to be. Upon that realization she begins to allow herself to appreciate the sweet spirit of Hoke—himself an elderly poor man who remains her truest friend even long after her health fails and she is forced to move to a nursing home. A technically excellent film, *Driving Miss Daisy* contains no violence, nudity, or sexually suggestive scenes. Unfortunately, it is marred by nine profanities, seven of which should be especially offensive to Christians because they are the taking of God's name in vain. ©1989

ECLIPSE OF REASON

CONTENT: ★★★★ ½   TECHNICAL QUALITY: ★★★ ½

PRIMARY AUDIENCE:	Jr. High–Adult
DIRECTOR:	R. Anderson
STYLE:	Documentary
DISTRIBUTOR:	American Portrait Films (800)736-4567, (216)531-8600
LENGTH:	27 min.

This award-winning pro-life documentary opens with a short introduction by Charlton Heston (who appeared without financial remuneration). Mr. Heston reprimands the television community for failing to better inform the public with regard to the abortion issue. The film is moderated by Dr. Bernard Nathanson, past director of the largest abortion clinic in the USA—a man ultimately responsible for over seventy-five thousand abortions. *Eclipse of Reason* focuses on "late abortions," those performed after the first three months of pregnancy. The film reveals many startling statistics and graphically documents the actual abortion of a five-month-old boy, pulled in pieces through the uterus of his mother. Also includes interviews with women who have been physically and emotionally scarred by their own abortions. Due to the very graphic nature of the material presented, the best uses of this very powerful film would be to those who have not had an abortion. A sad, sobering, excellent resource for the church's video library. (Also available on 16mm film.) ©1987

E.T. THE EXTRATERRESTRIAL

CONTENT: ★★   TECHNICAL QUALITY: ★★★★★

PRIMARY AUDIENCE:	Ages 13+
DIRECTOR:	Steven Speilberg
STYLE:	Live-Action Drama, Science Fiction
DISTRIBUTOR:	MCA Home Video
LENGTH:	1 hr., 55 min.
FEATURING:	Henry Thomas, Dee Wallace, Peter Coyote, Drew Barrymore
MPAA RATING:	PG

Billed as one of the two most-viewed modern film projects in the world, *E.T.* is exciting, humorous, and heartwarming. Unfortunately, several recurring elements make it inappropriate for preteens. The main story is about a stranded little alien who befriends a ten-year-old boy named Elliot. The longer that E.T. remains on earth, the more feeble he becomes. Because Elliot and E.T. share a type of telepathic oneness, Elliot also becomes very sick. Both are revitalized, however, when E.T.'s fellow extraterrestrials return to rescue him. Suspense is high when a group of government authorities seal off Elliot's house in order to capture and study the alien. E.T. and Elliot escape and—with help from several friends—outwit the police cars that chase their fleeing bicycles. Negative elements that should concern parents include profanities, frequent name-calling between siblings and friends, mystical levitation, and alcohol and drunkenness portrayed in a humorous light. The show also matter-of-factly portrays and reinforces the unfounded idea that there are creatures from other worlds. ©1982

EVOLUTION CONSPIRACY, THE

CONTENT: ★★★ ½   TECHNICAL QUALITY: ★★★★

PRIMARY AUDIENCE:	Jr. High–Adult
DIRECTOR:	Pat Matrisciana
STYLE:	Documentary
DISTRIBUTOR:	Jeremiah Films (800) 828-2290, (909)925-6460
LENGTH:	56 min.

While it is subtitled *A Quantum Leap into the New Age, The Evolution Conspiracy* really focuses on presenting a concise overview of the modern Creation/evolution controversy. This documentary points out that no truly valid transitional forms ("missing links") between various types of animals and man have ever been found in the earth's fossil record. It also briefly discusses the theory of "punctuated equilibrium," the Scopes Monkey Trial, and it very summarily shows the connection between Darwinian evolution and the New Age movement. "Evolution, whether biological or mystical, is man's way to explain away

God and His creation, and put man in God's place." Includes short interviews with many different creationists, evolutionists, and New Agers. While it does not develop the many evidences for creation, this film does succeed in packing a wide variety of information into one hour. For more depth and specific evidences in support of creation, see the six-part *Origins* series, which is reviewed later in this book. ©1988

FATHER OF THE BRIDE

CONTENT: ★★★★   TECHNICAL QUALITY: ★★★★

PRIMARY AUDIENCE:	Ages 12+
DIRECTOR:	Vincente Minnelli
STYLE:	Live-Action Drama (colorized)
DISTRIBUTOR:	MGM/UA Home Video
LENGTH:	1 hr., 33 min.
FEATURING:	Spencer Tracy, Joan Bennett, Elizabeth Taylor, Don Taylor
MPAA RATING:	Not Rated

In this original version of *Father of the Bride*, Dad is played by Spencer Tracy and the daughter bride by Elizabeth Taylor. This is a humorously portrayed story of the emotional turmoil that a father experiences in learning to let go of his beloved only daughter as she prepares for and finally enters into marriage. While this production is great fun to watch (especially for fathers and brides-to-be), it does include lots of "social drinking"—especially by the nervous father character. Spencer Tracy's delivery of his many humorous lines is great, but a bit drier feeling than that of Steve Martin, who plays the father in the 1991 remake. (While this reviewer prefers the lighter humor and heightened emotions of the 1991 version, it, unfortunately, includes both profanity and implied premarital sex.) There is no profanity in this 1950 version. Very good entertainment and more wholesome overall than the remake. ©1950

FIDDLER ON THE ROOF

CONTENT: ★★★★   TECHNICAL QUALITY: ★★★★★

PRIMARY AUDIENCE:	Ages 8+
DIRECTOR:	Norman Jewison
STYLE:	Drama
DISTRIBUTOR:	MGM/UA Home Video
LENGTH:	3 hr. (approx.)
FEATURING:	Topol, Norma Crane, Molly Picon, Leonard Frey
MPAA RATING:	G

Set in the Russian village of Anatevka sometime in the early 1900s, this musical drama is a wonderful film about love and tradition. Viewers empathize with the roller-coaster emotions of Tevye, a poor Jewish milkman, as he is forced to ask of himself, "When is it good to continue to observe tenaciously preserved cultural and religious traditions, and when is it better to allow the pressures of a changing society to dictate a different course?" In this Oscar-winning film, three of Tevye's daughters plead to be allowed not to have to enter the arranged marriages that tradition would dictate. Instead, they place a higher value on their desire to wed men whom they actually love rather than to observe such an antiquated tradition. (The marriage ceremony of Tevye's oldest daughter is a wonderful exhibit of some of the joys of Jewish culture, and the joy that can be experienced when certain traditions are broken.) This two-tape set contains much excellent humor, but it also reveals some of the heartache caused by anti-Semitic government policies. *Fiddler* portrays the peasant Tevye as a man who continually talks to God. However, he also celebrates to the point of drunkenness and sometimes "stretches the truth" to help achieve his goals. Excellent overall but not for children under the age of eight. ©1971

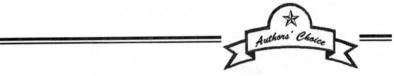

FIRST FRUITS

CONTENT: ★★★★   TECHNICAL QUALITY: ★★ ½

PRIMARY AUDIENCE: Jr. High–Adult
DIRECTOR: Dan Niedameyer
STYLE: Docudrama
DISTRIBUTOR: Vision Video (800)523-0226, (215)584-1893
LENGTH: 1 hr., 10 min.

This entertaining docudrama is more than just a historical look at the Moravian mission movement. It is a well-written and heartwarming challenge to deeper commitment in the Christian life and in our emotional, prayerful, and financial support of contemporary missionaries. With excellent cinematography, this multiple-award-winning production transports its viewers back in time more than 250 years. Viewers follow two young Moravian men who leave their comfortable European community convinced that they are called of God to preach to the ill-fated mistreated slaves of the West Indies. They are willing even to become slaves themselves. You will rejoice over the hard-won "first fruits" of their ministry and the worldwide impact of their commitment on the course of Christianity and world history. While it suffers from some poor acting, this film merits repeated viewing and should be in every church and Christian school video library. (Also available on 16mm film.) ©1982

FOCUS ON THE FAMILY (series)

Episode 6: "WHAT WIVES WISH THEIR HUSBANDS KNEW ABOUT WOMEN"

CONTENT: ★★★★ ½   TECHNICAL QUALITY: ★★

PRIMARY AUDIENCE: Adults
DIRECTOR: Earl J. Miller
STYLE: Lecture
DISTRIBUTOR: Word, Inc. (800)933-9673, (214)556-1900
LENGTH: 1 hr., 22 min.

This video should be viewed by every married couple. While the style is very simple (Dr. James Dobson speaking before a live audience in an auditorium), viewers soon see past the producer's lack of creativity. Dr. Dobson is a masterful speaker who uses humor and emotion-filled real-life stories to help communicate his excellent message. *What Wives Wish Their Husbands Knew about Women* deals primarily with the subject of depression in women, the ten main causes for it, and how men and women can work to avoid or cure it. Also reveals some of the primary emotional differences between men and women. Buy (don't just rent) this tape, so that you can have it on hand to help minister to others including neighbors, relatives, and church friends. Note: Clothing styles have changed since this tape was produced, but the emotional needs of women are the same today as they were then. ©1979

FLYING HOUSE, THE (series)

ABOUT THE SERIES: This series is another in the genre where modern youths are transported backward in time. Like cookies from the same mold, the main difference between this and other similar series (such as *Superbook* and Hanna-Barbera's *Greatest Adventures*) is simply the color of the frosting. All are cartoons based on popular Bible stories. All are intended for young viewers, and yet almost none is appropriate for that age group due primarily to two reasons: (1) Children up to five and even seven years of age do not readily separate fact from fiction, even when the differences are obvious to older children and adults, and (2) the Bible story itself is often diluted by liberal doses of "artistic license." Strongly consider the *Animated Stories from the Bible* series or even the lower (technical) quality *Greatest Stories Ever Told* series before investing time and money in this widely distributed misrepresentation of Scripture.

Volume 4: "THE PRIZE. . . " and "ANOTHER LIFE"

CONTENT: ★   TECHNICAL QUALITY: ★★★ ½

PRIMARY AUDIENCE:	Ages 5–8
DIRECTOR:	Unknown
STYLE:	Animation
DISTRIBUTOR:	Tyndale Christian Video (800)323-9400, (312)668-8300
LENGTH:	39 min.

In this volume, three children, a robot, a house, and a bumbling professor end up in two different time "zones." The first of the two episodes on this tape, "The Prize that Was Won and Lost," deals with the beheading of John the Baptist. The biggest problem here is that the dancer who asked for John's head on a platter is portrayed as an innocent ten-year-old who is an unwilling participant in the matter. The second episode, "Another Life," deals with Jesus' raising Jairus's daughter from the dead, as recounted in Mark 5:22, Matthew 9:23, and Luke 8:41. The episode is very entertaining but contains many inaccuracies. Don't view any episode from this poorly researched series without also seriously observing and then discussing the differences between the video version of the Bible story and the Bible record itself. ©1982

FREEMASONRY: FROM DARKNESS TO LIGHT

CONTENT: ★★★★   TECHNICAL QUALITY: ★★ ½

PRIMARY AUDIENCE:	Adults
DIRECTOR:	Unknown
STYLE:	Documentary
DISTRIBUTOR:	Jeremiah Films (800) 828-2290, (909)925-6460
LENGTH:	34 min.

Over five million American men are members of Masonic temples. The vast majority of its members—including several of this reviewers' own acquaintances—are of the opinion that Freemasonry is like a grown-up version of the Boy Scouts. This delusion is prevalent because most who become Masons do so with the intent of simply joining a nice fraternal order. Most never advance past the "third degree" of Freemasonry's *thirty-three* degrees—(a degree is a level within the organization). But this video uses on-screen testimonies of former Masons to reveal that there are many surprising similarities between Freemasonry and witchcraft. It shows from various past leaders' own writings—and manuals used today within the organization—that Freemasonry places Jesus Christ on an equal plane with Mohammed, Buddha, and other "great religious teachers." Discusses such topics as: the organization's history, facts about its founders, secret initiation rites (including their sacred bloodrite, the sword to the initiate's bare chest, and the wearing of a special white lambskin apron) plus the meaning of the Masonic "symbol," and the difference between a "craft Mason" and a "speculative Mason." The bottom line is: Freemasonry is a religion. Unfortunately, it is a religion that denies salvation by grace and strongly emphasizes "works" as the Mason's passport to heaven. Strongly recommended for anyone who presently is a Mason or is considering membership in a Masonic lodge. ©1991

FURY TO FREEDOM

CONTENT: ★★★★   TECHNICAL QUALITY: ★★★★

PRIMARY AUDIENCE:	Jr. High–Adult
DIRECTOR:	Erik Jacobson
STYLE:	Live-Action Drama
DISTRIBUTOR:	Gospel Films Video (800) 253-0413, (616)773-3361
LENGTH:	1 hr., 21 min.

This high-action drama tells an amazing true story. It is the story of the transformation of a violent, hateful young man into a God-loving, tender husband and father. Young Raul Ries is constantly in trouble at his southern California high school, but somehow he wins the affections of a popular Christian girl. Before long, she is pregnant. She is tremendously distraught and remorseful before God for the sexual sin into which she has fallen. However, her affections for this handsome young man again cause her to forget that a believer in Christ is not to be "unequally yoked" with a nonbeliever. The two marry, but Raul soon returns to his old self, sleeping around, and even eventually venting his frustrations by beating his wife. Raul also becomes increasingly interested in and skilled at martial arts. (There are several fight scenes in this film. Some are very intense and more graphic than prejunior-high kids should be exposed to.) Then, while standing one Sunday night with a loaded shotgun, waiting for his wife to return home so that he can kill her, a miracle changes the heart of Raul from intense rage to peace and brokenness before Christ. Raul begins to serve the God he once hated. An especially wonderful scene is that of Raul embracing and weeping with his father when the father (played by John Quade) accepts Raul's invitation to also accept Jesus Christ as his Savior. This film is an excellent example of both the depths from which God can save those who seek him and the ramifications of choosing not to obey God's commands. Great for teenagers but not suited for younger audiences. (Also available on 16mm film.) ©1985

GERBERT (series)

Volume 5: "SAFE IN HIS ARMS"

CONTENT: ★★★★   TECHNICAL QUALITY: ★★★★

PRIMARY AUDIENCE:	Ages 3–8
DIRECTOR:	David Freyss
STYLE:	Live-Action Puppetry
DISTRIBUTOR:	E Films (214)437-6575
LENGTH:	31 min.

In this fifth episode of the fast-paced *Gerbert* video series, the puppet star of the show, Gerbert, learns the value of protecting what is important. With a wide-ranging and quickly changing array of visuals (puppets, human actors, real-life outdoor footage, and cartoon illustrations), the message of this tape also includes a special song and choreography sequence about how helpful police-men are, footage of skillful skateboarders demonstrating why protective gear is important, and a story that helps youngsters appreciate people's uniqueness. A nice addition to any video library. Bright colors, upbeat music, and fast editing are sure to captivate young viewers. ©1988

GIANT OF THUNDER MOUNTAIN, THE

CONTENT: ★★★ ½   TECHNICAL QUALITY: ★★★★

PRIMARY AUDIENCE:	Adults (and kids 10+)
DIRECTOR:	James Roberson
STYLE:	Live-Action Drama
DISTRIBUTOR:	American Happenings (714)454-0270
LENGTH:	1 hr., 24 min.
FEATURING:	Richard Kiel, Noley Thornton, Bart the Bear, Marianne Rogers
MPAA RATING:	PG

This drama is a refreshing surprise, especially for those who desire a story with action, intensity, and depth. Set in a small mountain community in 1896, it depicts a man misunderstood by those around him. Pursued and even shot, he overcomes his raging desire for revenge by helping those who have hurt him. Though aided by including a tenderhearted eight-year-old girl (Amy), *The Giant of Thunder Mountain* cannot escape the fact that it is, at its core, a sad story of prejudice, greed, and injustice. Its redeeming message of forgiveness and reconciliation is all but overshadowed by the unjust actions of an entire town against an honest man. In the story, a greedy circus owner causes a disastrous chain of events when the town's residents act on their prejudice after a rumor is launched by a meddlesome woman. Very quickly the entire town believes that the "giant" who lives on Thunder Mountain (Eli) has harmed three children. In reality, the very tall mountain man has selflessly risked his own life and saved young Amy from an attacking bear while the circus owner and his two bumbling sons have kidnapped one child and injured another. This film upholds Christian values (such as prayer, Bible reading, and forgiveness), shows alcohol consumption in a negative light, and is thankfully devoid of profanity. It is unfortunate that several intense and violent scenes make this otherwise excellent film unsuitable for the preschool and early gradeschool children who would be its most enthusiastic viewers. ©1991

GOD OF CREATION

CONTENT: ★★★★   TECHNICAL QUALITY: ★★★ ½

PRIMARY AUDIENCE:	Ages 8–Adult
DIRECTOR:	Unknown
STYLE:	Documentary
DISTRIBUTOR:	Moody Institute of Science (800)621-5111, (312)329-2190
LENGTH:	28 min.

This "Sermons from Science" classic is hosted by the late Dr. Irwin Moon. Visually supported with high-quality photography, Dr. Moon opens with an explanation of how many stars there are in the universe and then uses wonderful scientific illustrations about lilies, caterpillars, and paramecium to illustrate that the same God who created the ten octillion stars also created and cares deeply for each one of us individually. The footage showing a caterpillar's actual transformation into a chrysalis and finally into a butterfly is amazing! Although the tape is dated by the 1940s style of background music, *God of Creation* continues to minister to young and old alike. Challenging evangelistic ending by Dr. Moon concludes this unique and educational production. (Also available on 16mm film.) ©1945

GOD'S OUTLAW: THE STORY OF WILLIAM TYNDALE

CONTENT: ★★★★ ½   TECHNICAL QUALITY: ★★★★

PRIMARY AUDIENCE:	High School–Adult
DIRECTOR:	Tony Tew
STYLE:	Docudrama
DISTRIBUTOR:	Vision Video (800)523-0226, (215)584-1893
LENGTH:	1 hr., 33 min.

This intense drama is a true story, describing how just one person can, by God's empowering, change the world for good. Well-written and well-acted, *God's Outlaw* also addresses international politics, false injustice, and a corrupt religious establishment. William Tyndale is burned at the stake at the end of the video. His crime: translating the Bible into English and publishing it for his fellow countrymen. High production values. A "must see" film for all Christian adults. (Also available on 16mm film.) ©1987

GOSPEL BILL (series)

Episode: "THERE IS NO SUCH THING AS MONSTERS"

CONTENT: ★★★ ½   TECHNICAL QUALITY: ★★★

PRIMARY AUDIENCE:	Ages 6–12
DIRECTORS:	Bruce Dinehart and S. Yaker
STYLE:	Live-Action Drama
DISTRIBUTOR:	Willie George Ministries (918)234-5656
LENGTH:	27 min.

The *Gospel Bill* show is a children's TV program. Often peppered with elements of Pentecostal theology or worship style, it is carried on many Christian stations across the USA. "There Is No Such Thing as Monsters" demonstrates biblical truths in a comical way by using an "Old West" studio setting and several humorous characters. In this episode, many residents of the town of Dry Gulch are afraid after hearing various monster stories. Mr. T. U. Tutwater initially laughs at the notion but soon is afraid to go to sleep at night because he fears a monster is stalking him. Gospel Bill, the town sheriff, tracks the "monster" and discovers that it is really nothing more than a prankster dressed in a costume trying to scare his friends. Gospel Bill then tells the young viewers that they should fill their minds with good thoughts "so there is no room for bad ones." ©1986

GREAT DINOSAUR MYSTERY, THE

CONTENT: ★★★★★   TECHNICAL QUALITY: ★★★ ½

PRIMARY AUDIENCE:	Ages 8–Adult
DIRECTOR:	Paul S. Taylor
STYLE:	Children's Documentary
DISTRIBUTOR:	FFC/Eden Communications (800)332-2261, (602)894-1300
LENGTH:	20 min.

This unique children's documentary actually appeals to adults and children alike. It's near timeless style effectively combines illustrations, simple animation, still photos, and outdoor cinematography to reveal evidence that dinosaurs have lived at the same time as man "in spite of the fact that evolutionists dogmatically say it is impossible." One of the highlights is the actual photograph of a recently dead plesiosaur carcass netted by a Japanese fishing vessel near New Zealand in 1977. This production also shows that dinosaurs fit into and are mentioned in the Bible. Effectively uses accounts of secular writers and historians to document intriguing dinosaur sightings of only several hundred years ago. While it is used primarily by churches, *The Great Dinosaur Mystery* was produced with public-school students in mind and has been used in thousands of public-school classes in America and other nations. (Also available on 16mm film.) ©1979

Hanna-Barbera's GREATEST ADVENTURE (series)

Episode: "THE CREATION"

CONTENT: ★★   TECHNICAL QUALITY: ★★★★★

PRIMARY AUDIENCE: Ages 5+
DIRECTOR: Don Lusk
STYLE: Animation
DISTRIBUTOR: Sparrow Home Video (800)877-4443, (615)371-6800
LENGTH: 27 min.

Oh that more Christian producers had enough money to make their productions sparkle as well as the creators of the Hanna-Barbera series. However, the technical qualities of this tape, even the top-rate animation, do not make up for the many scriptural misrepresentations that young viewers will mistakenly understand as truth (especially if viewed repeatedly). Studies have shown that children up through approximately five to seven years of age do not readily differentiate reality from fiction. "The Creation" is a well-produced entertainment tape, but it is not an accurate representation of scriptural narrative. Some of the problem areas include: modern youths interacting with Adam and Eve, how Eve was presented to Adam, Adam "unknowingly" eating the forbidden fruit, rain in the Garden, no Cherubim posted at the entrance to the Garden, and no movement of God's flaming sword (it is stuck in the ground instead). It would probably be better to present a parable than so much inaccurate information to such young, impressionable eyes. ©1988

Episode: "DAVID AND GOLIATH"

CONTENT: ★★★   TECHNICAL QUALITY: ★★★★★

PRIMARY AUDIENCE: Ages 5+
DIRECTOR: Ray Patterson
STYLE: Animation
DISTRIBUTOR: Sparrow Home Video (800)877-4443, (615)371-6800
LENGTH: 25 min.

Three modern youths witness David and Goliath's confrontation after passing through a "time portal." Excellent animation. However, like all other episodes in this series, this is a highly embellished representation of what is actually recorded in Scripture. In this story, the ground actually shakes when Goliath walks, Goliath is represented as three times taller than other men, and modern youths interact with David. While the writers included a line by David that his reason for going to battle is "to uphold the name and honor of the Lord," the overall emphasis of the story focuses on David's skill rather than God's choosing and using of this very unlikely young shepherd warrior (see 1 Sam. 17:36–37). Oversights and unreasonable additions are generally negligible, but viewers should reacquaint themselves with the biblical account prior to viewing since

---

there are some minor discrepancies. Challenge your children to locate these and then to describe them to you. ©1984

Episode: "JOSHUA AND THE BATTLE OF JERICHO"

CONTENT: ★   TECHNICAL QUALITY: ★★★★★

PRIMARY AUDIENCE: Ages 5+
DIRECTOR: Ray Patterson
STYLE: Animation
DISTRIBUTOR: Sparrow Home Video (800)877-4443, (615)371-6800
LENGTH: 25 min.

The basis for this animated adventure is found in Joshua 5:13–6:27. If the viewers are mature enough to be able to separate fact from scriptwriter's fantasy, they will find the basic message is fairly close to the Old Testament account of this amazing story. However, the inclusion of three time-traveling youths seriously deters from the usefulness of the tape. One of the three youths gets captured and taken inside Jericho but is later rescued by his two cohorts after they sneak into the city by climbing over the walls at night. All three then escape from Jericho by "surfing" on a board through an underground river passageway. Exciting? Yes. But very misleading for younger viewers. Some of the biblical problems: (1) Jordan River simply dries up rather than being cut off and standing in a heap (see Josh. 3:13); (2) Rahab is portrayed as a wholesome young woman rather than as a harlot as stated in Scripture. Poor attention to important details. Not recommended. ©1985

Episode: "THE NATIVITY"

CONTENT: ★★   TECHNICAL QUALITY: ★★★★★

PRIMARY AUDIENCE: Ages 5+
DIRECTOR: Don Lusk
STYLE: Animation
DISTRIBUTOR: Sparrow Home Video (800)877-4443, (615)371-6800
LENGTH: 30 min.

This tape begins with a scene of a Roman soldier reading a decree of Caesar Augustus. Everyone in Roman jurisdiction must return to his city of birth and register for a census. This now famous decree is the catalyst that sends Joseph and his pregnant wife, Mary, on their trip to Bethlehem. In this city Jesus was born (in a cavelike stable, according to what is presented here) in fulfillment of Old Testament prophecy. Like the other stories in this series, "The Nativity" is heavy on entertainment value but light on scriptural accuracy. Also, like so many "first Christmas" accounts, the writers of this script chose to misrepresent the clear account of Matthew 2:1–16 by having the three Magi arrive with their gifts of gold, incense, and myrrh on the very night of Jesus' birth rather than when he was about two years old, as the Bible intimates. Finally, while portions of several Christmas carols are sung by the voices of the Southern California Mormon Choir, no chorus of praise-giving angels is included with the announcement by the angel of the Lord to the shepherds of the Christ child's birth (see Luke 2:13–14). (It's odd that a choir from a religious group that doesn't acknowledge the deity of Christ—Mormons—plays an integral part of a video that is all about the deity of the baby Jesus.) Concludes with a very large crowd gathered under a huge bright star outside the stable where the newborn baby Jesus is sleeping. (The inclusion of the mischievous twentieth-century youths that plagues the other episodes of this series is not as detrimental here.) ©1987

Episode: "NOAH'S ARK"

CONTENT: ★★   TECHNICAL QUALITY: ★★★★★

PRIMARY AUDIENCE: Ages 5+
DIRECTOR: Ray Patterson
STYLE: Animation
DISTRIBUTOR: Sparrow Home Video (800)877-4443, (615)371-6800
LENGTH: 26 min.

This story of Noah and the ark is similar to the account recorded in Genesis, but there is not much attention to detail. The story is very entertaining but not appropriate for younger viewers since repeated viewing will ingrain inaccurate Bible knowledge. (Contrary to what is shown here, only eight people survived this awesome, earth-changing event, not eleven. No appreciation for the long 120 years needed to build the ark is portrayed, and certainly no feeling for the year that man and animal shared the vessel. Elephants and oxen did not slide up and down the aisles of the ship, and the horn of a hippopotamus was never used to plug a leak.) The episode features excellent animation and good intensity, but poor or often completely inaccurate history is presented. ©1985

Episode: "SAMSON AND DELILAH"

CONTENT: ★★ ½   TECHNICAL QUALITY: ★★★★★

PRIMARY AUDIENCE: Ages 5
DIRECTOR: Ray Patterson
STYLE: Animation
DISTRIBUTOR: Sparrow Home Video (800)877-4443, (615)371-6800
LENGTH: 27 min.

Samson and Delilah is based on chapters 13–16 of Judges, which shows the overwhelming physical strength and emotional frailty of this man whom God installed as Israel's leader for twenty years. While this episode does not distort the biblical record nearly as much as some of the other episodes, it does go overboard in its extrabiblical embellishments. (One of the three modern youths who have passed through a "time portal" to Samson's period in history even builds and flies a hangglider!) Also, the physical attributes of Delilah and other women are revealed more than many parents will appreciate. If you do rent or purchase this tape, you might play a family game by first reading aloud the entire Judges 13–16 account. Then, give each of your reading-aged children a Bible and challenge them to find the content problems in the video. In this way, the kids will become much more familiar with the true biblical account, and you will enjoy the family interaction and discussion. ©1985

Ken Anderson's GREATEST STORIES EVER TOLD (series)

Episode: "JONAH AND THE BIG STORM"

CONTENT: ★★★★   TECHNICAL QUALITY: ★★

PRIMARY AUDIENCE:	Ages 4–10
DIRECTOR:	Unknown
STYLE:	"Draw-On" Animation
DISTRIBUTOR:	Ken Anderson Films (800)458-1387, (219)267-5774
LENGTH:	25 min.

This production does more than just retell the traditional children's version of the story of Jonah and his adventure with the big fish. With respect for communicating the true realities of God's Word—an essential ingredient sadly missing from some of the flashier children's tapes—a fuller story is presented here. Using simple "draw-on animation"—an animation style that goes over great with preschoolers but can become downright monotonous for older kids and adults—the producer introduces Jonah, the obedient, God-honoring prophet in his earlier experiences with King Jeroboam (from 2 Kings 14:25). Then begins the exciting adventure of Jonah trying to run from God and eventually learning to accept God's grace when people truly change their lives. Includes well-woven, interesting information, such as how tall the walls around Nineveh were, what a prophet is, and the fact that the king of Nineveh's great-great-grandfather was Noah. This is a unique teaching tool that helps transform important biblical truths into applicable lessons for modern Christians. (Also available on 16mm film.) ©1984

Episode: "JOSHUA AND THE PROMISED LAND"

CONTENT: ★★★★★   TECHNICAL QUALITY: ★★

PRIMARY AUDIENCE:	Ages 4–10
DIRECTOR:	Unknown
STYLE:	"Draw-On" Animation
DISTRIBUTOR:	Ken Anderson Films (800)458-1387, (219)267-5774
LENGTH:	28 min.

This episode uses the life and events of Joshua to teach the importance of trusting God in all circumstances. It shows Joshua as Moses' special helper and eventually as the man who God chose to lead Israel into the Promised Land. A "draw-on animation" film, it is full of interesting details that help to transform stories most Christians have probably begun to take for granted into an entertaining and genuinely educational format for teaching Old Testament history. This true-to-Scripture series would be excellent for Christian elementary schools to integrate into their Old Testament history curriculums. Also super for VBS, Sunday school, family devotions, and general entertainment. (Also available on 16mm film.) © 1984

Episode: "MARY AND JOSEPH"

CONTENT: ★★★★ ½   TECHNICAL QUALITY: ★★

PRIMARY AUDIENCE:	Ages 4–10
DIRECTOR:	Unknown
STYLE:	"Draw-On" Animation
DISTRIBUTOR:	Ken Anderson Films (800)458-1387, (219)267-5774
LENGTH:	25 min.

This is an excellent film to show during the Christmas season, but it is super as an entertaining teaching tool throughout the rest of the year too. The producer has gone to extra effort to allow young viewers to get a glimpse into Jesus' earthly family, being forced to flee to Egypt, the visit by the gift-bearing Magi two years after His birth, being taken to the temple as an infant, and more. Provides details that even Mom and Dad will appreciate about King Herod, the census, shepherds, the child Jesus teaching in the temple, and other areas. The tape is good for repeated viewing at home and also as a children's Sunday school audiovisual teaching aid. No apologies whatsoever for content. We only wish the quality of animation were a little better to measure up to the excellent content. (Also available on 16mm film.) © 1985

Episode: "NOAH'S BIG ADVENTURE"

CONTENT: ★★★★ ½   TECHNICAL QUALITY: ★★

PRIMARY AUDIENCE:	Ages 4–10
DIRECTOR:	Unknown
STYLE:	"Draw-On" Animation
DISTRIBUTOR:	Ken Anderson Films (800)458-1387, (219)267-5774
LENGTH:	23 min.

This animated adventure takes the exciting story of Noah and the ark out of the realm of fanciful imagination and places it where it belongs—in the factual events of history. Opening with a cursory look at the creation of the world, Adam and Eve, and the effects of their sin on the pre-Flood world, it then reveals the story of the worldwide catastrophic judgment popularly known as the Flood. Noah's obedience to God in the face of ridicule from his contemporaries is emphasized. This video accurately presents facts generally overlooked or misrepresented in other Noah story tapes, and the ark itself is illustrated very similarly to what it probably looked like (a huge wooden barge) rather than a storybookish little boat with animal heads sticking out all over. "Noah's Big Adventure" is entertaining and wonderfully educational. (Also available on 16mm film.) © 1983

Episode: "PAUL'S ADVENTURES"

CONTENT: ★★★★★   TECHNICAL QUALITY: ★★

PRIMARY AUDIENCE:	Ages 4–10
DIRECTOR:	Unknown
STYLE:	"Draw-On" Animation
DISTRIBUTOR:	Ken Anderson Films (800)458-1387, (219)267-5774
LENGTH:	24 min.

"Paul's Adventures" introduces young children to a Bible personality whose adventures and teachings are generally reserved for older audiences. Thanks to this well-researched "draw-on animation" production, children can now have a visual overview of the life of Paul that will provide increased appreciation during future Sunday school lessons and sermons. The video includes many interesting details and integrates simple maps of Israel and the areas visited by Paul on his missionary journeys. It also depicts Paul's conversion, shipwreck, snakebite, beatings, and imprisonment. An excellent teaching aid for Sunday school classes, home schools, and family devotions. It closes with a challenge to follow Paul's example by sharing the story of Jesus with others. While it is best suited for children, teenagers and adults will find this one entertaining and interesting as well. (Also available on 16mm film.) © 1986

HEAVEN'S HEROES

CONTENT: ★★★★   TECHNICAL QUALITY: ★★

PRIMARY AUDIENCE:	Ages 8–Adult
DIRECTOR:	Donald W. Thompson
STYLE:	Docudrama
DISTRIBUTOR:	Russ Doughten/Mark IV (800)247-3456, (515)278-4737
LENGTH:	1 hr., 12 min.

In this wonderful true story, a series of flashbacks combine to reveal the life of Christian police officer Dennis Hill. Killed in the line of duty by a sniper, Officer Hill's marital and Christian life is an example and inspiration to all viewers. *Heaven's Heroes* shows the problems and humanity of those who patrol our city streets and demonstrates effective lifestyle evangelism as Officer Hill strives to win his partner to Christ. Though the story is sad in that a loving father and husband is torn from his family and friends, the need for Christians to rely on Christ to carry them through rough times is well developed. A great drama to add to any church's video lending library. (Also available on 16mm film.) ©1980

HELL'S BELLS: THE DANGERS OF ROCK AND ROLL

CONTENT: ★★★★   TECHNICAL QUALITY: ★★ ½

PRIMARY AUDIENCE:	Adult Supervision
DIRECTOR:	Eric Holmberg
STYLE:	Documentary
DISTRIBUTOR:	American Portrait Films (800)736-4567, (216)531-8600
LENGTH:	3 hr., 5 min.

Hell's Bells is an almost epic work on the effects of secular rock music. It concentrates on heavy metal but discusses "pop rock" as well. Hosted by former rocker Eric Holmberg, this documentary is divided into five parts. Viewers are warned against showing the material to younger viewers (includes footage from rock concerts and videos with explicit material of sexual and occultic natures). Groups and musicians covered include: Lionel Ritchie, Whitney Houston, Huey Lewis, Guns and Roses, (then) Prince, Ozzy Osbourne, AC/DC, Madonna, Michael Jackson, John Lennon, Bon Jovi, Heart, Twisted Sister—all of whom were very popular in the late eighties and early nineties. *Hell's Bells* includes a brief historical overview of music and provides a summary about the effects of various types of music on objects, people, and plants. Interesting segments with references to Anton LaVey's *Satanic Bible* (part 2) and "back masking" (part 4). If you have not previously been calloused by the images, lyrics, and fruits of the rock culture, you will probably find it hard to sit through this entire production. However, even if you must fast-forward through the first four segments, be sure to view part 5. Here Holmberg addresses the issue of "pop rock." Holmberg explains why "the middle of the road—in music as well as in many other areas of life—can sometimes be the most dangerous place of all." This hard-hitting but calmly presented look at the late 1980s music culture concludes with Holmberg inviting viewers to pray with him if they would like to accept Jesus Christ as their personal Savior. This is a large dose of bitter medicine, but medicine that is much needed by most Christian teens today. ©1989

HIDDEN KEYS TO LOVING RELATIONSHIPS (series)

CONTENT: ★★★★   TECHNICAL QUALITY: ★★★

PRIMARY AUDIENCE:	Adults
DIRECTOR:	Unknown
STYLE:	Lecture
DISTRIBUTOR:	Gary Smalley Seminars (800)982-6750
LENGTH:	45–60 min. each

This multisession seminar, marketed in the USA via late-night "infomercials," features the funny and down-to-earth best-selling author Gary Smalley. On-air endorsements by such celebrities as John Tesch, Connie Seleca, and Kathi Lee Gifford helped to sell many videos; but many more viewers undoubtedly kept their wallets securely shut. We may not have the famous smiles of Tesch or Gifford, but we do heartily add our enthusiastic endorsement to this professionally produced and simply staged series. Smalley's humor and transparency help viewers to feel at ease with a friendly counselor whose practical advice and examples are sure to enhance any relationship, especially that of husband and wife. Smalley uses word pictures and everyday objects to help communicate his topics, which include understanding the differences between men and women, knowing how to deal with stress and conflict in marriage, and developing better relationships with your children. Smalley is a Christian, but he intentionally avoids evangelical lingo and almost all references to God or the Bible. ©1994

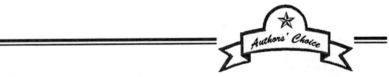

HIDING PLACE, THE

CONTENT: ★★★★★   TECHNICAL QUALITY: ★★★★★

PRIMARY AUDIENCE:	Jr. High–Adult
DIRECTOR:	James F. Collier
STYLE:	Docudrama
DISTRIBUTOR:	Broadman & Holman (800)251-3225, (615)251-2721
LENGTH:	2 hr., 25 min.

This intense story is a superbly produced drama about the lives, sufferings, and triumphant joys of the ten Boom family. Imprisoned in Nazi Germany's Ravensbrook concentration camp for helping to save the lives of Jews by harboring them in their Holland home, Corrie ten Boom and her sister, Betsie, suffer inhuman treatment at the hands of Nazi prison guards. The love between the two sisters and toward their God deepens as their trials intensify. Although *The Hiding Place* contains some brief scenes of violence and almost indiscernible cursing, it is extremely valuable and highly recommended. There is something very special and sobering about watching a show like this, always knowing that both the terrible sufferings and the triumphant joys were real. Try to provide an atmosphere as free from potential interruptions as possible. Doing so will greatly enhance this inspiring and timeless story. (Also available on 16mm film.) ©1975

HOMECOMING, THE

CONTENT: ★ ½   TECHNICAL QUALITY: ★★★★

PRIMARY AUDIENCE:	Ages 6–Adult
DIRECTOR:	Fielder Cook
STYLE:	Live-Action Drama
DISTRIBUTOR:	Fox Video
LENGTH:	1 hr., 38 min.
FEATURING:	Patricia Neal, Richard Thomas, Edgar Bergen, Ellen Corby
MPAA RATING:	Not Rated

Subtitled *A Christmas Story*, this classic drama inspired the long-running TV series *The Waltons*. The setting is Christmas Eve, 1933, in a snowy rural area of the Blue Ridge Mountains. The Great Depression has forced John Walton to live and work fifty miles from his beloved family, but he takes buses and hitchhikes the long trek home to be with the his wife (Olivia), seven children, and aged live-in parents this night. However, there will be no store-bought gifts unless Daddy arrives soon. Already anxious at the thought of greeting her husband again, Olivia is deeply concerned upon hearing via the big family radio that a bus has crashed, killing one man and injuring others. Hours drag by as Olivia and her parents-in-law keep the radio report to themselves and hope to see John arriving soon. Finally, John Boy (at age fifteen, the oldest child) is sent to try to find his father. The search is an adventure but proves fruitless. Tensions increase and emotions erupt, but Daddy does eventually arrive, even lugging a bag full of nicely wrapped gifts. This story is heartwarming and family-oriented overall, but is not high on our personal list of Christmastime "must see" movies. Note that the Walton family bases its standards on the Christian-based culture of their community, but none exhibit a personal relationship with Jesus Christ. This leads to a "moving target" form of morality, where certain actions are OK sometimes and inexcusable other times. Point out to young viewers that simply going to church or "being good" doesn't make one a Christian and can lend a false sense of spiritual security. (This tape includes several scenes of unchecked disrespect between bickering siblings, name-calling, overall promotion of the Santa Claus story and other Christmas myths.) ©1971

HOMEWARD BOUND: THE INCREDIBLE JOURNEY

CONTENT: ★★★   TECHNICAL QUALITY: ★★★★★

PRIMARY AUDIENCE:	Ages 6–Adult
DIRECTOR:	Duwayne Dunham
STYLE:	Live-Action Drama
DISTRIBUTOR:	Buena Vista Pictures
LENGTH:	1 hr., 24 min.
FEATURING:	Voices of Michael J. Fox, Sally Field, Don Ameche
MPAA RATING:	G

Homeward Bound is a humorous and heartwarming movie about acceptance, perseverance, and faithfulness. When Mom remarries, the new stepfather's job forces him to temporarily separate his new stepchildren from their beloved pets. A degree of resentment festers in the mind of the oldest son as a result. That resentment boils to the surface when the pets run away from the family friend who is temporarily caring for them. Unknown to the humans, the unlikely trio of domesticated beasts (wise old golden retriever, youthful bulldog, and always sarcastic Siamese cat) are struggling against many natural obstacles, including a bear, a waterfall, a mountain lion, and a porcupine in an all-out attempt to cross the mountain range that they believe separates them from their beloved owners. While the story is humorous throughout, it does include enough tension that it may be too scary for many preschool-aged children. (If necessary during the part where Sassy the cat is swept over a waterfall and assumed drowned, reassure your youngster that Sassy is only hurt and will get better and rejoin her friends soon.) After effecting the rescue of a lost little girl, Shadow, Chance, and Sassy are taken to an animal shelter and their owners are called. A happy reunion seems imminent, but the event is missed when Chance convinces his friends that they are all going to be killed unless they immediately escape. More challenges face the trio; however, they are eventually reunited with their humans in a touching final scene. (If you view this video, be sure to point out to your children that the sarcasm and crass words are inappropriate.) ©1993

HOOMANIA

CONTENT: ★★★★   TECHNICAL QUALITY: ★★★★

PRIMARY AUDIENCE:	Ages 4–10
DIRECTOR:	Rick Garside
STYLE:	Claymation and Live Action
DISTRIBUTOR:	Side by Side Films (213)698-6556
LENGTH:	37 min.

This unique children's adventure combines live action and colorful "claymation" to take a creative look at some simple lessons from the Book of Proverbs. After accidentally breaking a living-room window while playing baseball in his front yard, a young boy (Kris) escapes to the workshop of his grandfatherly friend, the inventor. The inventor offers Kris a chance to play an amazing board game that he has invented. The claymation portion of the video begins here as Kris accepts the offer and is immediately zapped into the game itself. As he strives to win the game by reaching Mount Wisdom, he makes some very foolish choices, including keeping bad company and disregarding instruction. Kris is chased by a daffy dodo bird, an army of chessmen, and tempted along his route by "goodie-gobbling sluggards." He finally learns from a wise old owl that wisdom means striving to please God. Awarded "Best Children's Film" by the Academy of Christian Cinemagraphic Arts for the year that it was released. (Also available on 16mm film.) ©1985

HOW SHOULD WE THEN LIVE

CONTENT: ★★★★★   TECHNICAL QUALITY: ★★★★

PRIMARY AUDIENCE: High School–Adult
DIRECTOR: Jan Bodzinga
STYLE: Documentary
DISTRIBUTOR: Gospel Films Video (800)253-0413, (616)773-3361
LENGTH: Ten 30-min. episodes

How Should We Then Live features the late Dr. Francis Schaeffer. It is a documentary series that contains a great deal of information about the philosophies that led to the degeneration of society, and it challenges Christians with suggestions about how we are to respond to our contemporary world. Schaeffer moderates all ten episodes on location in many different settings, principally throughout Europe. The scenes include a wide variety of illustrations and dramatizations and a unique style of cinematography. This is a series that requires serious viewers and is thus highly recommended. The episodes are well suited for use in college-aged through adult Sunday school or Bible study classes or for home viewing for personal enrichment. Nearly timeless content. This series should be a staple component in every church and upper-level Christian school library. (Also available on 16mm film.) ©1977

HOW THE BIBLE CAME TO BE

CONTENT: ★★★★   TECHNICAL QUALITY: ★★ ½

PRIMARY AUDIENCE: Adults
DIRECTOR: Jan Bodzinga
STYLE: Documentary
DISTRIBUTOR: Gospel Films Video (800)253-0413, (616)773-3361
LENGTH: 52 min.

Have you ever wondered how the sixty-six short books that we call the Holy Bible came to be? Who says that the Bible, the best-selling book of all time, is to be trusted as historically accurate? How do we know that the Bible wasn't written by a fraud who has perpetrated the greatest hoax of all time? Did Adam, Noah, Moses, and other men from the earliest books of the Old Testament participate in their actual writing? And what has recent archeological research revealed about the accuracy of both the New and Old Testaments? This documentary production contains a rich variety of visuals and excellent information. Don't let its slow European style of pacing deter you from using this great tool. Viewers will better appreciate how God has worked to make His written Word so easily available to you today. (Also Available on 16mm film.) ©1978

HOW TO KNOW YOU'RE IN LOVE

CONTENT: ★★★★   TECHNICAL QUALITY: ★★

PRIMARY AUDIENCE:	Jr. High–College
DIRECTOR:	Ken Glass
STYLE:	Lecture
DISTRIBUTOR:	Word, Inc. (800)933-9673, (214)556-1900
LENGTH:	65 min.

This is part 4 of the lecture series *Straight Talk about Love, Sex, and Dating.* Speaking before a live audience, popular youth speaker Dawson McAllister skillfully uses humor to reveal the difference between love and infatuation. He emphasizes that "love is both an emotional need and an act of the will based on a clear understanding of what the other person is like." He stresses to young men, "Don't get married unless you are willing to make your wife your second most important relationship" (God being #1). The message of this video is very good and worthy of being seen by every high school and college young person. The technical quality is satisfactory but uncreative (really nothing more than a large-group lecture sandwiched between a musical introduction and conclusion). *(For additional insight on this subject, consider tape #4 ["The Keys to a Lifelong Love"] in the LIFE ON THE EDGE teen-issues series from Focus on the Family, featuring Dr. James Dobson. It is more recent [1994], and of higher technical quality.)*©1985

HUMAN RACE CLUB (series)

Volume 1: "SELF-ESTEEM"

CONTENT: ★★ ½   TECHNICAL QUALITY: ★★★★

PRIMARY AUDIENCE:	Ages 6–10
DIRECTOR:	Steve Sheldon
STYLE:	Animation
DISTRIBUTOR:	Bridgestone Multimedia (800)523-0988, (602)940-5777
LENGTH:	22 min.

This animated story, based on the book by Joy Berry, is the first in the *Human Race Club* series. "The Letter on Light Blue Stationery" deals with the topic of self-esteem. Shows the dilemma of Pamela, a little girl who finds it hard to write a sympathy letter to the family of a classmate who has been killed in an auto accident. Pamela is encouraged by her mother to mention several of her friend's outstanding qualities in the letter, but she finds it hard to think of anything truly "special" about the average-looking, slightly pudgy girl. It isn't until a rather somber talk with her friends in the neighborhood clubhouse that Pamela finally recognizes and truly appreciates the caring, helpful attitude of her friend and recognizes the value of every person. This story is very good; however, it lacks any reference to God or Scripture (a strictly humanistic viewpoint). ©1989

HUMPTY

CONTENT: ★★★   **TECHNICAL QUALITY: ★★★ ½**

PRIMARY AUDIENCE:	Ages 3+
DIRECTOR:	George "Marty" Martsegis
STYLE:	Animation
DISTRIBUTOR:	Bridgestone Multimedia (800)523-0988, (602)940-5777
LENGTH:	24 min.

Humpty is the animated story of an inquisitive egg who discovers the value of good rules but learns this lesson the hard way. Deceived by a dragonlike serpent into believing that he is the best egg, Humpty becomes conceited and mean to his neighbors. He eventually disobeys the king's rule against climbing over a tall, protective wall that surrounds his city. While it is good Humpty learns that pride comes before a fall and that obedience is the real key to peace and contentment, the message of this film falls short in that the king (symbolic of God) freely forgives Humpty without any mention of atonement. ©1980

IMAGE OF THE BEAST

CONTENT: ★★★ ½   **TECHNICAL QUALITY: ★★★ ½**

PRIMARY AUDIENCE:	Jr. High–Adults
DIRECTOR:	Donald W. Thompson
STYLE:	Live-Action Drama
DISTRIBUTOR:	Russ Doughten/Mark IV (800)247-3456, (515)278-4737
LENGTH:	1 hr., 33 min.

The *Image of the Beast* is the third of four films in Russ Doughten/Mark IV's dramatic "prophecy series." This drama attempts to depict the events and emotions of the midyears of the seven-year Great Tribulation. The Antichrist has set up his one-world government, and anyone who has not taken his "mark" on the hand or forehead is hunted down and put to death. The first several minutes of this production are *extremely* intense and not recommended by this reviewer for young children or weak-stomached adults. The acting is good overall, but the production could have been helped by stronger performances from several of the supporting actors. While the story and special effects may seem like science fiction at times, this is primarily because we cannot fathom the terrible reality of the tribulation that is to come. It is difficult to visually represent events that even scholars do not understand. This series—based upon pretribulation rapture theology—is more than just good entertainment; it is a tremendous evangelistic tool. If possible, be sure to view *A Thief in the Night* and *A Distant Thunder* before seeing this film. (Also available on 16mm film.) ©1981

ISRAEL: GOD'S CHOSEN LAND

CONTENT: ★★★   **TECHNICAL QUALITY: ★★ ½**

PRIMARY AUDIENCE:	Adults
DIRECTOR:	Don Swingle, Jr.

STYLE:	Documentary
DISTRIBUTOR:	Christian Duplications International (800)327-9332, (407)299-7363
LENGTH:	35 min.

By combining scenes of modern-day Israel, Scripture reading, cutaways to maps of Israel, historical facts told by an unseen narrator, and a good selection of background music, this rather low-budget production is a good tape for anyone who is considering a trip to, or has already visited, "God's Chosen Land." It is a concise travelogue of the attractions most frequented by North American visitors to Israel (including the traditionally accepted tomb of Jesus, the garden of Gethsemane, the Jordan River, and the temple site). The inclusion of aerial photography provides a good feeling for the geography of the area. Although some scenes do not mesh with the narration or script reading, the tape is good overall. (If you have serious interest in Israel, and its applicability to today, you may wish to consider the 27-part series from Focus on the Family, *That the World May Know.*) © 1988

IT'S A WONDERFUL LIFE

CONTENT: ★★★★   TECHNICAL QUALITY: ★★★★ ½

PRIMARY AUDIENCE:	Ages 8+
DIRECTOR:	Frank Capra
STYLE:	Live-Action Drama
DISTRIBUTOR:	RCA/Columbia Pictures
LENGTH:	2 hr., 40 min.
FEATURING:	James Stewart, Donna Reed, Henry Travers, Thomas Mitchell
MPAA RATING:	Not Rated

It's a Wonderful Life is traditionally thought of as a Christmas film, but its powerful and emotionally uplifting message about the value of every individual life makes it excellent all year round. George Bailey (James Stewart) is a smart, ambitious young man who strongly dislikes the career that he has "inherited." He longs for the day when he can leave his hometown of Bedford Falls to travel the world. However, George's most endearing attribute—putting others ahead of himself—is also the greatest impediment to the fulfillment of his personal dreams. After a large sum of company money is lost by his employee/uncle, George hits bottom and, believing that his loving family would be better off if he had never been born, comes within seconds of committing suicide. Instead, a slightly dopey angel who is out to "earn his wings" shows George how the lives of those he loves would have been different had he never been born. This excellent drama shows that each person's life touches many lives. Each individual is important. Though there is no profanity and the fun and romantic subplot is kept wholesome, the film does include drinking and a distorted view of angels. A wonderful feel-good film overall. ©1946

JESSE OWENS STORY, THE

CONTENT: ★★★ ½   TECHNICAL QUALITY: ★★★ ½

PRIMARY AUDIENCE:	Ages 10+
DIRECTOR:	Richard Irving
STYLE:	Docudrama
DISTRIBUTOR:	Paramount Home Video
LENGTH:	2 hr., 54 min.
FEATURING:	Dorian Harewood, Debbie Morgan, George Brown
MPAA RATING:	Not Rated

This docudrama reveals important but little-known facts about the life of Jesse Owens, the black track star who won four gold medals for the USA at the 1936 Berlin Olympics while Hitler's white "supermen" embarrassed their feared leader. Jesse's life story is revealed piece by piece from the perspective of a court-appointed investigator who strives to understand why this quiet humanitarian and national hero ended up refusing to pay personal income taxes for four years in the 1970s. Because this drama contains lots of actual and reenacted Olympic track-and-field footage, it will appeal to most sports enthusiasts. Most important, viewers will be warmed and inspired as they watch Owens hold fast to his good values and principles though he endures a lifetime of terribly unfair racist attitudes. This is an entertaining way to brush up on American history and civics, but it does contain several profanities. No nudity or sexual situations. ©1984

JESUS

CONTENT: ★★★★★   TECHNICAL QUALITY: ★★★★★

PRIMARY AUDIENCE:	Family (Ages 4+)
DIRECTORS:	Peter Sykes and John Kirsh
STYLE:	Docudrama
DISTRIBUTOR:	FFC/Eden Communications (800)332-2261, (602)894-1300
LENGTH:	2 hours

This film was made entirely in Israel with a cast of over five thousand Israelis and Arabs. With a script taken entirely from the Book of Luke, this is clearly one of the most accurate Bible dramas ever produced. The story covers the angel's announcement to the Virgin Mary of the impending birth of Jesus, the main events of Jesus' life and ministry, a painfully realistic crucifixion, and it ends with His ascension through the clouds. It includes none of the standard Hollywood sensationalism usually written into Bible films of this financial magnitude ($6,000,000 in 1979 dollars). Wonderful attention to scriptural purity combined with excellent technical and cinemagraphic quality. This film moves slower than American viewers are used to, but it allows the many events depicted and the message imparted to "sink in" rather than simply being lost as nonapplicable entertainment. This film has been translated into over two hundred languages and is used as an evangelism tool throughout the world. Indoor and outdoor screenings of the 16mm version serve as the catalyst to introduce literally thousands each month to a personal relationship with Jesus Christ. (Also available on 16mm film.) ©1979

JESUS BICYCLE

CONTENT: ★★★★ ½   TECHNICAL QUALITY: ★★★

PRIMARY AUDIENCE: Ages 4–10
DIRECTOR: J. Ron Byler
STYLE: Live-Action Drama
DISTRIBUTOR: Cathedral Films (800)338-3456, (818)991-3290
LENGTH: 21 min.

This children's drama is filled with the warmth of people helping other people. A mentally retarded and physically handicapped teenage boy (Dirk) rides his special three-wheeled bicycle to the rescue of a six-year-old girl (Emily) who is lost. Because of Dirk's handicaps he is unfairly ridiculed by other boys, but the ridicule doesn't dim his spirit. Dirk's positive attitude, helpful spirit, and unassuming ways all combine to reveal the dignity and value of the disabled. The original score and lyrics remind viewers of the high value that our Creator places on *all* of His creation—whether "normal" or "special." This is good entertainment, but it is also valuable in that the story helps young viewers to understand and accept the disabilities of others. Includes brief discussion guide. Great for Sunday school or family devotions. (Also available on 16mm film.) ©1985

JESUS' LIFE (series)

Tape 1: "HIS BIRTH"

CONTENT: ★★★★ ½   TECHNICAL QUALITY: ★★ ½

PRIMARY AUDIENCE: Ages 5–Adult
DIRECTOR: Keith R. Neely
STYLE: Filmation
DISTRIBUTOR: Biblevision (209)825-5645
LENGTH: 35 min.

Improperly titled, this is much more than just a story about the birth of Christ. The first in a seven-part series of visualized Scripture reading, this video tells the story of Jesus Christ with the purity of actual word-for-word Scripture (NIV translation). It is unique in that it achieves excellence without cartoons or Hollywood-style distortions. While the animation is simple (only pans and zooms, no actual character movement), the viewer is drawn into a visual presentation of God's Word that features lifelike paintings rather than cartoonish characters. Both the narration and orchestral music and sound effects are superb. This is more than an ordinary children's video. Because it is broken down into many short stories, it is also excellent for family devotions and even for churches to use as a visual aid when teaching adult and youth Bible studies on the life and ministry of Christ. ©1986

Tape 2: "HIS MINISTRY"

CONTENT: ★★★★★   TECHNICAL QUALITY: ★★ ½

PRIMARY AUDIENCE:	Ages 5–Adult
DIRECTOR:	Keith R. Neely
STYLE:	Filmation
DISTRIBUTOR:	Biblevision (209)825-5645
LENGTH:	56 min.

The realistic caricatures, excellent narration, and rich music enhance this well-produced video that is based on sections from the NIV Bible. The producer has packed twenty-six stories of Jesus' ministry onto the fifty-six-minute tape. (This is the longest of the seven tapes in the *Jesus' Life* series.) More than entertainment and education, this tape and the series of which it is part is very edifying—honoring God through its visually enhanced Scripture readings. This is the same simple—but effective—animation style as that used in this same producer/director's *Acts* series. Both the *Jesus' Life* series and the *Acts* series received the enthusiastic personal endorsement of respected Bible teachers, like Dr. John MacArthur. ©1986

JIMMY AND THE WHITE LIE

CONTENT: ★★★★   TECHNICAL QUALITY: ★★★★

PRIMARY AUDIENCE:	Ages 3–8
DIRECTOR:	Unknown
STYLE:	Animation
DISTRIBUTOR:	Family Films/Concordia (800)325-3040, (314)664-7000
LENGTH:	20 min.

This animated adventure is great to share with children at home, church, or school. A baseball-loving young boy (Jimmy) accidentally breaks the window of a cranky neighbor and then lies to his parents about what happened. His lie becomes an obnoxious, visible white blob that expands and becomes difficult to hide. Jimmy learns that lies tend to grow and become uncomfortable to live with. He also learns that admitting to a lie is usually much better than being found to be a liar by someone else. Introductory and concluding comments by a real-life animation artist add a valuable, personalized quality. ©1985

JOHN HUS

CONTENT: ★★★★★   TECHNICAL QUALITY: ★★★ ½

PRIMARY AUDIENCE:	Jr. High–Adult
DIRECTOR:	Michael Economou
STYLE:	Docudrama
DISTRIBUTOR:	Vision Video (800)523-0226, (215)584-1893
LENGTH:	55 min.

Historically based drama of the beliefs and teachings that led adversaries of John Hus to burn him at the stake in 1415. Hus taught that salvation comes by faith, apart from works. He also introduced congregational singing into his church, departing from Latin mass in favor of presenting the Bible in the language of the Bohemian people to whom he preached. His relentless pursuit of God's truth planted the seeds of the Reformation one hundred years before Martin Luther. This well-acted and well-scripted motion picture should be a part of every church and school media library. *John Hus* is an inspiring example of one man's commitment to and faith in Jesus Christ. Refusing to compromise his beliefs, Hus died singing as he was burned at the stake for heresy. Don't be concerned about the year of release (1977) because this drama is not dated in any way; it is a period film whose material will always be current. ©1977

JOHN WYCLIFFE: THE MORNING STAR

CONTENT: ★★★★   TECHNICAL QUALITY: ★★★★

PRIMARY AUDIENCE: Jr. High–Adult
DIRECTOR: Tony Tew
STYLE: Docudrama
DISTRIBUTOR: Vision Video (800)523-0226, (215)584-1893
LENGTH: 1 hr., 15 min.

Fourteenth-century scholar and cleric John Wycliffe is best known as the man who first translated the Bible into the English language. However, as this film reveals, Wycliffe also served as a champion of English nationalism against the power of the Pope. Wycliffe once asked "How can men live under the authority of God's Word if they don't even *know* God's Word?" These words ring as clearly in our modern society (where Christians take the availability of God's Word for granted and do not consistently read it) as they did in Wycliffe's own fourteenth-century England (where the Bible was not even available in the English language). The film features very good acting and well-researched history, but the production moves a bit slowly. Videos such as this should definitely be integrated into adult Sunday school curriculums. (Also available on 16mm film.) ©1983

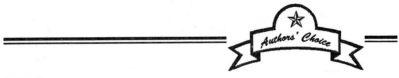

JONI

CONTENT: ★★★★ ½   TECHNICAL QUALITY: ★★★★ ½

PRIMARY AUDIENCE: Ages 10–Adult
DIRECTOR: James F. Collier
STYLE: Docudrama
DISTRIBUTOR: Broadman & Holman (800)251-3225, (615)251-2721
LENGTH: 1 hr., 50 min.

Set in the rural New England, this docudrama opens with a reenactment of the tragic 1967 diving accident that broke the neck of Joni (Eareckson) Tada. She was instantly transformed from an athletic seventeen-year-old into a wheelchair-bound quadriplegic. Joni endures the physical trauma of spine-fusion surgery and lengthy rehabilitation before reentering the "normal" world by living with her sister on the family's Maryland farm. Through various people that God brings into her life, Joni begins to submit her will to His and eventually becomes a vehicle through which God ministers to others. Viewers are drawn into this well-written, technically excellent story as it reveals the physical, emotional, and spiritual struggles that Joni was forced to endure, but always with support from loving family members. *Joni* asks the questions, "Why does God allow suffering?" and "Why doesn't He always heal those who ask in faith?" but it provides no pat answers. This excellent film stresses, instead, God's sovereignty, His plan for our lives, and our need to trust Him completely, even when He doesn't make sense. This is a sensitive drama that provides insights into the emotions and frustrations of what it is like to be unable to control the functions of one's own body. Entertaining, inspiring, and challenging. ©1979

JOURNEY OF LIFE

CONTENT: ★★★★ ½   TECHNICAL QUALITY: ★★★★★

PRIMARY AUDIENCE:	All ages
DIRECTOR:	Ladd Allen
STYLE:	Documentary
DISTRIBUTOR:	Moody Institute of Science (800)621-5111, (312)329-2190
LENGTH:	40 min.

Young and old alike will be captivated by the beautiful photography, rich soundtrack, and fast pacing of this Creator-honoring production. It is an eye-opening and awe-inspiring look at how plants have been designed to reproduce and replenish themselves through the incredible voyage of their seedlings. A refreshing and educational examination of some of nature's intricacies, without a single reference to evolution or "millions of years." The movie falls short, however, in that the producer did not use this excellent opportunity to uphold and endorse the Genesis account of creation (specifically, that plants were created "according to their kinds" on day three of the six days of creation). Contains a mild evangelistic ending that urges viewers to examine God's plan for their lives. Purchase this one for your personal video library because one viewing simply is not enough. ©1985

KIDS PRAISE 4: *SINGSATIONAL SERVANTS*

CONTENT: ★★★★   TECHNICAL QUALITY: ★★ ½

PRIMARY AUDIENCE:	Ages 3–8
DIRECTOR:	Richard Eisleben
STYLE:	Live-Action Musical
DISTRIBUTOR:	Word, Inc. (800)933-9673, (214)556-1900
LENGTH:	44 min.

While this video's package may mislead buyers into thinking that the style of presentation is animation, it is really a very good, live-action children's musical, well staged with a colorful set and great costumes. In this story, Charity Churchmouse (seeking fame and fortune on her way to California to become a Gospel music singing star) learns the value of serving others instead of just herself. She finds that serving others puts a song in her heart. If we follow the Lord's example, we will be servants of all and great in God's kingdom. Constant movement, excellent camera angles, great choreography, and a large number of sing-along songs all add to the attention-holding power of this tape. ©1984

KINGDOM CHUMS, THE (series)

Episode 1: "LITTLE DAVID'S ADVENTURE"

CONTENT: ★   TECHNICAL QUALITY: ★★★★ ½

PRIMARY AUDIENCE: Ages 6–10
DIRECTORS: Colin Chilvers and B. Deyries
STYLE: Animated, Live Action
DISTRIBUTOR: Word, Inc. (800)933-9673, (214)556-1900
LENGTH: 52 min.

Originally telecast during prime time on ABC, "Little David's Adventure" is a combination of high-quality animation, live-action drama, great songs, and well-executed special effects. Unfortunately, it is an excellent tool to begin the process of subtly indoctrinating impressionable young minds with New Age and humanistic religious concepts. In this video, three modern-day youths are magically changed into cartoon characters after having been transported through a computer screen and a moving rainbow (the "Love Light Beam") to Israel three thousand years ago. The children watch as a raccoon (David) slays the giant bulldog (Goliath). (King Saul is a cat, and the enemy Philistine army is made up of a variety of ugly rodents.) The raccoon refers both to Jesus and to "the power within," but it is unclear whether the power within is the Holy Spirit or some sort of mystical "force." While this tape admittedly provides fifty-two minutes of spirited entertainment, it is a poor example of good Bible storytelling. Not recommended. ©1986

Episode 2: "THE ORIGINAL TOP TEN"

CONTENT: ★★★   TECHNICAL QUALITY: ★★★★★

PRIMARY AUDIENCE: Ages 4–10
DIRECTOR: Rick Reinert
STYLE: Animated Musical
DISTRIBUTOR: Word, Inc. (800)933-9673, (214)556-1900
LENGTH: 48 min.

Congratulations to ABC for this exceptionally positive program. The writers of this colorful animated musical are to be commended for investing their energies into creating a very entertaining program that has appeal to Christians and non-Christians alike. While "The Original Top Ten" includes the same animated "stars" as its predecessor ("Little David's Adventure"), the writers of this episode wisely chose to devise a new way of encouraging youngsters to obey the Ten Commandments rather than butchering another important event of Bible history. Here, three young music lovers are magically transported to the land of the rainbowlike "Love Light Beam." Their experiences convince them why the Ten Commandments are truly *the* top ten and most important "hits" ever recorded. Teaches values such as love, courage, joy, loyalty, and perseverance.

The contemporary, fast-paced storyline will go over well with the intended audience. ©1989

LASSIE COME HOME

CONTENT: ★★★★   TECHNICAL QUALITY: ★★★★ ½

PRIMARY AUDIENCE:	Family (Ages 3+)
DIRECTOR:	Fred M. Wilcox
STYLE:	Drama
DISTRIBUTOR:	MGM/UA Home Video
LENGTH:	1 hr., 30 min.
FEATURING:	Lassie, Roddy McDowall, Elizabeth Taylor, Donald Crisp
MPAA RATING:	G

Set in picturesque England and Scotland, *Lassie Come Home* is the story of a well-bred Collie and her insatiable desire to be reunited with the boy master who dearly loves and misses her. The boy's impoverished parents have been forced to sell the beloved family pet to a wealthy duke in order to be able to buy food to eat. After being relocated some one thousand miles, to Scotland, Lassie escapes from the duke's mean-spirited dog handler. During her adventure-filled trek back home, the caring canine touches the lives of a traveling peddler and an elderly couple. But Lassie's desire to return to her young "master" drives her onward. After overcoming mountains, treacherous rivers, unfamiliar forests, and rocky ocean beaches, this amazing dog is inevitably reunited with the family and the boy who raised her. Though predictable, it is an emotional story that children love. (Point out to young viewers near the film's end that the boy's parents lie to the duke by saying that they have not seen Lassie. Aware that the parents are not telling the truth, the kind-hearted duke feigns that he doesn't recognize his dog. Point out that the same result—giving the dog back to its original owner—could have resulted from honesty.) ©1943

LAST CHANCE DETECTIVES (series)

Episode 1: "MYSTERY LIGHTS OF NAVAJO MESA"

CONTENT: ★★★ ½   TECHNICAL QUALITY: ★★★★

PRIMARY AUDIENCE:	Ages 8–13
DIRECTOR:	Stephen Stiles
STYLE:	Mystery-Adventure Drama
DISTRIBUTOR:	Tyndale Christian Video (800)323-9400, (708)668-8300
LENGTH:	46 min.

The Arizona desert sets a unique backdrop for this slightly scary mystery/adventure. From their clubhouse inside an old B-17 bomber that stands next to a roadside diner, the Last Chance Detectives (LCD) are four young teens who strive to solve their town's small mysteries. However, their desire to get an important, hard-to-solve case leads them headlong into the middle of the biggest crime that the town's sheriff has ever investigated. Priceless Aztec artifacts have been stolen from the town library, and mysterious voices are heard on the B-17's recently repaired radio. When the kids ride their all-terrain cycles into the desert to check things out, mysterious nighttime lights (designed to make viewers suspect UFOs) add a twist to the investigation. The thieves turn out to be smugglers, well hidden in an abandoned mine shaft; and the "UFO" is a supersecret, superquiet FBI helicopter. The message of this film is: don't hold onto grudges because you can't let your feelings guide you; rather, the Bible should be your guide. (In this case, Ephesians 4:32 is taken to heart by Mike, the leader of the LCD, after he has been wronged by his best friend.) Includes appearances by several Hollywood actors. Very good but too intense for preschool through six-year-olds. ©1994

LAUREL WITH A MORAL

CONTENT: ★★★★★   TECHNICAL QUALITY: ★★★ ½

PRIMARY AUDIENCE: Ages 2–5
ANIMATOR: Rod Harris
STYLE: Animation
DISTRIBUTOR: Tyndale Christian Video (800)323-9400, (708)668-8300
LENGTH: 32 min.

Laurel's animated short stories (there are twelve on this tape) are both educational and thoroughly entertaining. Her stories are told in rhyme and deal with self-esteem, obedience, kindness, generosity, and God's love. You won't mind your children watching this video again and again. An excellent addition to any parent's or grandparent's video library, especially for preschoolers and young grade-schoolers. © mid-1980s

---

LEARNING ABOUT SEX (series)

Ages 6–8: "WHERE DO BABIES COME FROM?"

CONTENT: ★★★★   TECHNICAL QUALITY: ★★

PRIMARY AUDIENCE: Ages 6–8 (With Parents)
DIRECTOR: Unknown
STYLE: Filmation
DISTRIBUTOR: Family Films / Concordia (800)325-3040, (314)664-7000
LENGTH: 10 min.

This simple video tactfully and with just the right amount of information for six- to eight-year-olds answers the question, "Where do babies come from?" Best of all, it does so from a biblical point of view in the context of our relationship to the God who created us and His plan for reproduction. Reveals the way in which a baby grows inside the mother's womb. Stresses the sanctity of marriage. Also, a "user's guide" that is included with the video is very helpful. The entire *Learning About Sex* series (of which this is the second segment) would be an excellent resource for every church to have on hand to aid parents in properly communicating this important subject to children of any age. ©1988

Ages 8–11: "HOW YOU ARE CHANGING"

CONTENT: ★★★★   TECHNICAL QUALITY: ★★

PRIMARY AUDIENCE: Ages 8–11 (With Parents)
DIRECTOR: Unknown
STYLE: Filmation
DISTRIBUTOR: Family Films / Concordia (800)325-3040, (314)664-7000
LENGTH: 15 min.

The third in the five-part *Learning About Sex* series, this segment is also simply but colorfully animated. *How You Are Changing* provides support, encouragement, and accurate, up-to-date medical and physiological information on a level well suited for eight- to eleven-year-olds. Very interesting and educational. This production is designed to help parents open a channel of communication that will prove to be even more important as the child enters the teen years. As with other segments in the series, sex education is provided from a Christ-centered point of view. Helpful "parent guide" is included. ©1988

LIFE FLIGHT

CONTENT: ★★   TECHNICAL QUALITY: ★★ ½

PRIMARY AUDIENCE: Jr. High–Adult
DIRECTOR: Donald W. Thompson
STYLE: Drama
DISTRIBUTOR: Vision Video (800)523-0226, (215)584-1893
LENGTH: 1 hr., 26 min.

The main plot in *Life Flight* is supposed to be that of a Vietnam veteran's emotional struggle to regain the courage he needs to be able to become part of an emergency medical team that uses a helicopter as a flying ambulance. However, some of the subplots (insufficient hospital funds to expand the helicopter program, "do things my own way" attitude of a young helicopter pilot, and keep handguns out of the reach of children) vie with the main theme for preeminence. The viewer is often confused as to the primary message, which appears to change frequently. This story is wholesome, generally well acted, and contains some good special effects, but the intensity level associated with these special effects somehow never meets the viewer's expectations. On the positive side, one of the best aspects of this film is its challenge to Christians to be knowledgeable about God's Word and to be ready to give an answer to those who ask tough questions. Non-Christians are often interested in knowing a biblical basis for our opinions, a point which is brought out in the movie. There is nothing truly outstanding about this film—too bad since it had the potential for much more. ©1987

LIFE ON THE EDGE (series)

CONTENT: ★★★★ ½   TECHNICAL QUALITY: ★★★★

PRIMARY AUDIENCE:	Jr. High–College
DIRECTOR:	Ed Flanagan
STYLE:	Lecture
DISTRIBUTOR:	Focus on the Family (800)232-6459, (719)531-3312
LENGTH:	Seven 50-min. segments

This seven-part series featuring Dr. James Dobson (and special guests) deals sensitively yet forthrightly with some of the most important issues facing teens today. Each segment is preceded by a mountain-climbing sequence and then cuts to the Great Hall at "Glen Eyrie," international headquarters of The Navigators in the mountains of Colorado. From behind a modest wooden podium, Dr. James Dobson (founder of Focus on the Family ministries) speaks to an audience of approximately one hundred teens. The information conveyed is of immense importance both to teens and to the adults charged with guiding them. This is the type of series that parents should view long before their children ever reach the potentially tumultuous junior high through college years, and one that youth pastors should definitely view and discuss with their youth groups at least once every two to three years. The titles of the seven videos in this series are: "Finding God's Will for Your Life" / "The Myth of Safe Sex" / "Love Must Be Tough" / "The Keys to a Lifelong Love" / "Emotions: Can You Trust Them?" / "When God Doesn't Make Sense" / "Pornography: Addictive, Progressive, and Deadly." ©1994

LION KING, THE

CONTENT: ★ ½   TECHNICAL QUALITY: ★★★★★

PRIMARY AUDIENCE:	Ages 8–12
DIRECTORS:	Roger Allers, Rob Minkoff
STYLE:	Animation
DISTRIBUTOR:	Buena Vista (Disney)
LENGTH:	1 hr., 28 min.
FEATURING:	Voices of Whoopi Goldberg, James Earl Jones, Matthew Broderick, Jeremy Irons
MPAA RATING:	G

Disney's exceptional animation, voice acting, and soundtrack may tempt you to embrace this video without analyzing its hidden messages. On the surface it is the story of an animal kingdom once ruled by the wise and powerful lion, Mufasa, but whose throne is usurped by his evil brother, Scar, who secretly murders him. The kingdom is eventually restored upon the return of the rightful heir, Simba (the guilt-ridden, self-banished son of Mufasa). Upon deeper examination, however, this box-office smash reveals a mixed bag of good moral teachings and New Age religious beliefs. On the positive side, Mufasa and his cub son, Simba, portray a loving father-son relationship; the consequences of disobedience and irresponsibility are portrayed; the flattery and temptations of wicked Scar are revealed; and, in the end, Scar receives the just reward for his treacherous ways. Unfortunately, there are some very negative aspects to this film, as well, which are especially harmful if viewers become so caught up in the characters and surface plot that they hardly notice or choose to overlook the fact that the script includes a witch doctor who practices divinations, conjuring up the spirit image of Simba's dead father to "guide" him in time of need. This witch doctor is depicted as someone wise from whom to learn. Add to that the frequent dark and tense moods dur-

---

ing the four murder attempts on Simba's life, the murder of his father Mufasa, the eerie surroundings and evil characters of the hyenas and Uncle Scar, and the intense fight scenes. In spite of *The Lion King's* positive qualities and runaway popularity, we cannot recommend it. ©1994

LION, THE WITCH, AND THE WARDROBE, THE

CONTENT: ★★★★★   TECHNICAL QUALITY: ★★★★ ½

PRIMARY AUDIENCE:	Family (Ages 4+)
DIRECTOR:	Bill Melendez
STYLE:	Animation
DISTRIBUTOR:	FFC/Eden Communications (800)332-2261, (602)894-1300
LENGTH:	1 hr., 35 min.

Awarded with an Emmy as an outstanding animated program, this production of C. S. Lewis's famous novel includes full orchestration. The first tale in Lewis's acclaimed *Chronicles of Narnia* book series, "The Lion, the Witch, and the Wardrobe" is the story of two brothers and two sisters who mysteriously pass through a wardrobe closet into the world of Narnia, a land of talking animals and mystical creatures. This story is beautiful and heartwarming in the believability of its symbolism, designed by Lewis to remind us of Jesus' atoning death and resurrection and His future vanquishing of Satan and his followers. Your children and the neighborhood children will plead to view this one again and again. ©1985

LITTLE LORD FAUNTLEROY

CONTENT: ★★★★ ½   TECHNICAL QUALITY: ★★★★ ½

PRIMARY AUDIENCE:	Family (Ages 4+)
DIRECTOR:	Jack Gold
STYLE:	Live-Action Drama
DISTRIBUTOR:	Family Home Entertainment
LENGTH:	1 hr., 38 min.
FEATURING:	Ricky Schroder, Alec Guinness, Connie Booth, Colin Blakely
MPAA RATING:	Not Rated

The entire family will enjoy this wonderful remake of the 1936 classic, *Little Lord Fauntleroy*. One day Seddy is a young boy who enjoys playing kick the can in the streets of his destitute New York City neighborhood. The next day his world is turned upside down when a messenger arrives with what he and his American friends consider horrible news. Seddy is to immediately move to England where he will live in a castle with his grandfather and assume his rightful place in English society as young "Lord Fauntleroy." Upon his arrival in England, his unpretentious demeanor and genuine compassion for others quickly endear him to his crotchety old grandfather, a man whom he had never before met. In time, the grandfather is changed by the love and admiration of this young, naive boy. While the *plot* weaves a humorous and heartwarming account of one boy's journey from rags to riches, the *message* is a well-crafted reminder that believing in and expecting the best of someone can inspire that person to strive to live up to your ideal of them. The film also reveals the hurt that can be wrought by prejudice. (In this case, the English grandfather, the Earl of Dorincourt, is prejudiced against his "commoner" American daughter-in-law.) Includes one mild expletive. ©1980

LITTLE TROLL PRINCE, THE

CONTENT: ★★   TECHNICAL QUALITY: ★★★★★

PRIMARY AUDIENCE: Ages 3–10
DIRECTOR: Ray Patterson
STYLE: Animation
DISTRIBUTOR: Sparrow Home Video (800)877-4443, (615)371-6800
LENGTH: 46 min.

According to its producer, this animated Hanna-Barbera production "tells the story of the once-frozen heart of the Little Troll Prince melting with joy upon receiving the greatest Christmas gift of all—God's love." But the video is weak on this key point; it should have shown him as actually receiving Christ as Savior rather than being transformed simply by the *realization* that God loves us. But (the Little Troll Prince) bravely battles the evil ways of the Royal Troll Family and their world, where bad is good and no word for love exists. The Royal Troll Family presumably is intended to symbolize Satan and his followers. Excellent with regard to technical aspects, but this well-intentioned production does not communicate the true way to salvation. Better materials dealing with Christmas are available. ©1987

LITTLE VISITS WITH GOD (Volume 1)

CONTENT: ★★★★★   TECHNICAL QUALITY: ★★★ ½

PRIMARY AUDIENCE: Ages 4–10
DIRECTOR: Unknown
STYLE: Drama, Puppets, Animation
DISTRIBUTOR: Family Films/Concordia (800)325-3040, (314)268-1000
LENGTH: 1 hr., 8 min.

The box in which this videocassette is packaged is really a treasure chest in disguise. Ten individual short stories make up this seventy-minute tape, and each is a valuable family resource. The great puppetry, real-life dramas, and simple animation segments all combine to reveal God's way to deal with some of life's not-so-smooth situations. Each story covers a specific subject, such as gossiping, being thankful, not looking down on others, and how God gives strength. The package also includes a simple devotional guide that is ideal for either one- or two-parent households to lead exciting family devotions. Each discussion in the devotional guide includes a short memory verse, questions to discuss, a suggested short Bible reading, and a suggested prayer. Now there is no excuse to skip family devotions! ©1985

MAN CALLED PETER, A

CONTENT: ★★★★★   TECHNICAL QUALITY: ★★★★ ½

PRIMARY AUDIENCE: Ages 8+
DIRECTOR: Henry Koster
STYLE: Docudrama
DISTRIBUTOR: Gospel Films Video (800)253-0413, (616)773-3361
LENGTH: 1 hr., 57 min.
MPAA RATING: Not Rated
FEATURING: Richard Todd, Jean Peters

This Hollywood release contains excellent Christian content. Beginning in Peter Marshall's native Scotland, *A Man Called Peter* reveals the events that led this dynamic young man to America in the 1920s; it then concentrates on his unorthodox courtship of the admiring young Catherine and his ensuing years of ministry—especially in Washington, D.C., at the prestigious Church of the Presidents in the 1930s and 40s—and as chaplain to the United States Senate prior to his untimely death. Marshall is a caring husband and father. But what is most impressive is his strong relationship with God and his desire to turn any who will listen toward a proper understanding of the one true Savior. Though appropriate for all ages, this docudrama is usually most appreciated by adult viewers. *A Man Called Peter* poignantly reminds us of the importance of making God's priorities our own and not allowing hallowed man-made traditions or personal pride to sway us from that course. A great biography that communicates the essentials of the gospel message. ©1955

MAN FROM SNOWY RIVER, THE

CONTENT: ★★   TECHNICAL QUALITY: ★★★★ ½

PRIMARY AUDIENCE: Ages 10+
DIRECTOR: George Miller
STYLE: Live-Action Drama/Adventure
DISTRIBUTOR: CBS/FOX
LENGTH: 1 hr., 44 min.
FEATURING: Kirk Douglas, Tom Burlinson, Sigrid Thornton, Jack Thompson
MPAA RATING: PG

Young viewers enjoy this picturesque Australian movie because of its strong subplot about a young man, a young woman, and a herd of wild horses. But adults are drawn into the story by mystery. A nearly destitute gold miner (Spur), and his brother, a wealthy cattle rancher, have not spoken for twenty years. Their long-broken relationship was caused by their competing love of the same young lady. The rancher brother eventually married that young lady and fathered a girl by her; however, his wife soon deserted him due to his over-whelming jealousy and suspicions of her possible interest in Spur. Now the rancher's twenty-year-old daughter meets Spur (both brothers are played by Kirk Douglas) and simultaneously falls in love with a strong-willed young man, Spur's good friend. The girl almost dies in a fall over a mountain but is rescued by her young beau. Against her father's stern wishes, the young woman eventually leaves her father's comfortable ranch to follow her newfound love. This popular film is hindered by a sometimes slow-moving script and five profanities, meriting our lackluster endorsement. ©1982

McGEE and ME! (Series)

ABOUT THE SERIES: This live-action dramatic series includes just the right amount of contemporary animation and tastefully upbeat music to excite both young children (ages four to six) and young grade-school kids (up to about twelve-years-old). Nicholas and his alter ego—represented by a comical cartoon named McGee—learn important life lessons while also learning to treat others the way that they would want others to treat them. Kudos to Focus on the Family and the creators of these much-acclaimed—and much-needed—children's films that are fun, wonderfully wholesome, and Bible-based at the same time!

Episode 1: "THE BIG LIE"

CONTENT: ★★★★★   TECHNICAL QUALITY: ★★★★★

PRIMARY AUDIENCE:	Ages 4–12
DIRECTOR:	Mark Cullingham
STYLE:	Animation, Live Action
DISTRIBUTOR:	Tyndale Christian Video (800)323-9400, (708)668-8300
LENGTH:	28 min.

This well-written story uses both animation and drama. The message is clear: Even what you may believe to be just a harmless little fib can grow until it reveals itself as a very harmful lie. The film shows clearly that lies hurt not only the one whom the lie is directed against but also the one doing the lying. Nicholas (a new boy in the neighborhood) and McGee (a cartoon character who gives Nicholas advice) discover that telling lies is a sure way to hurt others. Nicholas bows to peer pressure and spreads a fanciful story about an elderly Indian man who lives alone in his neighborhood. As a result, the school bully and his gang vandalize the home of the Indian man. Nicholas apologizes to the man for the damage his lie has caused and then acts on his apology and remorse by cleaning up the massive mess created by the gang. The portrayal of Nicholas's Christian father is sensitive and a good model of a godly head-of-household. The music track is upbeat and contemporary but not overpowering. A discussion guide for parents accompanies each video in this series. ©1989

Episode 3: "THE NOT-SO-GREAT ESCAPE"

CONTENT: ★★★★★   TECHNICAL QUALITY: ★★★★★

PRIMARY AUDIENCE: Ages 5–12
DIRECTOR: Mark Cullingham
STYLE: Animation, Live Action
DISTRIBUTOR: Tyndale Christian Video (800)323-9400, (708)668-8300
LENGTH: 28 min.

"The Not So Great Escape" is fast paced, humorous, and intense. It imparts excellent biblical principles by stressing the value of obedience, wisdom when making decisions, and carefully guarding what is allowed to enter our minds. The young star of the series, Nicholas, sneaks out of his house to view a forbidden movie with a friend. Nicholas finds the horror film to be grotesque and revolting. At home, his disappointed mother and father sternly but lovingly confront him with his disobedient actions and explain their desire to protect him from detrimental images that become permanently impressed on his mind. Nicholas is given an appropriate punishment. Parents, especially the father, are very well represented. "The Not So Great Escape" is this reviewer's personal favorite in the original nine-part *McGee and Me21!* series. ©1989

Episode 4: "SKATE EXPECTATIONS"

CONTENT: ★★★★★   TECHNICAL QUALITY: ★★★★★

PRIMARY AUDIENCE: Ages 4–12
DIRECTOR: Chuck Bowman
STYLE: Animation, Live Action
DISTRIBUTOR: Tyndale Christian Video (800)323-9400, (708)668-8300
LENGTH: 27 min.

This fourth episode of the original *Mcgee and Me!* series contains something that parents will appreciate: an eleven-year-old role model whose selfless actions are based on a desire to live what the Bible teaches. The tape opens with a very humorous animated adaptation of the Luke 10 story of the good Samaritan. Then, Nicholas is presented with an opportunity to be a modern-day good Samaritan when he comes repeatedly to the aid of a younger boy who is being taken advantage of by the school bully. Exciting skateboard sequences, upbeat tasteful music, and Nicholas's animated sidekick, McGee, all combine to make this a truly top-quality show. It teaches that cheating doesn't pay while encouraging viewers to look for ways that they can be good Samaritans themselves. ©1989

Episode 5: "TWISTER AND SHOUT"

CONTENT: ★★★★★   TECHNICAL QUALITY: ★★★★★

PRIMARY AUDIENCE: Ages 5–12
DIRECTOR: James Gardner
STYLE: Animation, Live Action
DISTRIBUTOR: Tyndale Christian Video (800)323-9400, (708)668-8300
LENGTH: 25 min.

In this episode, Nicholas learns that when your trust is in God, you don't have to worry about being alone. Mom and Dad have gone out for the evening and left big sister in charge of her siblings. During Mom and Dad's absence, a tornado cuts off all electrical power and the phones go dead. A tree limb even crashes through the living-room window. This small group of squabbling, sarcastic kids learns that God has given them to one another to help each other in times of need. Big sister learns that she isn't quite as self-sufficient as she thought. A wonderful drama with excellent animation sequences interspersed throughout and a great music soundtrack. (Also available on 16mm film.) ©1989

Episode 10: "IN THE NICK OF TIME"

CONTENT: ★★★   TECHNICAL QUALITY: ★★★ ½

PRIMARY AUDIENCE: Ages 8–12
DIRECTOR: Virgel W. Vogel
STYLE: Animation, Live Action
DISTRIBUTOR: Tyndale Christian Video (800)323-9400, (708)668-8300
LENGTH: 43 min.

Filmed in the majestic Sierra Nevada mountains of California, this first "New Adventures" episode features many of the same actors that were in the preceding nine episodes, but it lacks the energy and dynamic intensity that made the earlier videos so popular. In "In the Nick of Time," Nick and two friends are given a surprise wilderness rock-climbing vacation with their fathers. All learn important lessons about themselves or one another, but it is Nick's struggle with a near-crippling fear and his eventual victory over that fear—by trusting God to help him rescue his injured father—that is the main plot of this story. Unfortunately, there are too many instances where important elements of the story are not developed thoroughly enough to make what are supposed to be serious situations and discussions truly believable. Mediocre editing and the screenplay itself are the weakest technical elements of this well-intentioned production. (Also available on 16mm film.) ©1992

MAN CALLED NORMAN, A

CONTENT: ★★★★★   TECHNICAL QUALITY: ★★★ ½

PRIMARY AUDIENCE: High School–Adult

DIRECTOR:	Stephen Stiles
STYLE:	Lecture, Drama
DISTRIBUTOR:	Focus on the Family Films (800)232-6459, (719)531-3400
LENGTH:	46 min.

Mike Adkins is now a gifted speaker and mild-mannered evangelist, but he was a coal miner living in a small southern Illinois town when this story took place. Adkins never dreamed that offering to try to fix the lawnmower of his neighbor would so drastically impact both of their lives. But his neighbor was no normal man; he was the elderly "town weirdo," *A Man Called Norman*. This is the humorous yet heartwarming story of how God guided Adkins into an uncommon friendship with Norman, a mumbling, smelly, dirty, rejected old man. It tells how God used Adkins's simple acts of loving-kindness to help win Norman's heart for Christ. The average-looking Mike Adkins stands alone on a modest stage before several thousand audience members to encourage folks of all ages to look past the surface attributes, deep down to the inner beauty of our neighbors and fellow man. This is a wonderful example of true lifestyle evangelism. (Also available on 16mm film.) ©1988

MARRIAGE: GOD'S STYLE

CONTENT: ★★★★   TECHNICAL QUALITY: ★★

PRIMARY AUDIENCE:	High School–Adult
DIRECTOR:	Fred Hollis
STYLE:	Lecture
DISTRIBUTOR:	Moody Institute of Science (800)621-5111, (312)329-2190
LENGTH:	46 min.

Featuring popular black author Dr. Anthony Evans—professor of evangelism at Dallas Theological Seminary and pastor of Dallas's Oakcliff Bible Fellowship—*Marriage: God's Style* lays the groundwork for a loving husband/wife relationship. Recorded as a sermon before Dr. Evans's own congregation, this video is a challenge to Christian couples (especially to inner-city couples) to acknowledge and assume God's intended roles for their genders. If you are not an inner-city minority, don't be intimidated by the culture gap. The scriptural basis of this humorous but hard-hitting message is solid and one that should span all ethnic backgrounds. ©1986

MARTIN LUTHER

CONTENT: ★★★★ ½   TECHNICAL QUALITY: ★★★★

PRIMARY AUDIENCE:	Jr. High–Adult
DIRECTOR:	Irving Pichel
STYLE:	Docudrama
DISTRIBUTOR:	Vision Video (800)523-0226, (215)584-1893
LENGTH:	1 hr., 45 min.

This docudrama on the life of Martin Luther was originally released in theaters worldwide in the 1950s. Although it is black-and-white and moves along a little slower than more recent films, it is technically excellent in almost every respect and was nominated for an Academy Award. *Martin Luther* documents the father of Protestantism's uncompromising convictions and intense, lifelong questioning of the Catholic church's fund-raising techniques and its traditionally accepted interpretations of Scripture. Seriously consider making this video a part of your video lending library because it provides an excellent historical perspective of the birth of Protestant denominations from their pre-Reformation "parent," Roman Catholicism. (Also available on 16mm film.) © 1950s

MARTIN LUTHER–HERETIC

CONTENT: ★★★★★   TECHNICAL QUALITY: ★★★★★

PRIMARY AUDIENCE: Jr. High–Adult
DIRECTOR: Norman Stone
STYLE: Docudrama
DISTRIBUTOR: Family Films / Concordia (800)325-3040, (314)664-7000
LENGTH: 1 hr., 8 min.

This production is superb in every respect. It very effectively communicates the historical facts and theological upheaval that surrounded Martin Luther during the Reformation. We witness his quest for truth as it leads him to discover the doctrine of "salvation through grace alone"—a concept in direct conflict with his own Catholic church, and the state! This production challenges its viewers to examine their own convictions and to strengthen their commitment to the same Lord that Luther so deeply loved. A wonderful church-history film. ©1981

MORMON DILEMMA, THE

CONTENT: ★★★★   TECHNICAL QUALITY: ★★

PRIMARY AUDIENCE: High School–College
DIRECTOR: Christopher Krusen
STYLE: Drama
DISTRIBUTOR: Bridgestone Multimedia (800)523-0988, (602)940-5777
LENGTH: 1 hr., 7 min.

While this low-budget drama leaves a bit to be desired in terms of technical and acting quality, it nonetheless deserves viewing. *The Mormon Dilemma* shows a young Mormon couple confronting their Christian neighbor (Jim) because the Christian church he attends has just shown a film that they understand to be an attack against their faith. During an exchange later that evening, both the Mormon couple and Jim discover the deep differences between Mormonism and evangelical Christianity. If you have Mormon friends or acquaintances, you *need* to view this video—probably more than once. While the technical quality leaves much to be desired, this is an entertaining and eye-opening attempt to educate both Christians and Mormons. ©1988

MR. SMITH GOES TO WASHINGTON

CONTENT: ★★★★ ½   TECHNICAL QUALITY: ★★★★ ½

PRIMARY AUDIENCE:	Ages 8+
DIRECTOR:	Frank Capra
STYLE:	Drama (B&W)
DISTRIBUTOR:	RCA/Columbia Pictures
LENGTH:	2 hr., 9 min.
FEATURING:	James Stewart, Jean Arthur, Claude Rains, Edward Arnold
MPAA RATING:	Not Rated

Mr. Smith Goes to Washington is a film about ideals, compromise, and honesty. With a wholesome romantic subplot, it shows the importance of refusing to compromise an honorable ideal or belief, even in the face of visibly insurmountable odds. In this wonderful Hollywood classic, an upstanding young man is appointed by his state's governor to fill the remaining term of a senator who has suddenly died. Once in Washington, he stumbles headlong into the ugly realization that a powerful political machine controls both the politicians and the media of his home state. When he stands against injustice, Smith is nearly crushed by a man that he has idolized since childhood and a corrupted version of the political system that he so deeply loves. In the end he shows that democracy, in the hands of men and women of honorable character, *can* make a difference for good. (Smith's marathon filibuster on the senate floor is the highlight of this film.) If you know of a "lost cause" that is worth fighting for, be careful; this profoundly inspiring production may just prompt you to buck the odds and enter the fray! Includes a couple of scenes with alcohol and drunkenness, but they are important to the overall script. ©1939

MUSIC BOX, THE

CONTENT: ★★★ ½   TECHNICAL QUALITY: ★★★★

PRIMARY AUDIENCE:	Jr. High–College
DIRECTOR:	James Ford Robinson
STYLE:	Live-Action Drama
DISTRIBUTOR:	Word, Inc. (800)933-9673, (214)556-1900
LENGTH:	28 min.

If you are in the mood for some lighthearted, silly entertainment designed to put joy back into the Christian life, see this production! Though dated by clothing styles, this is probably the most creative, upbeat representation of "ministering spirits" ever filmed. In this story a factory worker whose life is filled with drudgery is visited by five dancing, singing, tuxedo-clad angels. They leave him a gift—a music box—which brings great joy and totally changes the factory worker's attitude toward life. Being afraid to share the gift with others, he is again visited by the angels; he learns that the gift must be shared and not hoarded or kept to himself. The parabolic message, to share the joy-filled message of salvation, is great! However, these frolicking angels border on sacreligiousness. Don't watch this one unless you are prepared to smile! ©1980

Authors' Choice

NATION ADRIFT, A

CONTENT: ★★★★ ½   TECHNICAL QUALITY: ★★★★

PRIMARY AUDIENCE:	Jr. High–Adult
DIRECTOR:	Brian Barkley
STYLE:	Documentary
DISTRIBUTOR:	Heritage/New Liberty Videos (913)681-1080
LENGTH:	90 min. (Approx.)

If you're like many adults, you may wish you had paid more attention during high school history class. Or, if you are presently parenting a high schooler, you may wish that your child would *not* pay attention during history class—since the Christian basis of so much of American history has been deleted or rewritten. This video is an answer to your yearnings! *A Nation Adrift* is a chronological view into the discovery, founding, development, and internal workings of America. You will hear portions from Christopher Columbus's personal diary, learn about the character and religious leanings of the Founding Fathers, understand the events leading up to and ending the Civil War, see some of the changes wrought by the Industrial Revolution, see footage of the Wright brothers' early flights, Henry Ford's first assembly line, Thomas Edison's first recorded words, the ravages of the Great Depression, the roots of the ACLU and Margaret Sanger's Planned Parenthood, the atomic bombing of Japan to end WW II, and many other significant changes all the way up to modern times. This video should be seen by every American because it contains information that will probably never again be presented in the secular classrooms of this "nation adrift." ©1994

ODYSSEY, ADVENTURES IN (series)

ABOUT THE SERIES: Born out of the success of Focus on the Family's *Odyssey* radio dramas, *Adventures in Odyssey* communicates welcome Bible-based morals in a way that kids love to watch over and over again. The main character—John Avery Whittaker, owner of Odyssey's youth center (Whitt's End) and inventor extraordinare—is a great role model for kids of any age. While you won't go wrong with any of the *Odyssey* videos, you still need to be mindful of the recommended age categories.

Episode 1: "THE KNIGHT TRAVELERS"

CONTENT: ★★★   TECHNICAL QUALITY: ★★★★ ½

PRIMARY AUDIENCE: Ages 5–10
DIRECTORS: Mike Joens and Ken C. Johnson
STYLE: Animation
DISTRIBUTOR: Word, Inc. (800)933-9673, (214)556-1900
LENGTH: 26 min.

While this first episode has a bit too much slapstick violence, and therefore should probably not be shown to children under five years old, it is still much better than anything that Saturday morning TV has to offer. Here, a scary villain, Faustus, steals Whitt's "Imagination Station" and tries to turn it into a "Manipulation Station" for his own evil desires. (The Imagination Station allows kids to witness historical events firsthand.) Faustus is foiled by a young boy, Dylan Taylor, and a determined dog named Sherman. Parents may be disappointed by scenes that are unnecessarily scary for small children, but they will appreciate Mr. Whittaker's quick prayer for God's help before he attempts to recover his stolen property. ©1991

Episode 2: "A FLIGHT TO THE FINISH"

CONTENT: ★★★★★   TECHNICAL QUALITY: ★★★★ ½

PRIMARY AUDIENCE: Ages 3–10
DIRECTORS: Mike Joens and Ken C. Johnson
STYLE: Animation
DISTRIBUTOR: Word, Inc. (800)933-9673, (214)556-1900
LENGTH: 27 min.

This is a fast-moving story about showing Christian love, even in the face of intense competition with a not-so-lovable adversary. Young Dylan has entered a soapbox derby race, the Tri-County Junior Grand Prix, and discovers that his new neighbor, Holly Ferguson, is going to be driving her fast derby car against his. After going to Whitt's End for advice from his sponsor (John Avery Whittaker), Dylan unwittingly treats his tires with Whitt's newest invention—a black compound that produces high energy on whatever it touches. During the big race, Dylan uses the speed produced by the secret compound to rescue his arch rival, Holly, rather than blasting to an easy victory. ©1991

Episode 4: "SHADOW OF A DOUBT"

CONTENT: ★★★★★   TECHNICAL QUALITY: ★★★★ ½

PRIMARY AUDIENCE: Ages 3–10
DIRECTORS: Mike Joens and Ken C. Johnson
STYLE: Animation
DISTRIBUTOR: Word, Inc. (800)933-9673, (214)556-1900
LENGTH: 27 min.

The fourth episode in Focus on the Family's fast-paced *Adventures in Odyssey* series, "Shadow of a Doubt," shows that being a faithful friend is important, especially if your friend has been falsely accused. Several homes in Odyssey have been burglarized and seemingly indisputable evidence points to John Avery Whittaker as the culprit. Young Dylan doesn't know what to do until his father shares a secret from his own past that inspires Dylan to trust and believe in Whittaker—a faithful Christian whose life and actions have been beyond reproach until the recent accusations. Dylan and his faithful dog win Mr. Whittaker's freedom when they reveal that a master of disguises is the real cat burglar. Best suited to young children, but this exciting adventure is genuinely enjoyable for all ages. ©1993

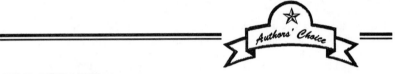

OLD YELLER

CONTENT: ★★★★★   TECHNICAL QUALITY: ★★★★★

PRIMARY AUDIENCE:	Family (Ages 4+)
DIRECTOR:	Robert Stevenson
STYLE:	Live-Action Drama
DISTRIBUTOR:	Walt Disney Home Video
LENGTH:	1 hr., 24 min.
FEATURING:	Fess Parker, Dorothy McGuire, Chuck Connors
MPAA RATING:	G

Even if your family has already seen *Old Yeller,* this Disney classic is worth watching again. Set on a rural Texas farm in the 1860s, a large stray dog becomes a trusted and lifesaving friend to the materially poor Coats family. Travis Coats, a young teen responsible for the homestead while his father is away, learns valuable lessons about growing up while also growing extremely close to his canine companion. This well-written movie starts out happy, becomes extremely sad when Travis has to kill Old Yeller because he has become rabid, and then ends with satisfying warmth when Travis finally begins to love and accept the frolicking puppy of his beloved friend. Younger children will probably need comforting during one of several intense scenes. Otherwise, there is nothing objectionable. ©1957

ONE HUNDRED AND ONE DALMATIANS

CONTENT: ★★★   TECHNICAL QUALITY: ★★★★ ½

PRIMARY AUDIENCE:	Family (all ages)
DIRECTOR:	Wolfgang Reitherman
STYLE:	Animated
DISTRIBUTOR:	Walt Disney/Buena Vⁱ
LENGTH:	1 hr., 19 min.
FEATURING:	Voices of Rod Taylor, Lisa Davis, Cate Bauer, Ben Wright
MPAA RATING:	G

What better way to capture and hold the attention of children than to bring a lovable newborn litter of cuddly puppies into their house, give the pups time to win the children's hearts, and then allow the children to witness the theft of the pups and the ensuing desperate search for them by their papa and mama? That's exactly the tact taken in this extremely popular Disney classic about a newlywed London couple, their family of Dalmatians, and an evil woman intent on acquiring as many of the black and white whelps as possible to kill and turn into fur coats. As you probably expect, the paranoid polka-dot parents do eventually locate their litter of fifteen, plus eighty-four *additional* spotted pups! But their escape from the angry, fearsome "Cruella De Ville" and her two hired, bumbling thugs is fraught with tense twists and turns and punctuated with numerous humorous situations. The film ends with the happy reunion of the greatly enlarged Dalmatian family and their human owners. Young children love to watch this one again and again, but do your family a favor the *first* time (or before the next time) it is inserted into your VCR. Pop some popcorn and enjoy this movie *together*. Also, be sure to point out that the insulting words (idiot, imbecile, shut up, etc.) spoken even by the sweet lead female are inappropriate and shouldn't be a normal part of a Christian family's vocabulary. ©1961

ORDINARY GUY

CONTENT: ★★★★ ½   TECHNICAL QUALITY: ★★★ ½

PRIMARY AUDIENCE: Family (Ages 4+)
DIRECTOR: Fred Herren
STYLE: Drama
DISTRIBUTOR: Daystar Productions (800)743-7700, (708)541-3547
LENGTH: 1 hr., 20 min.

Delightfully humorous, this award-winning drama has proven itself as a classic among Christian film productions. The timeless message challenges "ordinary" Christians to be rich in good works and share the message of God's love. *Ordinary Guy* shows how the Lord can use all of us, even if we're not famous athletes, musicians, or politicians. It is a well-written reflection of real life. In terms of the message communicated, this has got to be one of the top Christian family films of all time. NOTE: Includes very short, carefully handled scenes of gang violence. (Also available on 16mm film.) ©1979

ORIGINS: HOW THE WORLD CAME TO BE

CONTENT: ★★★★★   TECHNICAL QUALITY: ★★★★ ½

PRIMARY AUDIENCE:	High School–Adult
DIRECTORS:	Paul Taylor and Jan Bodzinga
STYLE:	Documentary
DISTRIBUTOR:	FFC/Eden Communications (800)332-2261, (602)894-1300
LENGTH:	Six 30-min. episodes

This is the most thorough and easy-to-understand series of films yet produced on the Creation/evolution controversy. A multiple-award-winning series, it consists of six episodes. The titles are: "The Origin of the Universe," "The Earth: A Young Planet?," "The Origin of Life," "The Origin of Species," "The Origin of Mankind," and "The Fossil Record." Moderated by the internationally respected Christian scientist Dr. A. E. Wilder-Smith (recipient of *three* earned doctorates), the production style is similar to that of a National Geographic special—but from a six-day scientific creationism perspective rather than the standard evolutionary point of view. The refreshing, attention-holding visuals include nature photography, animation, interviews, and dramatizations shot in many beautiful settings throughout the world. The *Origins* series should be a staple component of every church's video library because it provides a tremendous defense for the trustworthiness and infallibility of God's Word. NOTE: While this series has repeatedly been broadcast on national network television in the former Soviet Union and other nations, American networks—even PBS—have refused to transmit this important material in the USA. (Also available on 16mm film.) ©1982

ORPHAN TRAIN, THE

CONTENT: ★★★   TECHNICAL QUALITY: ★★★★

PRIMARY AUDIENCE:	Ages 12+
DIRECTOR:	William A. Graham
STYLE:	Live-Action Drama
DISTRIBUTOR:	Prism Entertainment
LENGTH:	2 hr., 24 min.
FEATURING:	Jill Eikenberry, Kevin Dobson, Melissa Michaelson
MPAA RATING:	Not Rated

The first part of this film slowly breaks your heart. The last part brings a smile to your face as lonely, outcast children are united with loving families. Set in 1854, this is the true story of Miss Emma Symms, a caring young woman who rescues about twenty orphans from the stark realities of survival-of-the-fittest New York street life. With help from a newspaper photojournalist, Miss Symms convinces a railway owner to transport a train car of orphans to the western frontier where families are anxious to adopt them. Many obstacles are faced, and most are overcome. This unrated made-for-TV-movie includes one profanity, a brief but intense segment where an adolescent boy is hanged for stealing, full backside nudity of a young boy who stands up to dry himself after a bath, and scenes in a brothel. (The brothel scenes are not visually revealing, but the segment is definitely not appropriate for young children.) Educational and very entertaining overall, but abide by the recommended age group unless you are willing to fast-forward through both the hanging and the brothel. ©1979

OUR DWELLING PLACE (series)

Volume: "THE TRIALS OF JESUS"

CONTENT: ★★★★   TECHNICAL QUALITY: ★★ ½

PRIMARY AUDIENCE: Ages 4–7
DIRECTOR: Ray Cioni
STYLE: Animation
DISTRIBUTOR: Chariot Family Publishing (800)437-4337, (616)245-5985
LENGTH: 24 min.

This biblically accurate video contains four story segments: "The Last Supper," "The Garden of Gethsemane," "The Crucifixion," and "Easter Appearances." Each segment is only a few minutes long and is separated by brief cutaways to animated conversations between several modern-day orphan children. This tape is a good possibility as an enhancement for family devotions. Note in advance that there is very little character movement; the story segments consist mainly of pans, zooms, and dissolves between various rough illustrations. Animation is simple, but quick editing helps to keep the viewer's attention. ©1988

PAPA WAS A PREACHER

CONTENT: ★★★★   TECHNICAL QUALITY: ★★★★ ½

PRIMARY AUDIENCE: Family (Ages 4+)
DIRECTOR: Steve Feke
STYLE: Live-Action Drama
DISTRIBUTOR: Rosie Productions (214)980-4228
LENGTH: 1 hr., 40 min.

The message of this refreshing feature-length drama is that it isn't enough just to believe, you have to live out your beliefs as well. Set in a small Texas town during the Korean War era, *Papa Was a Preacher* is the true story of a Methodist minister's family that leaves the comfort of a big city church to try to save a small, fledgling congregation in a little town many miles away. Two touching subplots add wholesome youthful romance and entertaining mystery. This film helps viewers to understand the stresses and pleasures of life in the family of a pastor who loves serving God by serving the people of his not-always-lovable community. The film features excellent acting by recognizable Hollywood actors and a beautiful theme song performed by Sandi Patti. (Also available on 16mm film.) ©1985

Volume 4: PARABLES, THE (series)

CONTENT: ★★★★★   TECHNICAL QUALITY: ★★★

PRIMARY AUDIENCE: Ages 3–8
DIRECTOR: Unknown
STYLE: Animation
DISTRIBUTOR: Tyndale Christian Video (800)323-9400,
                      (708)668-8300
LENGTH: 25 min.

Eleven short cartoons, each with a different message, make up this volume of the *Parables* series. Each cartoon was originally broadcast in Canada and the USA as a part of the *Circle Square* Christian children's television series. The quality of animation is good, consisting of rather simple yet colorful full-movement animals, people, and objects. The moral of each short segment (one to four minutes) is excellent and always biblically based. The brevity of each cartoon makes them perfect as visual illustrations of Bible parables for family devotions. ©1983

Volume 5: PARABLES FROM NATURE (series)

CONTENT: ★★★★★   TECHNICAL QUALITY: ★★★

PRIMARY AUDIENCE: Ages 3–8
DIRECTOR: Unknown
STYLE: Videostrip
DISTRIBUTOR: Cathedral Films (800)338-3456, (818)991-3290
LENGTH: 32 min.

This series is an upgraded video edition of some excellent Sunday school filmstrips that many parents will recognize from their own growing-up years. Because this is a "videostrip," it does not contain camera movement of any kind. However, the colorful illustrations are well done and the use of friendly animals clearly communicates to preschool and early elementary-aged children. There are three animal "parables" on every video in the series. This tape contains "Peppy the Pup/The Prodigal Son," "Chuckie the Chipmunk/The Good Samaritan," and "Bushy the Squirrel/The Foolish Rich Man." Each animal parable is immediately linked to a lifelike illustration and a quick summary of Jesus' original parable. Excellent for Sunday school, family devotions, and as wholesome entertainment communicating biblical principles. Includes a study guide to assist in leading follow-up discussions. ©1987

PERFECT PEACE

CONTENT: ★★★★   TECHNICAL QUALITY: ★★★★★

PRIMARY AUDIENCE: All Ages

DIRECTOR:	Ladd Allen
STYLE:	Live Action
DISTRIBUTOR:	Moody Institute of Science (800)621-5111, (312)329-2190
LENGTH:	28 min.

From the series of *Praise and Worship* videos produced by Moody in cooperation with Maranatha Music, this video combines beautiful songs, breathtaking nature photography, and moving passages from God's Word. Top-notch technical aspects include footage of thousands of beautiful monarch butterflies, a large variety of animals in their natural habitats, fast-moving cloud formations enhanced with time-lapse photography, and a kayak running dangerous river rapids. Wonderfully interesting and awe inspiring for adults, but also sure to captivate and relax even the rowdiest youngster. The stereo soundtrack is tremendous, especially if shown on a stereo VCR and TV. ©1989

PILGRIM'S PROGRESS

CONTENT: ★★★★   TECHNICAL QUALITY: ★★

PRIMARY AUDIENCE:	Ages 8–Adult
DIRECTOR:	Unknown
STYLE:	Animation
DISTRIBUTOR:	Gospel Films Video (800)253-0413, (616)773-3361
LENGTH:	38 min.

In the 1950s, pioneer Christian filmaker C. O. Baptista produced a colorful, animated version of John Bunyan's novel, *Pilgrim's Progress.* In the mid-1970s, the production was updated with the addition of contemporary Christian music written and performed by Chuck Girard. The novel is an excellent allegory of the Christian life both as it should be lived and as it actually is lived generally.This visual abbreviation of the book does a good job of illustrating the fact that prayer and the armor of God (Eph. 6) are necessary to stand against the fiery darts of Satan throughout our "pilgrimage" through this world. The animation is good, but transitions between various segments of the story are often abrupt. This particular production has a lower intensity level than *Dangerous Journey* (another animated version of Bunyan's novel, also reviewed in this book), so it is probably better suited for young children. (Also available on 16mm film.) ©1976

PISTOL, THE

CONTENT: ★★★★   TECHNICAL QUALITY: ★★★★

PRIMARY AUDIENCE:	Ages 8+
DIRECTOR:	Frank C. Schroeder
STYLE:	Docudrama
DISTRIBUTOR:	Columbia/Tri-Star

LENGTH:	1 hr., 44 min.
FEATURING:	Adam Guier, Nick Benedict, Boots Garland, Mike Perkins
MPAA RATING:	G

Don't let the title fool you. This video is not about guns. In fact, it is not even violent. To the contrary, this is one of the best family dramas to have been released by Hollywood in the 1990s. Subtitled *The Birth of a Legend*, this is the true story of the young "Pistol" Pete Maravich. Set in the southern USA in 1959 and 1960, Pete Maravich is a 5-foot 2-inch, ninety-pound nine-year-old who has a dream. Pete wants to be the best basketball player in the world. This dream has been handed down by his biggest fan, his loving father. The appeal and beauty of this film is that it is more than a story about basketball—*The Pistol* is an inspiring reminder of how parents have the unique opportunity to "coach" and mold their children. All viewers will be challenged to keep pursuing their dreams, and they will be encouraged by this story which shows that—with persistence and patience—even very lofty dreams can come true. Very good overall, but some viewers may wonder how *The Pistol* achieved a G rating when it includes a couple of slightly embarrassing scenes (joke about jock strap being too big and a basketball hitting a guy in the crotch) plus three instances of mildly crude language. ©1990

PRODIGAL, THE

CONTENT: ★★★★   TECHNICAL QUALITY: ★★★★

PRIMARY AUDIENCE:	Ages 10–Adult
DIRECTOR:	James F. Collier
STYLE:	Drama
DISTRIBUTOR:	Broadman & Holman (800)251-3225, (615)251-2721
LENGTH:	1 hr., 46 min.

The Prodigal is a drama based on a well-written, realistic script. It is the story of Greg, a talented twenty-one-year-old tennis player, who is under so much pressure from his highly successful businessman father to conform to the father's expectations that emotionally charged sparks inevitably fly whenever the two are together. At one point Greg lashes out against his father's worldly, hypocritical brand of Christianity. The intense honesty of this late-night confrontation causes the father (and all Christian viewers) to begin to examine seriously the true depth of his relationship with Christ. While the film moves a little slowly during the first twenty minutes, it soon captures all viewers for the duration. Excellent screenplay, great acting, and super in all technical aspects. Consider sponsoring this one for your church's video lending library. (Also available on 16mm film.) ©1983

PRODIGAL PLANET, THE

CONTENT: ★★★   TECHNICAL QUALITY: ★★★

PRIMARY AUDIENCE:	Ages 10–Adult
DIRECTOR:	Donald W. Thompson
STYLE:	Drama
DISTRIBUTOR:	Russ Doughten/Mark IV (800)247-3456, (515)278-4737
LENGTH:	2 hrs., 7 min.

The Prodigal Planet is the fourth in the dramatic prophecy series produced by Russ Doughten/Mark IV (other episodes are *A Thief in the Night, A Distant Thunder,* and *The Image of the Beast*). This is a futuristic film that attempts to portray some of the true events that will take place during the seven-year reign of the Antichrist on earth. It depicts a world devastated by nuclear holocaust toward the end of the Tribulation. Seeing the seven-year Tribulation lived out in the three final films of this series throws a powerful light on what is yet to come although no one can know *exactly* how things will happen. This film answers some of the basic questions of the Christian faith through dialogue during the film, and its greatest strength lies in its usefulness as an evangelistic tool. Its greatest weakness is its length (too long). Intriguing introduction and good special effects. (Also available on 16mm film.) ©1983

Authors' Choice

QUIGLEY'S VILLAGE (series)

Episode: "BE KIND TO ONE ANOTHER"

CONTENT: ★★★★ ½   TECHNICAL QUALITY: ★★★★

PRIMARY AUDIENCE: Ages 3–8
DIRECTOR: Jim Maguire
STYLE: Puppets, Live Action
DISTRIBUTOR: Zondervan Consumer Sales (800)727-1309, (616)698-3336
LENGTH: 36 min.

Each segment in the *Quigley's Village* series combines live actors and puppets. It is very similar in style to *Sesame Street,* but it has a biblically-based rather than humanistic approach to communicating values. Mr. Quigley is a friendly man upon whom the animal puppets rely for sound advice. In this episode, it's time for the "World Champion Hide-and-Seek Contest," and Danny Lion and Spike the Porcupine both want to be the champ. When Danny breaks his arm, Spike thinks it serves him right for thinking that she won't win the championship. But when Danny needs Spike's help, they both learn a little more about what being kind really means. From the examples of the puppets and the good advice given by Mr. Quigley, children will understand why it is important to be kind to each other. Contains three very good sing-along songs that every parent will be happy to hear their children singing throughout the day. This episode is well written (age-appropriate script), has excellent original music, impressive sets, and very good video effects. ©1987

Episode: "FUN AEROBICS FOR KIDS"

CONTENT: ★★★★   TECHNICAL QUALITY: ★★★★

PRIMARY AUDIENCE: Ages 3–8
DIRECTOR: Jim Maguire
STYLE: Puppets, Live Action
DISTRIBUTOR: Zondervan Consumer Sales (800)727-1309, (616)698-3336
LENGTH: 22 min.

This children's exercise video is an excellent solution to the problem of "couch potato" kids. Tie on the tennis shoes, turn on this video, and get out of one another's way! Integrating the people and puppets from the *Quigley's Village* series, and adding the talents of certified aerobics instructor Cheryl Merrill, "Fun Aerobics for Kids!" is both entertaining and energetic. Two adults and several children do various creative exercises, leading viewers in an aerobic workout. A good use of video special effects and Christian children's music combine to create an exercise routine that even Mom will want to join! Parents will also appreciate the fact that no skimpy or expensive aerobics outfits are used. Children wear normal, loose-fitting shirts along with shorts and sneakers. A good video to include as a regular part of children's exercise schedules, especially on rainy or snowy days. ©1988

RED RUNS THE RIVER

CONTENT: ★★★ ½ TECHNICAL QUALITY: ★★★

PRIMARY AUDIENCE: Jr. High–Adult
DIRECTOR: Katherine Stenholm
STYLE: Docudrama
DISTRIBUTOR: Unusual Films/Bob Jones University (803)242-5100, ext. 103
LENGTH: 1 hr., 26 min.

Set on the battlefields of America's Civil War, this docudrama "is the story of two wars—one in the heart of General Richard Ewell and the other on the battlefields of Manassas and Bull Run. It traces the influence of General 'Stonewall' Jackson's vigorous faith upon the profane, unbelieving Ewell." Provides interesting insights into the lives of these two Confederate military generals that viewers will probably never be exposed to by secular history textbook writers. "Stonewall" Jackson was a devout Christian who lived out his faith, even on the battlefields. At first annoyed by Jackson's praying and hymn singing, the hardhearted, General Ewell eventually surrenders his heart and life to Christ. Excellent cinematography and music score. All actors are students or staff of Bob Jones University. (Also available on 16mm film.) © 1970s

REVELATION REVEALED (series)

CONTENT: ★★★★ TECHNICAL QUALITY: ★★★

PRIMARY AUDIENCE: Adults
DIRECTOR: Unknown
STYLE: Lecture
DISTRIBUTOR: Jack Van Impe Ministries (313)852-5225
LENGTH: Five 2-hr. tapes

This five-part series is, effectively, a "video commentary" on the entire Book of the Revelation. It is directed at the average layman but "meaty" enough to challenge theologians. Using newsroom-style staging, Dr. Jack Van Impe enthusiastically and convincingly reveals that Revelation is *not* a deep, mysterious book—as so many people think—but one that can be understood and should be studied to achieve that understanding. Dr. Van Impe is a knowledgeable spokesman for the pretribulation rapture and presents an excellent case for that perspective. Viewers will appreciate the fact that a wide array of paintings and video graphics, plus segues between subjects by Rexella Van Impe (Dr. Van Impe's wife) are included to help break up what would otherwise be a visually monotonous ten-hour, single-location video series. Best suited for small study/discussion groups or for personal enrichment. ©1991

RIGHT TO KILL, THE

CONTENT: ★★★★   TECHNICAL QUALITY: ★★★★

PRIMARY AUDIENCE:	High School–Adult
DIRECTORS:	Jack Dabner and Donald Smith
STYLE:	Docudrama
DISTRIBUTOR:	American Portrait Films (800)736-4567, (216)531-8600
LENGTH:	56 min.

Webster's dictionary defines *euthanasia* as the act or practice of killing hopelessly sick or injured individuals in a "painless way for reasons of mercy." The producers of this thought-provoking documentary define it as *wrong*. Hosted and narrated by William F. Buckley, Jr., *The Right to Kill* opens with a scene of a lethal injection at a hospital in the Netherlands, then utilizes a variety of scenes—especially interviews with theologians, medical doctors, and lawyers—to present a well-reasoned (biblical?) case *against* "mercy killing." Statements by Dr. Jay Adams of Westminster Seminary are especially good. An excellent resource tool for any church video library. ©1989

ROCKETEER, THE

CONTENT: ★ ½   TECHNICAL QUALITY: ★★★★★

PRIMARY AUDIENCE:	17+
DIRECTOR:	Joe Johnston
STYLE:	Live-Action Drama
DISTRIBUTOR:	Walt Disney Home Video
LENGTH:	1 hr., 49 min.
FEATURING:	Timothy Dalton, Jennifer Connelly, Alan Arkin
MPAA RATING:	PG

This sci-fi/drama is so unbelievable that some portions are downright corny. However, that corniness doesn't significantly deter from *The Rocketeer's* ability to entertain. Set in southern California in 1938, a young pilot finds a top-secret rocket jet pack that was hidden by a gangster who stole it from billionaire Howard Hughes. The jet pack is sought both by federal agents and a popular movie star who is actually a secret agent for Hitler's Nazis. *The Rocketeer* contains a significant amount of gunfighting, fistfights, and other violence. Also, though there is no nudity or bed scenes, the female star is at times portrayed provocatively (close-ups of her putting on nylons and her tight, low-cut dress). At least nine profanities are thrown in for good measure. In the early 1970s, this same program may well have received an R rating. (According to society's common application of the MPAA "PG" rating standard, this is basically sanctioned viewing for adolescents and most young gradeschoolers. But what about the standards of the B-I-B-L-E?) ©1991

SAMMY

CONTENT: ★★★★   **TECHNICAL QUALITY:** ★★★

PRIMARY AUDIENCE:	Family (Ages 4+)
DIRECTOR:	Russ Doughten
STYLE:	Live-Action Drama
DISTRIBUTOR:	Russ Doughten/Mark IV (800)247-3456, (515)278-4737
LENGTH:	1 hr., 8 min.

Sammy is a heartwarming story that explores the tensions, conflicts, and triumphs of a young crippled boy and his financially stressed family. This award-winning movie will appeal to parents and children alike. A variety of animals, especially one particular kitten, add a soft touch to the story and really hold younger viewers' attention. (Also available on 16mm film) ©1977

SARAH, PLAIN AND TALL

CONTENT: ★★★★½   **TECHNICAL QUALITY:** ★★★★★

PRIMARY AUDIENCE:	Family (Ages 4+)
DIRECTOR:	Glenn Jordan
STYLE:	Live-Action Drama
DISTRIBUTOR:	Republic Pictures
LENGTH:	1 hr., 38 min.
FEATURING:	Glenn Close, Christopher Walken
MPAA RATING:	G

Set in rural Kansas in 1910, *Sarah, Plain and Tall* is refreshingly wholesome family-friendly fun. Originally released as a part of the *Hallmark Hall of Fame* collection, this excellent production presents the story of Jacob Witting, a Kansas farmer whose wife died soon after the birth of their second child. Several years have passed and Jacob senses the need to remarry, primarily for the good of his two children. He places a newspaper advertisement for a bride. Eventually, it is answered by Sarah, a beautiful, strong-willed woman from Maine. Sarah travels to Kansas to live with the family for thirty days. If she is able to "make a difference," she and Jacob will marry. However, this is not a normal courtship. Sarah and Jacob have very different expectations for Sarah's role in the family. Also, both Jacob and his ten-year-old daughter (Anna) have to adjust to the reality that Sarah will never be a duplicate of Jacob's deceased wife. Adjusting is difficult, but this well-scripted drama makes the process fun to watch. Sarah contains no objectionable scenes or course language and is appropriate for all ages, if viewed in a family setting. ©1990

SATANISM UNMASKED

CONTENT: ★★★ ½   TECHNICAL QUALITY: ★★ ½

PRIMARY AUDIENCE:	High School–College
DIRECTOR:	Stephen Yake
STYLE:	Documentary
DISTRIBUTOR:	Infinity Video (918)582-2126
LENGTH:	1 hr., 48 min.

Satanism Unmasked is a startling, humorous, and sometimes frightening revelation of modern Satanism in the USA. This video has been produced in a way
that is guaranteed to capture and hold the attention of its intended audience,
but which is also guaranteed to turn off many adults. Opens with an excellent
attention-grabbing black-and-white music video. Uses high-energy contemporary Christian music, interviews with famous former Satanists (Johanna
Michaelsen, Lauren Stratford, Sean Sellers), and several silly but message-carry-
ing skits to emphasize that born-again Christians have absolute power over
Satan and his demons through our position in Jesus Christ. Makes an attempt
at instructing viewers in how to exercise our authority (cast out a demon), but
the film is weak on this point. Consider watching this show as a group and then
discussing it afterward to more fully comprehend and enhance what has been
seen. ©1988

SEASONS OF THE HEART

CONTENT: ★★★★★   TECHNICAL QUALITY: ★★★★ ½

PRIMARY AUDIENCE:	Ages 8+
DIRECTOR:	T. C. Christensen
STYLE:	Live-Action Drama
DISTRIBUTOR:	Feature Films for Families (800)347-2833
LENGTH:	1 hr., 34 min.

Set in a stark yet picturesque Oregon mountain valley during the 1860s, *Sea-
sons of the Heart* portrays the emotion-touching story of Jed and Martha Richards,
homesteaders who are asked by their minister (Claude Akins) to adopt a boy
whose parents have recently died. Though seven-year-old Daniel is readily
accepted and deeply loved by Jed, Martha is unable to see how desperately the
boy needs and desires her acceptance. This is because Jed and Martha's own
children, two lovely young girls, were stricken with cholera and abruptly died on
the wagon train only a few months previously. Because Martha's heart has not
yet healed when Daniel arrives, his boyish ways are hard for her to accept. Martha has stopped reading her Bible and feels abandoned by God until she realizes—by overhearing Daniel's loving telling of the story of the first Christmas to
his farm animal friends—that her girls are being taken care of much better than
she can imagine. Includes an excellent father figure and several humorous

scenes with a neighbor lady who talks almost nonstop. (This great all-family video is also an excellent choice for a snuggly "date night" with your beloved. Pop some corn, turn down the lights, and don't forget the Kleenex!) Nothing objectionable. ©1993

SECRET ADVENTURES (series)

Episode 1: "SPIN—TRUTH, TUBAS, AND GEORGE WASHINGTON"

CONTENT: ★★★   TECHNICAL QUALITY: ★★★★ ½

PRIMARY AUDIENCE: Ages 4–12
DIRECTOR: Jim Drake
STYLE: Drama
DISTRIBUTOR: Broadman & Holman (800)251-3225, (615)251-2721
LENGTH: 30 min.

With the feeling of a fun-after-school TV special, "Spin" combines live-action drama with cartoon animation to emphasize the importance of honesty. In this fast-paced first episode of the *Secret Adventures* series, the thirteen-year-old star of the series, Drea Thomas, reluctantly agrees to run for seventh-grade class president. But both Drea and her opponent, the most popular girl in school, are quickly caught up in negative campaign tactics, openly belittling one another at every opportunity. Uncomfortable with the tone of the campaign, Drea is soon inspired by an incident with one of the two young children that she baby-sits and by the honest character of George Washington (whom she is studying in history class) to publicly apologize for her actions. She even goes so far as to withdraw from the campaign. "Spin" is wholesome, feel-good entertainment that communicates biblical values, yet (unfortunately) makes no reference whatsoever to the Bible, God, or Jesus Christ. ©1993

SEX, LIES, AND THE TRUTH

CONTENT: ★★★★ ½   TECHNICAL QUALITY: ★★★★ ½

PRIMARY AUDIENCE: Ages 12+
DIRECTOR: Ed Flanagan
STYLE: Documentary
DISTRIBUTOR: Focus on the Family (800)232-6459, (719)531-3400
LENGTH: 35 min. (approx.)

This hard-hitting award winner makes an excellent case for sexual abstinence prior to marriage. It combines interviews obtained from ordinary (sometimes very humorous) teens and adolescents, Christian athletes, and entertainers with alarming facts from concerned health-care professionals. Together, they emphasize that saving sexual intimacy until marriage, and then remaining faithful to

---

your spouse, is the only *truly* protected way to avoid the many physically and emotionally devastating STDs (sexually transmitted diseases). Encourages teens who have already been sexually active to begin reserving themselves by launching their "secondary virginity." This title has been released in both a "secular" and a "Christian" version. The Christian version is the full-length one and includes good Bible-based counsel from several of the mid-1990s best-known American Christian role models (Kirk Cameron and Chelsea Noble, Orel Hersheiser, Kathy Troccoli, A. C. Green, Michael W. Smith, and others). ©1993

SHEFFEY

CONTENT: ★★★★   TECHNICAL QUALITY: ★★★ ½

PRIMARY AUDIENCE:	Ages 8–Adult
DIRECTOR:	Katherine Stenholm
STYLE:	Drama
DISTRIBUTOR:	Unusual Films / BJU (803)242-5100
LENGTH:	2 hr., 15 min.

Robert Sheffey was a simple, inspiring circuit-rider preacher of the Appalachian mountains from the mid- to late 1800s. This feature-length production traces Sheffey's life all the way back to his unorthodox conversion and his hilariously embarrassing first preaching experience. It then follows his life all the way to the devastating arson fire that destroyed his beloved open-air camp meeting facility and caused the death of his wife. This film emphasizes Sheffey's very personal relationship with God and his conversational style of praying. It reveals a man wholly devoted to evangelizing and aiding his fellow mountain-region neighbors. The film contains some beautiful cinematography, an extensive diversity of locations, a rich instrumental soundtrack, and a large cast with excellent period wardrobes. Unfortunately, it is seriously encumbered by too many mediocre actors and editing constantly reminding the viewer that this is a *long* film. See *Sheffey* because it is good, but be aware that it falls short of most adult viewers' expectations in some key areas. (Also available on 16mm film, but to qualifying fundamental Baptist churches only.) ©1988

SMOKEY MOUNTAIN KIDS

CONTENT: ★★★   TECHNICAL QUALITY: ★★

PRIMARY AUDIENCE:	Ages 2–7
DIRECTOR:	Greg Page
STYLE:	Kid's Musical Video
DISTRIBUTOR:	Brentwood Music (800)333-9000, (615)373-3950
LENGTH:	23 min.

What do you do if you have several nice audio recordings of kids singing fun Sunday school songs that are popular throughout the Smokey Mountain region of the USA? Well, if you are an executive at Brentwood Music, you hire someone to write a slightly corny story about a new boy in small-town Cedar Creek. In the dramatized story that is the vehicle to move from one song to the next, the new boy is befriended by a small group of cute church kids. Together, they do their best to lip-sync to Brentwood's songs while walking and running all over the

Smokey Mountain countryside. This simple, silly, low-budget music video is sure to appeal to its target audience (young children) and will probably raise them from the couch and get them square dancing around the TV room. (In addition to the good soundtrack, kids will also enjoy seeing basket weavers and pottery makers, plus lazy-feeling views of mountain vistas that are seen throughout the presentation.) ©1991

SOUND OF MUSIC, THE

CONTENT: ★★★★★   TECHNICAL QUALITY: ★★★★★

PRIMARY AUDIENCE:	Ages 4+
DIRECTOR:	Robert Wise
STYLE:	Live-Action Drama, Musical
DISTRIBUTOR:	CBS Fox Video
LENGTH:	2 hr., 52 min.
FEATURING:	Julie Andrews, Christopher Plummer, Richard Haydn
MPAA RATING:	G

Turn down the lights, take the phone off the hook, and get your family situated for an evening of wholesome cinemagraphic excellence. *The Sound of Music* has just the right blending of tender emotions, suspenseful action, and great music to please all age groups. Filmed in the breath-taking scenery of Austria, this classic is interspersed with now-famous songs as it portrays a few memorable months in the life of the Von Trapp family during the Nazi occupation of their homeland. Maria (Julie Andrews) is a young woman who is uncertain about her decision to enter a religious order. To give her time to decide, her convent sends her to serve as governess for a widowed ex-naval officer's seven children. Although she has a difficult start of it, she soon endears herself to all the children and—much to her surprise—the handsome autocratic captain Von Trapp as well. They struggle with their feelings but are soon married. An intriguing adventure ensues as the Von Trapp family strives to evade the captain's forced subscription into the navy of Hitler's Third Reich. This rich musical is well worth your time. It has everything: romance, adventure, and wholesome values. ©1965

SPACE SHUTTLE JOURNEY

CONTENT: ★★★★   TECHNICAL QUALITY: ★★★★

PRIMARY AUDIENCE:	Ages 3–10
DIRECTOR:	Unknown
STYLE:	Animation
DISTRIBUTOR:	Ken Anderson Films (800)458-1387, (219)267-5774
LENGTH:	25 min.

The basic story of this Christian cartoon is that of two children and their fathers who go on a space-shuttle flight to conduct a "comet search" experiment that the boys developed as a school project. While this is not too realistic, it certainly captures the imaginations of children and provides an exciting story into which the producer has woven an important biblical lesson: Don't be disappointed if things don't seem to go the way you want them to go; God is nevertheless in control, and He knows what is best for you. ©1985

SPIRIT OF ST. LOUIS, THE

CONTENT: ★★★★   TECHNICAL QUALITY: ★★★★

PRIMARY AUDIENCE:	Family (Ages 6+)
DIRECTOR:	Billy Wilder
STYLE:	Docudrama
DISTRIBUTOR:	Warner Home Video
LENGTH:	2 hr., 17 min.
FEATURING:	James Stewart
MPAA RATING:	Not Rated

This docudrama is about Charles A. Lindbergh, a twenty-five-year-old airmail pilot who followed his dream to be the first person ever to solo an airplane across the Atlantic Ocean. The outstanding actor James Stewart reenacts some of the more significant and humorous events of Lindbergh's life, including his historic flight in May of 1927. While this history-based film is well worth seeing, it portrays this American hero as a man with an "I can do it alone; I don't need God" type of attitude. Lindbergh evidently based his pride on and attributed his successes to his own skill. He did not credit God for helping and protecting him. Point out to younger viewers Lindbergh's self-reliant attitude. Emphasize that God *did* answer his last-minute, lifesaving plea as he landed, totally exhausted, in Paris. ©1957

ST. JOHN IN EXILE

CONTENT: ★★★★   TECHNICAL QUALITY: ★★★

PRIMARY AUDIENCE:	Adults
DIRECTORS:	Dan Curtis and Lory Jones
STYLE:	One-Man Stage Play
DISTRIBUTOR:	Bridgestone Multimedia (800)523-0988, (602)940-5777
LENGTH:	1 hr., 35 min.

This one-man stage play features Dean Jones as the apostle John at age eighty-six. The setting is that of a cave prison cell on the isle of Patmos. As such the stage props are few and simple, just enough to enhance the excellent performance of Jones. The thrust of the presentation is that of a very animated John relating his life story directly to the theater audience as if they are visitors to his cave. With each story he recounts, John "becomes" many other characters: Jesus, John the Baptist, Peter, a servant girl, a Roman soldier, a Pharisee, Mary Magdalene, and others. Overflowing with emotion, *St. John in Exile* reminds viewers of the humanity of the disciples by building logical character descriptions and embellished stories from the bits of information scattered throughout the Bible and extrabiblical writings. Viewers will have a better understanding of the culture and the men and women whom Jesus impacted during His time on earth. They will also better understand the actions and attitudes of the disciples. ©1986

STORMIE OMARTIAN'S FIRST STEP WORKOUT VIDEO

CONTENT: ★★★★★   TECHNICAL QUALITY: ★★★★ ½

PRIMARY AUDIENCE: Ages 10–Adult
DIRECTOR: Roseanna Giordano
STYLE: Exercise
DISTRIBUTOR: Sparrow Home Video (800)877-4443, (615)371-6800
LENGTH: 32 min.

This workout video is great for beginners or for anyone whose physical condition prohibits them from strenuous exercise. Low impact, low stress, low sweat, but high quality and nonintimidating. Features singer/songwriter Stormie Omartian with several smiling friends, all of whom are conservatively dressed (in terms of workout attire, that is). The video builds from tension-relaxing exercises to toning and stretching warm-up exercises to seven minutes of low-impact aerobics, and then it gradually works the exerciser back down through firming and strengthening exercises through final stretching exercises. No complicated exercise maneuvers. If you can walk and move your arms at the same time, you can benefit from this tape. The workout is accompanied by beautiful instrumental renditions of Christian music. (Other video workouts have been produced since Stormie's pioneering work on this tape. Check your local Christian bookstore for additional options.) ©1988

STORY KEEPERS (series)

ABOUT THE SERIES: This technically excellent series recounts events from the earthly ministry of Jesus while also imparting an awareness of the terrible persecution faced by Christians during the first century A.D. The main teaching aspect of the series is that it features frequent flashbacks to brief, animated "Jesus stories," as a middle-aged baker, who witnessed many of the miracles of Jesus when he was a boy, tells of those events whenever he has opportunity, thereby propagating the good news of salvation at a time when the Bible as we know it was not available.

Volume 1: "BREAKOUT"

CONTENT: ★★ ½   TECHNICAL QUALITY: ★★★★ ½

PRIMARY AUDIENCE:	Ages 6–10
DIRECTOR:	Don Bluth
STYLE:	Animation
DISTRIBUTOR:	Zondervan Consumer Sales (616)698-3336
LENGTH:	25 min. (approx.)

A lovable, roly-poly baker, Ben, joyously tells his first-century contemporaries of the life and message of Jesus. Together with his caring wife Helena, Ben takes in children orphaned by the awful fire that almost consumed Rome in A.D. 64 In this episode Roman soldiers capture Cyrus, a young street juggler, along with many other followers of Christ. They are sentenced to certain death in the Roman arena, so Ben and the other children must save them. Though totally unbelievable, the rescue is successful and very exciting. Unfortunately, Nero—a licentious, blood-thirsty ruler whose callousness and hatred for Christianity led to the most terrible persecution that the Church has ever known—is portrayed in a somewhat humorous manner. Further, the story's most fearsome gladiator, "Giganticus," is also presented in a humorous fashion. The creators are to be applauded for the fact that they chose not to include reenactments or explicit verbal descriptions of the horrible tortures that so many first-century Christians suffered, but they must also be chastised for softening the historical record so much that even a few simple-minded children could outsmart and outmaneuver the highly trained Roman army. Our recommendation: read to your child(ren) about this period of Christian history. Then, view the video *and discuss it with them.* Doing so will help it to mean much more to all who see it. ©1995

SUPERBOOK (series)

Volume 5: "THE TEST" and "HERE COMES THE BRIDE"

CONTENT: ★ ½   TECHNICAL QUALITY: ★★★ ½

PRIMARY AUDIENCE:	Ages 5–10
DIRECTOR:	Unknown
STYLE:	Animation
DISTRIBUTOR:	Tyndale Christian Video (800)323-9400, (708)668-8300
LENGTH:	40 min.

The *Superbook* series is another in the genre of animated Bible stories that, unfortunately, injects contemporary children into each episode. The problem with this type of storytelling is that young viewers (those five to seven years of age and younger) cannot readily separate fiction from reality. Studies indicate that they soon come to believe that the fictional characters are as much a part of the scriptural record as the Bible characters themselves, or they assume that because the children's part is fictional the Bible story must be fiction too. Although *Superbook* episodes are very entertaining and excellent attention holders, younger viewers would be better off watching animated Bible stories such as Ken Anderson's *Greatest Stories Ever Told* series. This tape—one of dozens available in this series—contains "The Test" (Abraham's willingness to sacrifice

Isaac) and "Here Comes the Bride" (Abraham sends his servant to find a wife for Isaac). Both episodes contain more scriptural inaccuracies and oversights than a reasonable amount of "artistic license" should allow. Read the stories to your children directly from the Bible, or find a better Bible-story video, rather than exposing them to these poorly researched representations of important historical events. ©1982

SUPERCHRISTIAN

CONTENT: ★★★★   TECHNICAL QUALITY: ★★★

PRIMARY AUDIENCE:	Jr. High–College
DIRECTOR:	John Schmidt
STYLE:	Live-Action Drama/Comedy
DISTRIBUTOR:	Gospel Films Video (800)253-0413, (616)773-3361
LENGTH:	28 min.

Awarded "Best Christian Youth Film" of 1980 by the Academy of Christan Cinemagraphic Arts, *SuperChristian* contains just the right balance of humor and seriousness to be entertaining and challenging. This drama allows Christians both to laugh at themselves and to take an introspective look at their own relationship to Christ. The story of this film raises the question, "Are you an actor playing the role of a Christian, or are you a servant of the Most High God?" The star of the show, Clark Cant, throws away his "Christian costume" after being confronted by another brother in the Lord who also used to act Christian on Sundays but lived like the rest of the world throughout the other six days of the week. The film is especially well suited for junior high through college youth, but it has a message that Christian adults would do well to see too. (Also on 16mm film.) ©1980

SWAN PRINCESS

CONTENT: ★★★ ½   TECHNICAL QUALITY: ★★★★★

PRIMARY AUDIENCE:	Ages 6–Adult
DIRECTOR:	Richard Rich
STYLE:	Animated Drama
DISTRIBUTOR:	Turner Home Entertainment
LENGTH:	1 hr., 30 min.
FEATURING:	Voices of Michelle Nicastro, Howard McGillin, Jack Palance
MPAA RATING:	G

This animated romance is similar in style and music to *Beauty and the Beast* and other classics. In *Swan Princess,* a young prince (Derek) and a beautiful princess (Odette) fall in love and want to marry. But an evil magician (Rothbart) wants Odette for himself so that he can become king. To try to force her to marry him, Rothbart kidnaps Odette and casts a spell that causes her to turn into a swan (regaining human form each night when touched by moonlight). Derek, meanwhile, searches unceasingly for his love, eventually overcoming all odds to find and rescue her. *Swan Princess* emphasizes that physical beauty is not as important as true love and that love and commitment can overcome even the most formidable of obstacles. Its emphasis in both story and song of "everlasting love" may connote the Mormon doctrine of eternal marriage (a belief held by some of the film's primary creators, and contrary to the teachings of the Bible). Christians will be glad to see that parts of the story can be understood symbolically as representative of Christ, the church, and our struggle to overcome the adversary, Satan. Consider viewing this video as a family and searching together for these elements. Can you find a scene(s) reminiscent of Christ's everlasting commitment to and love for the church? What else do you feel may be represented? Enjoy! ©1994

SWISS FAMILY ROBINSON

Volume 1: THE TERRIBLE TYPHOON

CONTENT: ★★★★   TECHNICAL QUALITY: ★★★ ½

PRIMARY AUDIENCE:	Entire Family
DIRECTOR:	Yoshio Kuroda
STYLE:	Animation
DISTRIBUTOR:	Eden Communications (800)332-2261, (602)894-1300
LENGTH:	25 min.

This dramatic cartoon series will be enjoyed and appreciated by the entire family, Mom and Dad, too! *The Terrible Typhoon* is the first of many episodes in this rather substantially revised version of the classic novel, *Swiss Family Robinson.* In this segment, the viewer is introduced to the Robinson family while they are aboard a luxury sailing ship headed for Australia. They are a loving, praying family with three children (two boys and a girl). Several humorous and heart-warming scenes lead up to the sudden eruption of a fierce storm that lasts for several days and finally causes the ship to run aground on a reef. Four of the five members of the Robinson family are left stranded without a life raft aboard the shipwrecked vessel while the oldest son, Fritz, has been blown overboard by the howling typhoon. This volume ends at this point. ©1988

Volume 4: SAD REUNION

CONTENT: ★★★★   TECHNICAL QUALITY: ★★★ ½

PRIMARY AUDIENCE:	Entire Family
DIRECTOR:	Richard Epcar
STYLE:	Animation
DISTRIBUTOR:	Eden Communications (800)332-2261, (602)894-1300
LENGTH:	22 min.

It is the morning of the Robinson family's second day on the island. They are thrilled to find a man lying on the beach, but they are soon terribly saddened to discover that it is their ship's captain—dead. Later, at the family's funeral for their deceased friend, the father prays and asks God to help the family accept and deal with the sorrows of life. God gives the opportunity to have more sorrows to deal with very soon. They watch their grounded ship finally become dislodged from the reef and sink. Excitement and adventures follow as father and Fritz leave on a three day "discovery" exploration of the island. Ends abruptly after a dream sequence of a giant crab. (This dream could be disturbing to very young children). ©1989

Volume 6: WOLF ATTACK

CONTENT: ★★★   TECHNICAL QUALITY: ★★★ ½

PRIMARY AUDIENCE: Entire Family
DIRECTOR: Richard Epcar
STYLE: Animation
DISTRIBUTOR: Eden Communications (800)332-2261, (602)894-1300
LENGTH: 22 min.

Mother, Becca, and Jack busily work to ready their campsite on the beach for the return of father and Fritz from their three-day exploration of the island. Before they return, however, a ferocious pack of white-fanged jackals attack but are kept at bay by Mother's makeshift fence and her shooting of one of the animals. In the meantime, Father and Fritz have had their own near-death scare while falling into quicksand. Due to the more frightening aspects of this episode, *not* showing it to preschool children should seriously be considered. Also, some family leaders will not appreciate its initial portrayal of the mother as a "wimp" while little Becca appears fearless (until the jackal attack, that is!). ©1989

TANGLEWOOD'S SECRET

CONTENT: ★★★   TECHNICAL QUALITY: ★★★

PRIMARY AUDIENCE: Ages 5–Adult
DIRECTOR: Mike Pritchard
STYLE: Live-Action Drama
DISTRIBUTOR: Children's Media Productions (800)448-3456, (818)797-5462
LENGTH: 1 hr., 20 min.

Fireworks! That's what you get when you mix one strong-willed eight-year-old girl (Ruth) with one strict aunt (Margaret). The mischievous Ruth and her well-behaved brother, Philip, have temporarily been placed in their aunt's care at her country home. One naughty antic follows another until Aunt Margaret declares that Ruth is an unmanageable child. Miserably, Ruth wishes she could be as good as her brother but doesn't know how, until one day she runs away and is found by a kind pastor. He tells her of Jesus Christ the Good Shepherd who rescues straying sheep like Ruth and draws them to Himself. With a changed heart she returns home. Not only does her behavior begin to improve, but she is eager to share her new hope in Jesus with a dying friend. Beautiful cinematography of the Scottish countryside enhance this film. Unfortunately, viewers may be distracted during the otherwise commendable production by slightly out-of-sync lip movements and light, infrequent scratches that appear on the film. This European production is good overall, but its pacing is slower than most Americans are used to. (Also available on 16mm film.) ©1980

THIEF IN THE NIGHT, A

CONTENT: ★★★★   TECHNICAL QUALITY: ★★★

PRIMARY AUDIENCE:	Jr. High-Adult
DIRECTOR:	Donald W. Thompson
STYLE:	Live-Action Drama
DISTRIBUTOR:	Russ Doughten Films/Mark IV (800)247-3456, (515)278-4737
LENGTH:	1 hr., 9 min.

This classic film was the first and continues to be the most popular of what eventually became a four-part dramatic prophecy series written from a pretribulation rapture point of view. The other three titles are: *A Distant Thunder, The Image of the Beast*, and *Prodigal Planet*. This particular production weaves the story of a young woman (Patty) who awakes one morning to find that her husband and millions of other Christians have all simultaneously disappeared from the face of the earth. As dramatic, earthshaking events begin to unfold around her, Patty realizes she is living in the end time spoken of in biblical prophecy. It concludes with a thought-provoking cliffhanger that serves well to end this film and to provide a bridge into the next (*A Distant Thunder*). While the film is dated by early-1970s clothing and hairstyles, the story is generally well written and acceptably acted overall. Clearly presents the way of salvation. Entertaining, evangelistic, and educational all at the same time. (Also available on 16mm film.) ©1972

THOUSAND HEROES, A

CONTENT: ★★★ ½   TECHNICAL QUALITY: ★★★★

PRIMARY AUDIENCE:	Ages 12+
DIRECTOR:	Lamont Johnson
STYLE:	Docudrama
DISTRIBUTOR:	New Horizons Home Video
LENGTH:	1 hr., 35 min.
FEATURING:	Charlton Heston, James Coburn, Richard Thomas
MPAA RATING:	"PG"

In an age when so many rebellious rock stars and immature athletes have been elevated by marketers and Madison Avenue moguls to superstar status, it is easy to understand why modern culture as a whole doesn't know the difference between a "star" and a true hero. *A Thousand Heroes* is a brief reparation for that unfortunate social condition. This tense reenactment of the 1989 crash of United Airlines flight 232 in Sioux City, Iowa, shows that ordinary people—firefighters, air traffic controllers, pilots, medical professionals, and others—in the face of extreme danger and even certain death, often work together to overcome the unalterable circumstances that threaten them. Though this made-for-TV movie includes over twenty-five instances of profanity and conveys the somber truth that almost 100 of the 296 people on board died during the horrible crash, it is especially good in that it transforms one of many matter-of-fact nightly news stories into an emotional realization that this and so many similar tragedies are real, affecting many individuals and families. Plus, as this film so aptly reminds us, most heroic deeds are performed by folks just like you. ©1992

THROUGH GATES OF SPLENDOR

CONTENT: ★★★ ½   TECHNICAL QUALITY: ★★

PRIMARY AUDIENCE: Adults
DIRECTOR: Unknown
STYLE: Documentary
DISTRIBUTOR: Gospel Films Video (800)253-0413, (616)773-3361
LENGTH: 36 min.

This color documentary tells the story of five North American missionaries who were viciously murdered by the very people whom they were trying to reach—the Auca Indians of Ecuador. Narrated by Elizabeth Elliot—wife of Jim Elliot, one of the men martyred on that fateful day in 1956—the film is certainly no technical masterpiece. It consists of silent footage and still photos shot by the missionaries with Mrs. Elliot telling the powerful, effective account. *Through Gates of Splendor* is enlightening, even inspirational, for those interested in missions, and it reveals a sovereign God at work during a key time in contemporary missions history. NOTE: Contains several scenes of native nudity. ©1963

TREASURE CHEST (series)

Episode: "ZACCHAEUS–LITTLE MAN UP A TREE"

CONTENT: ★★ ½   TECHNICAL QUALITY: ★

PRIMARY AUDIENCE: Ages 2–5
DIRECTOR: Dave Adams
STYLE: Live-Action drama
DISTRIBUTOR: Christian Duplications, Inc. (800)327-9332, (407)299-7363
LENGTH: 14 min.

You can't judge a book by its cover, and that goes for videos too. The colorful cardboard box in which this tape is contained misleads the customer into expecting an animated adventure when, in fact, it contains no drawings or animation whatsoever. A picture or word description of the actual production style could easily have been included on the package but was not. While the message itself is good, this episode of the series is a low-budget, live-action drama (acted out by a cast of children). It opens with Zacchaeus unmercifully collecting exorbitant taxes. He is hated by those whom he defrauds. The story then progresses to a scene at Zacchaeus's home where his children wish that their father would find a more respectable job so that they could have more friends. Ends by showing a repentant Zacchaeus who meets and seeks to please Jesus by vowing to repay, in quadruple, everyone from whom he has stolen. This video's low purchase price is attractive, but its low technical quality is not. Let the buyer beware! ©1988

TREASURES OF THE SNOW

CONTENT: ★★★★★   TECHNICAL QUALITY: ★★★★ ½

PRIMARY AUDIENCE: Family (Ages 4+)
DIRECTOR: Mike Pritchard
STYLE: Live-Action Drama
DISTRIBUTOR: Children's Media Productions (800)448-3456, (818)797-5462
LENGTH: 1 hr., 48 min.

You probably won't find a better Christian family film than this one! Shot on location in the Swiss Alps, *Treasures of the Snow* is a dynamic production that shows how harboring an unforgiving spirit only ends up bringing pain to yourself and the ones you love. Granting forgiveness, on the other hand, brings emotional and spiritual healing. Based on the powerful book by Patricia M. St. John, young Lucien's careless act of childish teasing turns into tragedy when the boy he is teasing falls over a steep mountain cliff and seriously injures his leg. The tragedy leads to bitterness as Annette, the sister of the child whose leg Lucien has damaged, refuses to accept Lucien's attempts to win forgiveness. Eventually, Annette's bitterness drives her to brokenness, and, finally, to a willingness to forgive. Other subplots are equally compelling. If at all possible, get your church to have a Sunday evening showing of this one in its 16mm format. Then, buy the video and invite non-Christian neighbors over to see it with you. But be sure to have a box of tissues handy during this one. (Also available on 16mm film) ©1983

TRUCE IN THE FOREST

CONTENT: ★★★★ ½   TECHNICAL QUALITY: ★★★★

PRIMARY AUDIENCE: Family (Ages 4+)
DIRECTOR: Jim Lawrence
STYLE: Live-Action Drama
DISTRIBUTOR: Family Films / Concordia (800)325-3040, (314)664-7000
LENGTH: 38 min.

Four German and three American soldiers ironically spend Christmas Eve, 1944, together in a small house in the German woods. Earlier that day they pursued and fired deadly rifle bullets at one another. Now one American's life hangs by a thread, and his buddies join his enemies in singing "Silent Night" and other Christmas carols. Based on an actual event at the Battle of the Bulge, *Truce in the Forest* is a moving drama of how a frightened German peasant woman reached out in the love of Jesus Christ and opened her humble home to the trio of lost, frightened Americans and to the cold, hungry, young Germans who had battled them. The story is great, and the acting and other technical aspects are all very well done. A wonderful picture of how Christian brotherhood, shared by enemies, transcended—for one night in a forest cabin—the war that raged around them. A fantastic video for the Christmas season, but great during any other part of the year as well. ©1976

VEGGIE TALES (series)

Episode 2: "GOD WANTS ME TO FORGIVE THEM"

CONTENT: ★★★ ½   TECHNICAL QUALITY: ★★★★

PRIMARY AUDIENCE:	Ages 3–8
DIRECTORS:	Phil Yischer and Chris Olsen
STYLE:	Animation
DISTRIBUTOR:	Word, Inc. (800)933-9673, (214)556-1900
LENGTH:	32 min.

This fast-paced video contains two extremely creative, computer-animated stories with sing-along songs that kids love. In the first story (based on Matthew 18:22), a family of grumpy grapes make fun of a young asparagus boy (remember, this is for kids!). The grape family learns that making fun of people is hurtful while the asparagus boy learns that Jesus wants us to forgive those who hurt us, even if they do it more than once. (A short "intermission story" defines sin and uses a very entertaining approach to explain how to obtain forgiveness.) In the second full-length story (based on Colossians 3:16), a three-hour cruise (a la "Gilligan's Island") leads to becoming stranded on a deserted island. Larry (the Gilligan character whose daydreaming led to the boat's crash) feels hurt and unaccepted that the Skipper and passengers won't forgive him for his mistake. But their own ensuing errors cause each to realize how terrible and unaccepted Larry must feel. They quickly forgive him and even ask his forgiveness for not forgiving him earlier. These stories are colorful and widely enjoyed by young children—to the great quandary of many too-serious-for-their-own-good adults! Don't supplant Bible storybooks with these wacky videos, but don't be afraid to laugh at the frivolity that they afford, either! ©1994

WAITING FOR THE WIND

CONTENT: ★★★★   TECHNICAL QUALITY: ★★★★ ½

PRIMARY AUDIENCE:	Family (Ages 4+)
DIRECTOR:	Don Schroeder
STYLE:	Live-Action Drama
DISTRIBUTOR:	Family Films/Concordia (800)325-3040, (314)664-7000
LENGTH:	22 min.

Waiting for the Wind is a creative story about a dying prairie farmer (Robert Mitchum), his faith in Christ, and his lifelong dream to build and sail a full-size sailboat—a promise he has made to his adoring young grandson and which he desperately wants to keep. Though the terminal illness that stalks him makes the

---

fulfillment of this promise impossible, a somewhat ethereal ending indicates that God provided for the grandson in a way that the farmer couldn't. This is great entertainment and can be used as a discussion starter for family devotions or small groups (on the subjects of dying or dealing with the death of a Christian). Our only complaint is that it is too brief and would be much more satisfying as a feature-length movie! ©1991

WAIT OF THE WORLD, THE

CONTENT: ★★★★★   TECHNICAL QUALITY: ★★★ ½

PRIMARY AUDIENCE:	Jr. High–Adult
DIRECTOR:	John Schmidt
STYLE:	Live-Action Drama
DISTRIBUTOR:	Gospel Films Video (800)253-0413, (616)773-3361
LENGTH:	1 hr., 25 min.

The producer/director of this film has wonderfully combined humorous situations with uncomfortably realistic examples of the *real* mission field. This film is unique—unequaled in its ability to entertain while revealing a whole new perspective on and appreciation for "missions." Here, three hotshot young reporters from a Christian magazine are each sent to different parts of the world in order to "get a good story." In the process, each reporter is enormously impacted by the intense need for Christian laborers, and each becomes personally involved in the lives of people as they realize the vast shortage of willing workers. Meanwhile, a retired missionary gentleman in the USA battles on his knees, vigilantly praying for each of the young reporters while they are in their foreign environments. Both his words and actions impress viewers with the fact that "prayer is what gives power to missions." Don't miss this powerful and unforgettable motion picture! (Also available on 16mm film.) ©1986

WENDY AND THE WHINE

CONTENT: ★★★★   TECHNICAL QUALITY: ★★★★

PRIMARY AUDIENCE:	Ages 3–8
DIRECTORS:	Dan Peeler and Bob Singleton
STYLE:	Animation
DISTRIBUTOR:	Family Films/Concordia (800)325-3040, (314)664-7000
LENGTH:	27 min.

This humorous children's musical cartoon effectively teaches that whining is very much disliked by all who come in contact with the whiner. In *Wendy and the Whine*, a "whine monster" escapes from little Wendy's mouth whenever she whines too much. She finds that people don't like being with a whiner and eventually even decides that she doesn't like whining herself. However, she doesn't know how to control her bad habit. She tries conquering it by whispering, not talking, and then by taping her mouth completely shut. Finally, she discovers that she needs to ask God to help her conquer her bad habit. Wendy climbs up on her grandmother's lap and together they pray for the Lord's help. Grandma has a good idea: "Think, 'A whine is a loathsome and troublesome thing' before you speak." The film concludes with a happy family around the dinner table. This entertaining tape would make a welcome gift for any family that has a child in the age category listed. ©1987

WHERE THE RED FERN GROWS

CONTENT: ★★★ ½   TECHNICAL QUALITY: ★★★

PRIMARY AUDIENCE:	Family (Ages 4+)
DIRECTOR:	Norman Tokar
STYLE:	Live-Action Drama
DISTRIBUTOR:	Vestron
LENGTH:	1 hr., 37 min.
FEATURING:	James Whitmore, Jack Ging, Stewert Peterson, Beverly Garland
MPAA RATING:	G

Though this film did not enjoy significant financial success when it was originally released, its good message about determination and "meeting God halfway" continues to inspire those who view it today. A praying, God-fearing family lives in the rural Ozarks region of Oklahoma in the 1930s. Twelve-year-old Billy desperately wants two puppies to train and raise as raccoon-hunting dogs, but because his family has no money with which to purchase "coon dogs," Billy quietly works scores of odd jobs to earn enough to purchase the dogs himself. It is the relationship that this sweet-spirited boy develops with his two award-winning dogs that drives the story. The message that we must "do our part" by working hard to attain our goals, while at the same time trusting God for the necessary courage and determination, sets the production apart from other secular releases. Very good overall, but it contains three mild profanities and a comforting but unsubstantiated statement by Billy's mama (after the death of his second dog) that "there is a heaven for dogs." ©1974

WHILE YOU WERE SLEEPING

CONTENT: ★★★ ½   TECHNICAL QUALITY: ★★★★ ½

PRIMARY AUDIENCE:	Adults, Older Teens
DIRECTOR:	Jon Turteltaub
STYLE:	Drama/Romance
DISTRIBUTOR:	Buena Vista/Disney
LENGTH:	1 hr., 38 min.
FEATURING:	Sandra Bullock, Bill Pullman, Peter Gallagher
MPAA RATING:	PG

While You Were Sleeping is a tender romantic drama whose unusual premise lends naturally to some very humorous sequences. When Lucy—a wholesome clerk at a Chicago train stop—saves the life of a handsome young man whom she has secretly adored from behind the glass of her token booth for several months, she follows his ambulance to the hospital and is assumed by hospital staff and family members to be his fiancée. Because the injured man (Peter) has fallen into a coma, Lucy delays informing his loving but sometimes quirky family that it is all a misunderstanding and that their son doesn't even know her. The week-long coma allows time for sweet-spirited Lucy to become accepted and even adored by Peter's family, but the continuation of her well-intentioned untruth creates complications that almost force her to miss out on the most meaningful relationship she has ever tasted. This fun "date video" is a great choice for any couple looking for a good drama devoid of bedroom scenes and violence. Unfortunately, the film is marred by about a dozen profanities, a few of which are spoken between family members during a disruptive conversation in the middle of Mass. Our "content" rating would otherwise have been higher. ©1995

WILD HEARTS CAN'T BE BROKEN

CONTENT: ★★★★ ½   TECHNICAL QUALITY: ★★★★ ½

PRIMARY AUDIENCE:	Family (Ages 6+)
DIRECTOR:	Steve Miner
STYLE:	Live-Action Drama
DISTRIBUTOR:	Walt Disney Home Video
LENGTH:	1 hr., 29 min.
FEATURING:	Gabrielle Anwar, Michael Schoeffling, Cliff Robertson
MPAA RATING:	G

This is a wonderfully entertaining movie about the gutsy determination of a teenage girl who sets out to fulfill the dream of her young, visionary heart. It is the true story of Sonara Webster, a daring runaway orphan who became the champion horse diver of the 1930s. Sonara's strong will and courage make viewers cheer when she finds a way to overcome the odds and continues performing her dangerous horse-diving act even after being blinded in a diving accident. This excellent film also includes two especially powerful subplots: a tender, wholesome love story, and the mending of a father/son relationship just prior to the father's death. It includes one profanity and one brief fistfight. An uncommon and welcome oasis among Hollywood's normal theatrical releases. ©1991

WILD WEST, THE (series)

Episode 1: "COWBOYS and SETTLERS"

CONTENT: ★★★   TECHNICAL QUALITY: ★★★ ½

PRIMARY AUDIENCE:	Adults
DIRECTOR:	Keith Merrill
STYLE:	Documentary
DISTRIBUTOR:	Warner Home Video.
LENGTH:	1 hr., 30 min.
MPAA RATING:	Not Rated

Until one sees a production such as this, contemporary television viewers are unaware of the extent to which Hollywood has incorrectly shaped America's impression of cowboy-era history. Gunslinging megastars like John Wayne and Clint Eastwood have helped drama producers to showcase fast-action gunfights and scenes of brutal Indian attacks on innocent settlers. But this very interesting production reveals a somewhat different perspective. By combining scenes of old black-and-white photographs and illustrations, unseen voice actors who quote from diaries of cowboys and wagon train settlers, and interviews with historians and other experts, this first episode in the five-part *Wild West* series will be much appreciated by those interested in the era that followed America's Civil War. It can even serve as a worthwhile educational enhancement for students *if* discretion is exercised to delete or fast-forward past a photo of three topless saloon girls. (We would have given this production a four and one-half-star content rating if this scene and three cowboy profanities were not included.) ©1993

WITNESSES OF JEHOVAH

CONTENT: ★★★★   TECHNICAL QUALITY: ★ ½

PRIMARY AUDIENCE:	Jr. High–Adult
DIRECTOR:	Unknown
STYLE:	Documentary
DISTRIBUTOR:	Bridgestone Multimedia (800)523-0988, (602)940-5777
LENGTH:	58 min.

This documentary is essential viewing for anyone currently in or considering association with the Watchtower Society (Jehovah's Witness). In an investigative style, the producer traces the history of the organization from its first days, penetrating the schemes, scams, and false prophecies used in this pseudo-Christian cult to maintain control over its 3.4 million members and to extend its worldwide empire. Churches should make this one available to their members to view in their own homes as they prepare for these inevitable door-to-door visitors. (Also available on 16mm film.) ©1986

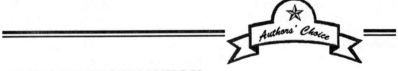

WITHOUT RESERVATION

CONTENT: ★★★★★   TECHNICAL QUALITY: ★★★★

PRIMARY AUDIENCE:	High school–Adult
DIRECTOR:	Fred Carpenter
STYLE:	Live-Action Drama

DISTRIBUTOR: Gospel Films Video (800)253-0413, (616)773-3361
LENGTH: 25 min.

The powerful message of this award-winning film is: "Don't assume that you have plenty of time to share Jesus with your friends. That assumption may cost your loved ones an eternity in hell!" Produced for youth but excellent for adults as well, *Without Reservation* is both deeply convicting and tremendously inspiring at the same time. Though this short drama is entertaining, don't expect light-hearted relaxation and warm fuzzies. Essentially, this is the story of six teens who are involved in a terrible auto accident that claims four of their young lives. Those who have died find themselves observing the friends they left behind. Temporarily suspended in a "time warp" somewhere between mortality and eternity, they are able to preview their individual destinies. This sobering story concludes with an unexpected turn that powerfully communicates the hope that is ours in Christ. It is not until you slip a video of this caliber into your video player that you appreciate the true value of owning a VCR. One tip: Turn off the lights, unplug the phone, and keep watching until the last credit has rolled. The potency of this film continues until the last moment. ©1988

WIZARD OF OZ

CONTENT: ★★ ½   TECHNICAL QUALITY: ★★★★★

PRIMARY AUDIENCE: Ages 8+
DIRECTOR: Victor Fleming
STYLE: Live-Action Drama
DISTRIBUTOR: MGM/UA Home Video
LENGTH: 1 hr., 59 min.
FEATURING: Judy Garland, Frank Morgan, Ray Bolger, Bert Lahr
MPAA RATING: G

Dorothy is a simple farm girl from Kansas. She learns—by way of a dream that lasts for the majority of the movie—that there is no place without trouble. Instead, happiness can be found right at home. According to *The Wizard of Oz*, you have the ability within yourself to improve your life. Dorothy is knocked unconscious during a Kansas tornado and while unconscious, she dreams that she and her dog are swept over the rainbow to the far away land of Oz. A "good witch" (there's an oxymoron!) directs her to the Emerald City, where the famed Wizard of Oz may be able to help her get back to Kansas. Along the way, she meets the Scarecrow, the Tin Woodman, and the Cowardly Lion. Each of these colorful characters also has a request to make of the great wizard. With help from one another they overcome the many evil schemes of the Wicked Witch. Dorothy awakens from her dream a wiser, abundantly contented girl. She now realizes that unknown people who appear amazingly courageous, smart, and philanthropic, are really just ordinary people like you and me. She learns to look for and appreciate those same qualities in the folks that are already around her. Very good overall but not recommended for younger children due to the evil witch character and some intense scenes. ©1939

WORLD THAT PERISHED, THE

CONTENT: ★★★★★   TECHNICAL QUALITY: ★★★★

PRIMARY AUDIENCE: Jr. High–Adult
DIRECTOR: Paul S. Taylor
STYLE: Documentary
DISTRIBUTOR: FFC/Eden Communications (800)332-2261, (602)894-1300
LENGTH: 33 min.

This award-winning documentary combines live action cinematography, animation, and special effects. Presents a well-researched concept of what the geography and climate of the earth was probably like prior to the worldwide Flood of Noah's day. The producer's use of a wide range of visuals adds entertainment value to the film and includes a reenactment of Noah building the ark, the ark on the stormy sea, the thirty-five thousand animal passengers housed in their cages and stalls on board the ark, erupting volcanoes, and modern-day search teams looking for remains of Noah's ark on Mount Ararat. It documents flood legends from tribes all around the world that are very similar to the actual scriptural record found in Genesis. This near timeless film is an excellent apologetic for the accuracy and trustworthiness of the first eleven chapters of Genesis. Viewers will appreciate the faith-strengthening evidences presented. Excellent evangelistic conclusion. This is a staple video for church and Christian school libraries. (Also available on 16mm film.) ©1977

YOUNG MR. LINCOLN

CONTENT: ★★★ ½   TECHNICAL QUALITY: ★★★ ½

PRIMARY AUDIENCE: Ages 8+
DIRECTOR: John Ford
STYLE: Docudrama
DISTRIBUTOR: 20th Century Fox/Key Video
LENGTH: 1 hr., 40 min.
FEATURING: Henry Fonda, Alice Brady, Richard Cromwell, Eddie Quillan
MPAA RATING: Not Rated

This biographical movie opens in front of twenty-three-year-old Abe Lincoln's backwoods general store in 1832. It ends in an Illinois courtroom where his self-taught legal skills and wonderful sense of humor are put to good use. Lincoln argues for and wins freedom for two young men who have wrongfully been charged with murder. This enjoyable but highly embellished docudrama is successful at showing something of the virtue and character of the mild-mannered lawyer who eventually became the sixteenth president of the United States.© 1939

Making Your Conviction Count

In an issue of his *Movieguide* newsletter, author/film critic Dr. Ted Baehr shared the following story. It is an eye-opener that underscores the need for concerned viewers to communicate their concerns in writing whenever possible. Baehr wrote that "Recently, I had breakfast with the head of Broadcast Standards at ABC television, who is trying to turn the network away from sex, violence, occultism, bigotry, and anti-family programming toward family programming. She noted that *she needs our letters to help her make her case to the programmers that the network must be sensitive to the concerns of Christians.* Within [the two years just preceding our meeting] she had only received *one* letter of concern, yet there are thousands of people who complain about programming every day." Baehr went on to ask the probing question: "Why do Christians complain, but fail to take a biblical stand for the good, the true, and the beautiful?"

While the emphasis of this book is to challenge and equip Christians to improve the way they manage TV in their own homes, we wholeheartedly join Dr. Baehr in his appeal: "When you see something on television . . . that you don't like, take a stand, be a witness, write (or phone) the appropriate parties."

To equip you toward that end, here are some important addresses, phone numbers and EMAIL. Mark this page so they will be easy to refer to later.

* ABC Television Network
  Attention: Broadcast Standards
  2040 Avenue of the Stars
  Sixth Floor
  Century City, CA 90067   Phone: (310) 557-6647

- NBC Television Network
  Attention: Broadcast Standards
  3000 West Alameda Avenue
  Burbank, CA 91523   Phone: (818) 840-3637

- CBS Television Network
  Attention: Broadcast Standards
  51 W. 52nd St.
  New York, NY 10019   Phone: (212) 975-3248
                                       EMAIL: marketing@cbs.com

- Fox Broadcasting Network
  Attention: Broadcast Standards
  10201 West Pico Boulevard
  Los Angeles, CA 90035   Phone: (310) 277-2211

- Federal Communications Commission
  Complaints and Investigations Office
  1919 "M" Street, NW   Fax: (202) 653-9659
  Washington, DC 20554   Phone: (202) 632-7048

APPENDIX B

Using This Book for Group Study

Has this book challenged or encouraged you? Do you wish that your family and friends could be exposed to the information and strategies described here? They can! This book can easily be used as a "curriculum" for any size study group (for instance, home fellowships, adult Sunday school classes, women's Bible studies, youth groups, and men's retreats).

While there are many ways you could use this publication to help enthuse and equip others for better TV management, the following sample plan is provided to get your creative juices flowing. It is for six "sessions" of approximately thirty to fifty minutes each.

For best results and to heighten enthusiasm, be sure to have one copy of this text for each household represented in your group. If possible, have the books available to hand out at your first session so group members can have a chance to read the suggested material before you come together again for session two.

Session Description

1. After introducing the subject and the text for your study (this book), take about five minutes to ask the following questions. Listen to everyone's responses, but be careful not to react negatively.

   • What were some of your favorite programs as you were growing up?
   • How many television sets did your parents own, and in what rooms were they located?
   • How many sets do you own today, and in what rooms are they located?

- What are some of the other electronic media prominently influencing society today?

Next, if the members of your group have not already done so prior to your meeting, select two or three people to take turns reading "Our Story" (chap. 1) aloud. Afterward, ask if anyone has experienced a similar situation in their home (that is, frustrated by the way they personally use TV or other media). Allow two or three brief personal stories to be shared. Then, read or summarize and discuss selected segments from chapter 2. If an overhead projector is available, project some of the interesting statistics and two or three key quotes from the chapter. (If no overhead projector is available, consider using poster board or a chalkboard.) End by praying together that God will help all the homes represented to reconsider the way that TV and related electronic media is used; pray that He will help each individual group member to be willing to change if their viewing habits or selections are discovered not to be in sync with God's standards for the Christian life.

Before next session: Read chapters 3, 4, and 5.

2. Summarize the contents of chapter 3. Then, ask group members to tell what they felt as they read the chapter on their own. Possible leading questions might include:

- Did you see yourselves in any of the Scripture verses cited in the chapter?
- If so, which verses, and how?

Next, take turns reading or summarizing selected segments from chapters 4 and 5, which deal with Hollywood's agenda and the effects of poorly managed TV on relationships. Allow the members of your group to discuss how they use TV and other electronic media. Encourage the group to constantly consider how the message of this book might apply to their own life first and their spouse or family second. What area of their *own* lives might God be encouraging them to reexamine? Challenge them to commit to strive toward better control in that problem area during the weeks to come.

Before next session: Read chapters 6 and 7.

3. Briefly (five to eight minutes) highlight the material covered in chapter 6. Next, set up a TV and VCR and practice evaluating programs. (In the days prior to this session, have someone record three to five minutes each from three or four of the most popular network TV dramas or situation comedies.) Hand out copies of the Program Evaluation Form, then use it to help analyze each recorded show segment. Use the discussion points noted in section 2 of the form to help get your group comfortable with evaluating and discussing programs. Next, hand out photocopies of the Viewing Inventory form from chapter 7. Challenge all persons to closely track their TV time until the next meeting (preferably for at least one week). Consider assigning each person a "buddy" and break off into subgroups of two at the beginning of session 4 to share how they did, and to pray for and encourage one another.

Before next session: Read chapter 8.

4. (Read the last sentence of session 3 above. Do this now if it applies to your group.) Prepare and bring a sample "TV Survival Kit" as described in chapter 8. Talk about the kit and allow group members to make their own lists of contents that would be good for a TV Survival Kit customized for their home. Give them the assignment of preparing and using their kit during the entire coming week or more. Also highlight and discuss several of the other survival ideas presented in that chapter. (Suggestion: challenge group members to the "Two Week Shutdown." For those willing to commit, have them complete a copy of the TV Viewing Contract. Have some sort of certificate or prizes available at the next session for those who successfully complete the commitment they made in their contract.)

Before next session: Read chapters 9, 10, and 12. Also, thoroughly scan chapter 11.

Require each person to choose and do at least 3 of the 151 TV alternatives from chapter 11 within the next week.

5. Read aloud the story about video seduction from chapter 9. Discuss the benefits and challenges of owning a VCR (or subscribing to cable television). Discuss the alarming facts that are included in the early pages of chapter 12. (If time permits and equipment is available to you, illustrate the fact that high-quality, Christ-centered videos are available by showing short clips from a few of the "Authors' Choice" videos that are noted in the VideoGuide section of chap. 12.) Tell your group where they can purchase or rent Christian videos locally. Suggest that your group donate tapes to your church library, and/or make a list of videos owned by your group and encourage sharing of the tapes.

Before next session: Read chapter 11.

6 . Show slides or share stories of members of your group who have enjoyed non-TV activities as a result of this study. Highlight and discuss ten to twenty of the TV-free activities described in chapter 11. Brainstorm and write down your own group's unique ideas. (Use an overhead projector to project the group's ideas as they are shared.) Finally, review highlights from what has been discussed in the previous sessions and encourage the group to continue the TV management skills that they have learned. Before ending, pray together for God's help in becoming ever-better media managers, so each household can be even more finely tuned!

Endnotes

CHAPTER 2

1. Carol Gentry, "Slaves to the Set," *Mesa Tribune*, 3 September 1990, A1.

2. Ibid., A6.

3. 107th Annual Statistical Abstract, U.S. Bureau of Vital Statistics.

4. Patti Doten, "Home Alone with Your TV?" *Mesa Tribune*, 16 April 1995, F1.

5. Joan Anderson Wilkins, "Breaking the TV Habit," *Readers Digest*, October 1987.

CHAPTER 3

1. M. Larson, "The One-Eyed Giant," *Moody Monthly*, October 1966, 26.

2. John W. Bachman, *Media—Wasteland or Wonderland* (Minneapolis: Augsburg, 1984), 33.

CHAPTER 4

1. *Aaron's Way*, originally broadcast by NBC, 4 May 1988.

2. Joshua Mooney and Matthew King, "What Hollywood Really Thinks," *Hollywood Reporter*, November 1995.

3. "CBS Mighty Mouse Sniffing Cocaine?" *American Family Association Journal*, July 1988, 4.

4. Donald Wildmon, *The Home Invaders* (Wheaton, Ill.: Victor Books, 1985), 45.

5. "The Gospel of Lucas," *Contemporary Christian Magazine*, August 1983.

6. Tom Hanks, "Double Takes," *New Dimensions*, June 1992, 13.

7. Kevin Perrotta, *Taming the TV Habit* (Ann Arbor, Mich.: Servant Publications, 1982), 116.

8. An excellent six-part series, *Origins-How the World Came to Be*, is listed in the video reviews section of this book. Though this award-winning production has been telecast in many countries, including the former Soviet Union, PBS has repeatedly turned down opportunities to broadcast it.

CHAPTER 5

1. Robert A. Mendelson, M.D., chairman of the TV Committee of the American Academy of Pediatrics, quoted in "TV Can Ruin Some Kids," *Journal Star*, Peoria, Ill., 20 April 1990, A4.

2. Dr. Jay Martin, "Caught in Fantasyland." *USA Today Magazine*, November 1983, 93.

3. *Mesa Tribune*, 18 December 1993, A8. "TV Violence Report Card" released in December 1993 by U.S. Senator Byron Dorgan revealed that Saturday morning cartoons contain almost eight times as many violent incidents as prime time.

4. Martin, "Caught in Fantasyland," 93.

5. Associated Press, "TV Violence Encouraged, Study Finds," *Tribune Newspaper*, 7 February 1996, AS.

6. Ibid.

7. Renee Stovsky, "'Sesame Street' Not A-OK," *Arizona Republic*, 20 January 1992, A1.

8. Ibid., A4.

9. Ibid.

10. Michael Conion, "High Fat Television Study: TV Lowers Youth's Metabolisms," *Phoenix Gazette*, 9 February 1993, A1, A4.

11. Associated Press, "High Cholesterol in Children Linked to Too Much Television," *Mesa Tribune*, 14 November 1990, A1.

12. Jane E. Brody, "Metabolism May Make TV Fattening," *Arizona Republic*, 5 April 1992, L6.

13. Ibid.

14. Ibid.

15. Bob Larson, *Larson's Book of Family Issues* (Wheaton, Il.: Tyndale House, 1986), 254, 260.

16. Robert S. Welch, "Making Your Family #1 . . ." *Focus on the Family* magazine, January 1987, 4.

17. "Time Bind Called Top Threat to Family," *Moody Monthly*, December 1989, 72.

18. Marie Winn, "The Plug-in Drug," *Saturday Evening Post*, November 1977, 40–41.

19. Patti Doten, "Home Alone with Your TV?" *Mesa Tribune*, 16 April 1995, F3. Poll conducted by "Children Now," a national Children's advocacy group. See also: Claudia Puig, "Kids: TV Harms Us," *Phoenix Gazette*, 27 February 1995, A1, A8.

20. Ellen De Franco, *TV On/Off* (Santa Monica, Calif.: Goodyear Publishing, 1980), 152.

CHAPTER 6

1. Gregg Lewis, *Telegarbage* (Nashville, Tenn.: Thomas Nelson, 1977), 117.

CHAPTER 7

1. *Glamour*, February 1988.

2. *Youthworker Update*, December 1991, 4. (*Youthworker Update* is a publication of Youth Specialties, El Cajon, California.)

3. *Parade*, 23 May 1993, 17. (Based on the findings of Nielson Media Research.)

4. *TV Guide*, 30 May 1987, 5.

CHAPTER 8

1. Nina Coombs, "Is Your Love Life Going Down 'The Tube'?" *Reader's Digest*, October 1987.

2. Gregg Lewis, *Telegarbage* (Nashville: Thomas Nelson Publishers 1977),102.

3. To order The Switch, contact the manufacturer: Sonic Technology, 120 Richardson Street, Grass Valley, CA 95945. Phone: (916)272-4257 or 1-800-247-5548. (At the time of publication, The Switch could be purchased for around $29.95, including postage and handling.)

CHAPTER 9

1. Anonymous, "Video Seduction," *Moody Monthly*, March 1995, 23–24.

2. Dr. William Fore, "Videocassettes Present a Challenge to the Church," *Christian Film & Video* (a newsletter of the Wheaton Graduate School of Communications), vol. 6, no. 1, 2.

3. Paul Thigpen, "Cleaning Up Hollywood," *Charisma*, December 1991, 40.

4. Fore, "Videocassettes Present a Challenge," 1.

CHAPTER 12

1. *Creation Science Foundation Prayer News*, April/May 1987 (Australia), p. 3.

2. Paul Thigpen, "Cleaning Up Hollywood," *Charisma*, December 1991, 40.

3. Ibid., 37.

4. Lee Grady, "The Censorship Smokescreen," *Charisma*, April 1991, 102.

5. The following services aid Christians in making decisions about what secular movies are most appropriate for viewing and what ones should be avoided.

- *Movieguide* (newsletter)
  An excellent parenting tool that is published twice each month, *Movieguide* provides detailed and insightful reviews of current secular movies plus articles about various special issues related to the movie industry. It helps readers decide which movies to see and which ones to avoid. *Movieguide* is probably the more widely circulated of the two newsletters listed here. Both provide a biblical perspective of each movie to help develop a biblical worldview and greater discernment. Editor and chief reviewer is respected author/film critic, Dr. Ted Baehr. A $40 donation is suggested for a one-year hard copy subscription (twenty-four issues), or $20 for six months.

- Request complimentary sample from: *Movieguide*, P.O. Box 190010, Atlanta, Georgia 31119. (Phone: 800-899-6684).

- As of this writing, *Movieguide* also offers a great way to get *immediate* reviews of current feature films and new video releases. "*Movieguide* Hotline" is a pay-per-call 900 number, available 24 hours a day, seven days a week. If you need to know about the content of a movie *now*, phone: 1-900-226-8224. At the time of the printing of this book, the charge was 99¢ per minute, with an average call requiring about three minutes.

- *Preview Family Movie and TV Guide* (newsletter)
  Published twice each month, this newsletter summarizes and rates all popular G, PG, PG-13 (and some R-rated) movies according to both entertainment value and content acceptability. Editor/Publisher, Mr. John Evans. A $30 donation is suggested for a one-year hard copy subscription (twenty-four issues). *Preview* also publishes and "on-line" version of the newsletter, making your ability to get a Christian based review of a new release simple. For subscription information and samples of recent reviews, visit *Preview's* Internet worldwide website. (URL:http://www.cyserv.com/preview)

- Request sample from: *Preview Family Movie and TV Guide*, 1309 Seminole Dr., Richardson, Texas 75080. (Phone: 214-231-9910).

6. Dr. Jerome K. Miller, *Video Copyright (Video usage rights) Guidelines: For Pastors & Church Workers* (Friday Harbor, Washington: Copyright Information Services, 1986), 6.

Index